CORPORATE AFFAIRS:
Nepotism, Office Romance, & Sexual Harassment

A BNA SPECIAL REPORT

Copyright © 1988

The Bureau of National Affairs, Inc.
1231 25th Street, NW
Washington, DC 20037

ISBN No. 0-8779-952-9

Extra copies of this report (BSP 78) are $75.00 each, and may be obtained by mail from BNA's Customer Service Center, 9435 Key West Ave., Rockville, Md. 20850; or by telephone from BNA's Response Center, toll free (800) 372-1033. The following quantity discounts are available: 6-10 copies, 10%; 11-25, 15%; 26-50, 20%; 51-500, 25%; 501-1,000, 30%; and more than 1,000 copies, 35%.

TABLE OF CONTENTS

Introduction

Love makes the world go round, or so the song goes, but in the world of work, love also can clog up the corporate machinery.

Co-workers engaged in office romance can spend more time becoming acquainted with each other and less time learning about their jobs. Budding sexual encounters can blossom not into corporate affairs but into corporate sexual harassment charges. And when co-workers are married or related to each other, employers may face even more problems.

Many employers are finding that these concerns can affect productivity and the bottom line. At the very least, corporations need to develop coherent policies on these issues — or risk expensive lawsuits, decreased morale, or reduced profits. Because, like it or not, the American workplace is becoming the American social place as well:

- *More women in the workforce.* One major reason for this trend is the influx of women into the workplace — particularly into more highly visible management and professional positions. The situation was different, said Helen Axel, director of The Conference Board's work and family information center, "when all the women were in the typing pool and the men were in the front office."

- *Chemistry at work.* A number of experts noted that when men and women work well together on interesting projects, spend large amounts of time together at the office, and travel together on business, it is easy to become sexually attracted to one another. Natasha Josefowitz, a management consultant who has written extensively on the subject, noted: "The most powerful aphrodisiac is common interests."

In addition, it has been pointed out that working with someone on a daily basis is a good way to get to know the person's strengths and weaknesses, rather than having to rely on superficial impressions gained by meeting someone at a social affair.

- *Changing social mores.* "With average age of first marriage increasing and incidence of divorce and remarriage increasing as well, it is now more likely that future spouses will meet at work than at school, social or neighborhood settings," noted the Boston University Study on Balancing Job and Home Life.

A 1987 survey of members of the American Society for Personnel Administration stated the basic dilemma to be faced more and more in American business: "The extent that Cupid is allowed to operate in the workplace reflects an important dimension of the tradeoff between employee and organizational rights."

Of the 245 respondents to ASPA's survey — most of them personnel administrators for private corporations — 51.4 percent agreed it is common to see professional compatibility turn into romantic attraction. But 69.8 percent also said that the organization can do nothing to stop romantic attractions.

Few employers have formal rules prohibiting dating among employees — a much larger number formally restrict situations in which husbands and wives can work together. In addition, the questions of what constitutes sexual harassment, how to counter it, and employers' legal liability for such harassment have progressed rapidly since the early 1980s. What was once a taboo subject now is discussed openly in both large and small corporations.

Major findings of the report are found in Chapter II. Chapter III covers the area of corporate nepotism policies, particularly as they pertain to husbands and wives working together. Chapter IV examines both the positive and negative effects of romance in the office, and different ways that companies address the issue. Chapters III and IV both contain summaries of major research and analyses of legal developments. Chapter V traces the development of sexual harassment as a major corporate problem, with particular emphasis given to the evolution of case law on the issue. Chapter VI includes four case studies of companies with differing policies on employing spouses and/or dealing with office romance.

The appendices include: four major court decisions; the employee sponsorship policy of Steelcase, Inc., which allows production employees with at least 15 years of service to the company to "sponsor" the hiring of a relative; the employment restriction policy of Rainier National Bank as it applies to both relatives and "close personal friends"; regulations and Federal Personnel Manual guidance setting out restrictions on hiring of relatives in the Federal Government; guidance for employers on nepotism, written for this report by Joan Wexler, associate dean and professor of law at Brooklyn Law School; guidance for employers on office romance, written for the report by Nancy Woodhull, president of Gannett New Media; and a model corporate policy on sexual harassment prepared by KJA Associates, a Cincinnati-based management consultant firm.

This special report was prepared by the Special Projects Division of The Bureau of National Affairs, Inc. Michael Levin-Epstein, associate editor of the unit, served as project manager. Sarah Crim, staff editor, served as principal researcher, writer and editorial coordinator of the report. Production coordinators were Jeff Day and Karen Newton.

Other BNA staff members contributing to the report included legal editors David Brandolph and Stephen S. Rappoport, staff correspondents Martha Kessler and Mark Wolski, and Jim Jasper, special correspondent.

* * *

Highlights

For many employees today, the workplace is also a social center. For some, this means working with relatives, making new friends, becoming romantically involved with co-workers, and perhaps finding a husband or wife.

For many employers, however, the increased connection between work and social life can create major headaches. When a superior has an affair with a subordinate, other workers can become jealous. When relatives work side by side, family problems can become work problems. When one worker is interested sexually in a co-worker, sexual harassment, not romance, may result.

In the last 10 years, the influx of women into the workforce, combined with the emergence of the workplace as a social center, have catapulted the issues of nepotism, office romance, and sexual harassment into increasing prominence.

From numerous interviews with employee relations specialists and extensive research, this special report reaches the following conclusions on these three volatile issues:

Office Romance

- Despite the potential problems that can arise when co-workers become involved romantically, the members of a panel of nine experts interviewed by BNA said that at best the effect of office romances on the workplace is positive or neutral, or at worst is negative only in certain specific cases.

- Most corporations do not have formal policies discouraging romances between employees of the same firm. Included in this count are those companies that do have formal policies against married couples working together. Only a few actively discourage dating between employees.

- The type of romance considered to be most disruptive of office routine and most negative in its consequences is an affair between a supervisor and a subordinate, especially when one or both of the lovers is married. On a parallel note, the restriction employers most often place upon married couples working together is that one spouse cannot supervise another.

- The executives, researchers, and other experts interviewed for this report had wide-ranging views as to what should be done when an office romance is affecting the workplace negatively. Suggestions ranged from "do nothing and hope for the best," to having group counseling sessions with a psychologist on the subject as a preventive measure, to transferring and sometimes even terminating one of the lovers. Very few thought that one solution could be applied to all situations.

- An office romance that is known to others can have a strong and negative influence on the careers of those involved. Natasha Josefowitz, a management consultant who has written extensively on the subject of male-female interactions at work, counseled that when the lovers are of unequal rank, to avoid co-worker charges of favored treatment, the lower-ranked partner should be passed over for promotions and choice assignments — even when such advancements are deserved.

Sexual Harassment

- Enactment of Title VII of the Civil Rights Act of 1964 has had a two-fold effect: It provided a basis for the development of legal principles to fight sexual harassment at the same time that it invalidated barriers to greater female participation in the labor market by increasing the opportunities to apply the principles. By making it easier for women to enter jobs formerly held only by men, the statute expanded the opportunities for conflict between the sexes.

- Courts generally agree that an employer is automatically liable for the untoward sexual harassment acts of its supervisors — even if higher management does not know about them — when the consequences are denial of a promotion or salary increase, an unwanted transfer, or a discharge. It is not yet settled legally whether actual knowledge by higher management of the supervisor's conduct is necessary to establish such liability. Furthermore, there is no judicial consensus on how much harassment there has to be before the requisite pattern of harassment can be said to exist.

- The Supreme Court's *Vinson* case established that sexual harassment by supervisors could subject an employer to liability. But the Supreme Court left open other questions, such as: What is harassment? When is it actionable? When is the employer liable?

- A workplace rule against sexual harassment has built-in weakness. Since sexual harassment arises out of a relationship between people, the conduct the law seeks to prohibit is not well-defined.

- One holding by the Supreme Court that provocative speech or dress can be relevant in determining whether particular sexual advances were unwelcome raised the question of whether an employer could also inquire into the employee's sexual history.

Nepotism

- Rules against nepotism are now applied more frequently in "situations not contemplated by their drafters," particularly when employees at the same workplace marry, a husband or wife seeks employment at the place where his or her spouse already works, or a married couple applies jointly for employment with the same employer.

- Some companies — such as Steelcase, Inc., in Grand Rapids, Mich., and Quad/Graphics in Pewaukee, Wis. — actively encourage hiring of relatives. Others, such as Greenwich, Conn.-based United Parcel Service, still have strong restrictions on hiring relatives. The trend, however, seems to be toward relaxing, rather than tightening, nepotism policies, because of the more frequent incidence of married couples wanting to work for the same company.

- Some industries have specialized concerns about nepotism. Many banks, for instance, will not hire both husband and wife, even if the two would work in separate departments, because of banks' great concern with security issues.

- In small communities, where there are only a few employers, related persons often work together because of the limited number of places where they can find jobs. For example, Jack Bramlage, director of recruiting and placement for Mead Corp., told BNA that Mead has many persons who are related working in its plants, many of which are in small communities. In several communities, he said, Mead "may be the only show in town" for employment.

- The most frequent restrictions placed on husbands and wives working together is that one spouse not supervise another. Also fairly common are restrictions on spouses working in the same department.

* * *

Nepotism

Strict anti-nepotism policies adopted by many U.S. corporations in the 1950s and early 1960s are being re-evaluated in the 1980s. As a result of the large influx of women into the workforce since the early 1970s, policies originally designed to prevent the hiring of male relatives of male employees are being applied to spouses who work for the same company. This chapter examines the origins of corporate nepotism rules, current trends, research, and legal developments.

Background

The word "nepotism," derived from "nepos," the Latin word for nephew, was coined to describe Pope Calixtus III's appointment of his young nephews as cardinals.

The first formal rules against nepotism also may have originated with the Roman Catholic Church, when resentment began to build against incompetents appointed to high clerical office during the Middle Ages and Renaissance.

According to Joan Wexler, associate dean and professor of law at Brooklyn Law School, nepotism was an accepted practice in American business until the 1950s. In a January 1982 *Boston University Law Review* article, Wexler cited a 1955 American Institute of Management survey finding that 7 percent of the 379 companies it rated as "excellently managed" had written policies banning or restricting the hiring of relatives, and a "somewhat larger" number had unwritten rules. By 1963, 28 percent of the 530 companies the institute surveyed had written anti-nepotism policies and 36 percent had unwritten ones.

Wexler noted that most of these rules originally were designed to prevent the hiring of incompetent male relatives. Furthermore, she noted that situations involving women were less noticeable in the 1950s and 1960s, when women "did not constitute a significant part of the professional or managerial workforce." Since "women have begun to enter the workforce in unprecedented numbers," she continued, "rules against nepotism are now applied in situations not contemplated by their drafters — for example, when employees at the same workplace marry, a husband or wife seeks employment at the place where his or her spouse already works, or a married couple applies jointly for employment with the same employer."

According to a 1985 report by The Conference Board, *Corporations and Families: Changing Practices and Perspectives*, the influx of women into the workforce — particularly into higher-level positions — has "altered the corporate landscape" so that "corporate positions on nepotism can no longer be drawn in black and white."

Several experts in personnel and corporate policy matters contacted by BNA said that employers generally appear to be relaxing their anti-nepotism rules, rather than tightening them.

Catherine Bower, a spokeswoman for the American Society for Personnel Administration, said "there used to be a lot more [anti-nepotism rules] than there are now."

Bower also noted that many ASPA members — most of whom are human resource executives in private industry — are asking the association to help them revise old policies on nepotism or develop new policies more consistent with the realities of the workforce of the 1980s.

Lisa Hicks, a senior associate at Catalyst, a New York City-based organization that promotes the advancement of women in the corporate hierarchy, also noted that many companies are relaxing their nepotism rules.

Helen Axel, director of The Conference Board's work and family information center, thinks "there are many gray areas" on the subject of how corporate nepotism policies should be structured.

The situation was different, she added, "when all the women were in the typing pool and all the men were in the front office."

Some companies, she said, "welcome family members" because "where we found one good worker, there might be another." Axel said employing members of the same family is often an accepted practice in companies that were started by families, or in isolated communities where a company might be the only employer or one of just a few employers.

As with other work and family issues related to the relatively recent infusion of women into the workforce — such as child care and maternity leave — U.S. companies appear to be in a state of flux on the issue of nepotism policies, particularly as they apply to husbands and wives.

Employer policies on hiring employees' relatives still vary widely, however. While many firms have relaxed their bans or restrictions on nepotism to accommodate the married couples who work for them, others have expanded such policies to cover not just married couples, but cohabitants or — as one corporate policy states — "close friends."

Research and interviews conducted for this special report indicate that the strictness of a company's nepotism policy depends on such factors as corporate culture, size of the firm, size of the community, security, and conflict of interest.

The federal government, for example, has limited restrictions on hiring of relatives. Section 3110 of title 5, United States Code, restricts the employment of relatives of a public official in the official's own agency or in an agency over which the official exercises jurisdiction or control. The restrictions apply throughout all three branches of the federal government.

Rationale for Hiring Relatives

Experts cite these arguments for hiring employees' relatives:

- Nepotism is good for the small, family-owned organization because it provides an efficient way to identify dedicated personnel to staff such organizations. Carol B. Gilmore, a professor of management at the University of Maine at Orono, noted that older industries, such as mills in New England, rarely have anti-nepotism policies because they have a tradition of having employed several generations of the same families.

- Allowing nepotism enables employers to consider all potential employees, and does not exclude some who might otherwise be the best candidates but who cannot apply simply because they are related by blood or marriage to an employee.

- Nepotism fosters a positive family-type environment that boosts morale and job satisfaction for all employees, relatives and non-relatives alike.

- The labor pool is shrinking in some parts of the United States, and employers shrink it even more when they exclude relatives of employees.

- Employers in remote areas or in one-employer communities are unable to attract talented employees who are part of two-career couples if they exclude spouses from employment.

- Employers that have made an investment in employees who meet and marry on the job lose that investment if an anti-nepotism policy forces one of them to leave.
- Employers that pay relocation expenses can hire two employees for the price of one move if they hire out-of-town professional couples.
- Companies that hire married couples also can save money because both are covered by one benefits package. In addition, some experts claim that couples often accept lower total wages than two single workers would accept.

Rationale for Not Hiring Relatives

These arguments are often cited for not allowing nepotism:

- Nepotism lowers the morale of people who supervise relatives of high-level executives, those who must work with them, and those who feel that promotions and rewards are given unjustifiably to a relative.
- Relatives of supervisors do not know whether they earn rewards or receive them because of who they are.
- Allowing nepotism exposes the organization to problems of family feuds and improper and sometimes costly intermingling of family business with company business.
- Workers react negatively when management disciplines or criticizes their relatives.
- When family emergencies arise, more than one family member often is absent from work.
- Nepotism policies that require the spouse with less seniority to transfer or quit when two employees in the same department marry can result in sex discrimination suits because the woman usually has less seniority.

Interviews by BNA for this special report and comments by corporate officers responding to various surveys on the topic indicate that many companies allow both spouses to be employed by the company, but often they are forbidden to work in the same department, or they cannot be in a supervisor/subordinate relationship. However, some companies, including United Parcel Service, still severely restrict hiring of any relatives. Other firms, such as Quad Graphics in Pewaukee, Wis. — where nearly half of the 3,500 employees are related to other employees — encourage employees to recruit their relatives.

Industries with Unique Concerns

Banking and newspapers have unique concerns that in many instances have resulted in more comprehensive or precise nepotism policies.

The Banking Industry

Helen Axel of The Conference Board observed that anti-nepotism policies are both "prevalent and under fire" in the banking industry, where prohibitions on hiring senior corporate officers' relatives are especially common.

According to Al Hinkle, manager for the American Bankers Association's human resources center, most banks also will not hire both husband and wife, even if the two would work in separate departments. Security issues are a great concern for banks, Hinkle noted. For example, banks would not want two relatives to have the combination to a safe, or the ability to approve each other's checks, he added.

Hinkle explained that banks are concerned about these issues in part because federal and state regulations require them to have more than one person control cash and other items.

In most cases where employees marry, he said, banks will let the individuals decide who leaves, rather than forcing the one with the least seniority to leave or ordering one or the other to leave.

Hinkle added that a large cadre of women in banking is about to break into senior management, and this may make banks "more sensitive to some of those issues ... clearly within the next five years."

Karen Hurst, senior vice president for the Bank of New England Corp. and a member of the human resources committee for the bankers association, said that at her bank, "we would not hire the relatives of senior VPs and above," because: the bank would not want it to appear that someone got his or her job because he or she knew a senior officer; the bank would not want to increase the chances that money would be stolen from the bank; and such hirings would create "decision-making opportunities for conflict of interest."

Rainier National Bank, which is the second largest commercial bank in Washington state and employs 5,500 persons, tightened its nepotism policy in mid-1986, according to James Liddell, vice president for personnel administration.

The policy, which previously applied only to employees related by blood or marriage, has been expanded to include unrelated personnel.

Although the policy states that Rainier "welcomes the opportunity to hire qualified relatives and friends of present employees," it adds that:

> Problems may arise ... when a new or existing employee works in an area in proximity to his or her relative or a person to whom he or she is closely attached. These problems relate to the strong emotional bonds which may exist between relatives or close friends. When such emotional bonds exist, the reality or appearance of improper influence or favor presents a problem.

Under Rainier's guidelines:

- Direct supervisor-subordinate relationships between relatives are prohibited.
- Indirect supervisor-subordinate relationships between relatives are prohibited unless approved by the division head.
- Relatives' job assignments that could jeopardize Rainier's security are prohibited. For example, an auditor could not audit a branch where a relative works.
- Working relationships between relatives that appear to present a potential or actual morale problem for the relatives or for other employees must be approved by the division head.

The policy says if "any of these situations occur" and the employees involved cannot resolve the problem "by a certain date," the company may transfer one or both employees, reorganize, or request a resignation.

Although the guidelines mention only relatives, the policy states, "similar actions may be required to separate close friends."

The Newspaper Industry

As in banking, the number of married couples applying for jobs with the same company and the number of co-workers marrying have increased greatly in the newspaper industry. Problems of having married couples working together are amplified in the newspaper industry. Meeting publication deadlines is high-pressure work, and many newsrooms are short on space, with employees working in close quarters.

Because many newspapers have gone out of business in recent years, reporters and editors often find that the number of places where they can get jobs is limited. Many small cities, and some large ones, have only one daily newspaper. There are increasing numbers of newsroom co-worker marriages and journalists being married to journalists at other publications. How newspapers are coping with the problems these marriages create has been the subject of recent articles in management-oriented publications such as *Editor & Publisher* and *Management* magazines.

In a July 18, 1987, article, *Editor & Publisher* noted that Pat Renfroe, manager of personnel relations for the American Newspaper Publishers Association human resources department, estimated that about half of the country's daily newspapers have formal or informal nepotism policies.

Four articles on "Newsroom Romance" in the February/March 1986 issue of *Management* detailed several instances where nepotism policies had forced one member of a couple to leave a job in journalism. *Editor & Publisher* noted that some well-known, large-circulation newspapers, including *The Wall Street Journal* and *The Chicago Sun-Times*, have nepotism policies, while others, including *The Philadelphia Inquirer* and *The Chicago Tribune*, do not.

The El Paso Times (see case study) accommodates the changing news staff demographics by allowing married couples to work together, and for several years had co-managing editors who were married.

Nepotism Policies in Smaller Communities

Several experts interviewed by BNA observed that employers in small communities with only a few places to work often employ people who are related because residents have no other place to work.

For example, Mead Corp., a major manufacturer of paper products headquartered in Dayton, Ohio, often employs people who are related in its approximately 350 offices and mills throughout the United States, according to Jack Bramlage, director of recruiting and placement.

Mead has 17,000 employees across the United States, most of them in small communities, Bramlage said. Having relatives working in the same location has "always been something we've lived with," he said, because often "we may be the only show in town" for employment.

In some situations, however, the firm does require husbands and wives to work in different parts of the company. Mead and 38 other major Ohio employers with offices on or near Interstate 75 organized the I-75 RATS (Relocation Assistance to Spouses) in 1979, in part, Bramlage explained, because of the increasing number of situations where couples who had met at work faced anti-nepotism rules after they got married. The I-75 RATS helps spouses of employees find jobs with other companies to avoid employment problems associated with nepotism.

Representatives of the member companies hold monthly luncheon meetings where they circulate resumes of employees' spouses who are job-hunting. The group holds day-long meetings twice a year. Bramlage said between 35 and 40 member-company employees' spouses are placed with jobs this way each year. I-75 RATS members include Armco Inc., NCR Corporation, and The Procter and Gamble Company.

Generational Influences

Many companies have long employed members of successive generations of the same family. According to The Conference Board, these include Kaiser Aluminum & Chemical Corp., Pitney Bowes, Pfizer Inc., The Quaker Oats Co., and Steelcase Inc.

Quaker Oats, for example, has no formal written policy prohibiting relatives from working together, but the company does not allow one relative to supervise another, according to Edward Kaplan, manager of human resources for the Chicago-based firm.

A September 1987 company newsletter article entitled "Quaker Couples" profiled several married couples who met at Quaker and still work there.

Kaplan said the company almost never makes employees resign because they marry co-workers. "They transfer or whatever," he said.

He thinks companies would find it extremely difficult to enforce rules governing non-marital romantic relationships between co-workers while they are at work. "I'm not smart enough to understand all the relationships we're trying to prevent," Kaplan said.

Nepotism or Else

In rare instances employees suffer adverse consequences at work because they do not practice nepotism. In 1986, a U.S. district court upheld the firing of the then-recently widowed executive director of the Elks National Home near Bedford, Va., because he did not remarry soon enough to suit the home's board of trustees.

Senior members of the Benevolent and Protective Order of Elks (BPOE) can retire to the home, which was founded in 1903. Executive directors of the home and their wives traditionally have functioned as a team, although only the director is paid. The plaintiff in the suit was married and was aware of the tradition when he took the executive director job in 1984.

In early 1985, the director's wife died unexpectedly of a brain hemorrhage. BPOE then pressured him to remarry, on the grounds that "a wife is essential in the exercise of an executive director's duties."

About 10 months after his wife's death, the director was fired, primarily because he had failed to remarry. He sued the BPOE Board of Grand Trustees, charging that BPOE intentionally had inflicted emotional distress on him, but the court ruled for the Elks. Noting that the director was an at-will employee, the judge noted that there is "no Virginia statute . . . which prohibits employers from requiring marriage as a condition of employment." (*Paul B. Woodring v. Board of Grand Trustees of the Benevolent & Protective Order of Elks,* USDC W. Va. Roanoke Div., Ca. No. 85-646(R), April 23, 1986)

Surveys, Studies, and Reports

Following are synopses of corporate nepotism studies and surveys conducted during the past 10 years.

- BNA PERSONNEL POLICIES FORUM SURVEY (1977) —
  This survey found that 60 percent of respondents had formal policies, with large firms (64 percent) somewhat more likely to have them than small ones (56 percent). The most common type of policy prohibited one relative from supervising another; about 50 percent of respondents with formal policies had this type. In 40 percent of companies with policies, relatives could not work in the same department. About 25 percent banned hiring any employee's spouse or relatives, or those of employees in certain positions.

The survey found that 41 percent of both small and large companies had problems with the employment of relatives. Problems were reported by slightly more respondents in non-manufacturing businesses (48 percent) than in manufacturing (39 percent) and non-business organizations (38 percent).

- INFORMAL SURVEY OF CORPORATIONS (1982) —
Joan Wexler, associate dean and professor of law at Brooklyn
Law School, conducted an informal survey of nepotism
policies at 45 corporations in 1982. Wexler wrote in the
January 1982 *Boston University Law Review* that most of the
corporations had written or informal policies concerning relatives, including spouses. Twenty-two respondents had rules
prohibiting employees from supervising relatives, 16 had rules
against relatives working in the same department, and seven
had both rules. Wexler found that none of the policies appeared to have been adopted because of particular problems,
but rather had been instituted years earlier to guard against
"traditional" nepotism abuses.

- AMERICAN SOCIETY FOR PERSONNEL ADMINISTRA-
TION STUDY (1986) — This survey, based on responses by
252 members of ASPA, a professional association of human
resource managers, found that 43 percent of the respondents'
employers had an actively enforced, formal policy against
nepotism; 17 percent had an informal policy against it; 30 percent had no policy, and 10 percent had either a formal or an informal policy encouraging nepotism. According to ASPA, nearly 90 percent of the companies that had policies said that they
had adopted them since 1970.

Of those firms that had nepotism policies, 78.2 percent said that
they covered spouses and 9.5 percent said that they applied to
divorced spouses. About 48 percent of the firms with policies made
exceptions for employees who married after they were hired and
41.5 percent exempted workers who were employed before the
policy was adopted.

The ASPA survey also found that the larger the company, the more
likely it is to have an anti-nepotism policy.

- BOSTON UNIVERSITY STUDY ON BALANCING JOB
AND HOME LIFE (1987) — Conducted by Boston University School of Social Work professors Dianne Burden and
Bradley Googins, this study covered a wide range of work and
family-related issues. The results were based on an extensive
survey of employees in eight different work settings at two
major corporations. The study had 1,565 respondents, 63 percent of those who were contacted.

The study found that nearly 25 percent of married respondents had spouses employed by the same company. The authors offered this explanation of the finding:

"With average age of first marriage increasing and incidence of divorce and remarriage increasing as well, it is now more likely that future spouses will meet at work than at school, social or neighborhood settings. The work setting may be rapidly replacing the friendship network in the support system of employees. The implications for management of larger numbers of married couples in the work force may be numerous and have yet to be considered in any systematic way."

Legal Developments

(Materials provided by Robert D. Papkin of the Washington, D.C., office of the national law firm of Squire, Sanders & Dempsey served as useful resources in preparing the legal discussion of pre-1985 cases.)

A highly qualified job applicant is denied employment at a company because her husband works there.

Two co-workers become friends, fall in love, and announce plans to marry. The boss congratulates them, then tells them that one of them must leave the company or be transferred.

Corporate anti-nepotism policies may seem harsh and unfair to employees or prospective employees in situations such as these. The consensus of major court cases in this area, however, is that such rules serve a legitimate business-related function.

Major Trends

These major trends have emerged in the development of law affecting anti-nepotism rules:

- The more narrowly such rules are prescribed, the more likely they are to be upheld.

- No-spouse rules are the most likely type of anti-nepotism rules to be challenged successfully in court.

- Rules that clearly discriminate against women are unlawful unless it can be shown that the nature of the job requires such discrimination.

- Rules that have a more negative effect on women than on men are unlawful unless the employer can show a compelling need for them and is able to show that they are designed to increase the safety or efficiency of its operations.

- No-spouse rules have not been found to interfere with the fundamental right to marriage under the Fifth and Fourteenth Amendments to the U.S. Constitution, and courts therefore have been unwilling to apply a strict scrutiny standard in assessing the constitutionality of such rules.

- In jurisdictions that prohibit employment discrimination based on "marital status" grounds may exist to attack a no-spouse rule. However, even if the jurisdiction is willing to extend the protection of such laws to no-spouse rules, the employer may defend its policy by asserting a business justification for its rule.

- Employers that continue to engage in nepotistic practices may be subject to liability if such activity discriminates against a protected class, or if it ignores the employer's own anti-nepotism rule.

Anti-nepotism rules are used by public and private employers to prohibit or restrict the hiring and/or retention of employees who are related by birth or marriage. Under these rules, applicants for employment may be rejected solely because a relative already is employed where the applicant is applying, and employees who marry co-workers may be asked to resign or transfer to another department or division.

These rules have been attacked in the courts under theories alleging violation of federal or state sexual discrimination laws, under state laws prohibiting discrimination against the status of marriage, and under the Constitution. The success of such attacks increases where these rules are broadly prescribed, are not consistently applied, and where the purpose for the rule cannot be justified.

Generally, the larger the employer — the more employees, departments, divisions, and facilities — the more difficult it will be to justify a rule prohibiting the employment of relatives in the workforce. In large firms, relatives are less likely to come in contact with each other, and employers have more opportunity to place relatives in positions where little or no conflict is likely. In such situations, rules limited to prohibiting relatives from working in the same department or within the same chain of supervisory command, but that do not exclude all relatives from employment, will be better able to survive judicial scrutiny. To avoid liability, an employer must be prepared to show that application of its rule serves to combat real or potential problems in its work environment.

However, even narrowly prescribed anti-nepotism rules may be struck down if they produce a result that appears to discriminate against a protected class. Rules that affect women are the type most often found unlawful in court actions, since if an employer's present workforce already is male-dominated, the rule may perpetuate this male domination.

Employees who marry co-workers in contravention of no-spouse rules often are given the opportunity by their employer to decide which spouse will resign or transfer from his or her current job. If the employees are unable to decide, the employer usually will retain the more senior of the two. Nevertheless, even such innocuous rules may result in charges of sexual discrimination if it can be shown that the policy substantially affects women more than men. Proving such a charge, however, remains difficult.

Sexual Discrimination

Although many anti-nepotism policies limit the employment of spouses and other relatives, the no-spouse portions of such policies are most frequently and successfully attacked in the courts. No-spouse rules often are challenged by married women alleging that they are the victims of sexual discrimination.

Title VII of the federal Civil Rights Act of 1964 makes it unlawful for an employer to discriminate in employment on the basis of an individual's sex, unless gender is shown to be a "bona fide occupational qualification" reasonably necessary to the employer's business operation. (42 U.S.C. sec. 2000e-2(a), (e)(1)). Most states also prohibit employment discrimination based on sex unless a business necessity is established.

A no-spouse rule prohibiting the employment of the "wives" of employees but not the "husbands" of employees would constitute direct evidence of discrimination against women under Title VII (EEOC Dec. 70453, EEOC, 1970, 2 FEP Cases 429). Similarly, an employer would be guilty of direct discrimination against women if it told a female employee that she and not her employee-husband was being discharged under the company's anti-nepotism policy because her husband is the "head of the household." (*George v. Farmers Electric Cooperative,* CA 5, 1983, 32 FEP Cases 1801)

An employer that applies its anti-nepotism policy by using stricter standards to assess female applicants than it uses to assess similarly situated male applicants, who generally are "not subjected to any consideration under the policy," is committing intentional sexual discrimination. *(McDowell v. Mississippi Power & Light*, DC SMiss, 1986, 44 FEP Cases 1088) However, in another case, an employer's discharge of a female spouse under its rule prohibiting relatives from working together in the same department did not discriminate intentionally against the woman. This was so, even though other relatives of hers continued to work in the department after she was fired, and despite the fact that all of these other relatives were males. In this case, the court found the rule to be legitimate and non-discriminatory because the female spouse was the only relative in the group who had access to confidential information. *(Slater v. Guest Services, Inc.*, DC DC, 1981, 33 FEP Cases 886)

Disparate Impact

With few exceptions, anti-nepotism policies are worded so that, on their face, they will apply equally to either spouse. Such gender-neutral policies are free from a direct attack alleging intentional discrimination. However, they remain subject to attack if the impact of the policy results in statistical discrimination against women.

This "disparate impact" theory was set out by the U.S. Supreme Court in *Griggs v. Duke Power Co.* (1971, 3 FEP Cases 1175). There, the Court ruled that a plaintiff can establish a *prima facie* case of discrimination upon a showing that facially neutral standards result in a significantly discriminatory pattern. To counter the plaintiff's *prima facie* case, the Court held that the employer must show that its rule or requirement has "a manifest relation to the employment in question." Once this is shown, the plaintiff's only recourse is to demonstrate the existence of non-discriminatory alternatives that will satisfy the employer's production goals. Although *Griggs* involved racial discrimination, the disparate impact theory was later extended by the Court in *Dothard v. Rawlinson* (1977, 15 FEP Cases 10) to encompass allegations of sexual discrimination.

The disparate impact theory was applied to a no-spouse rule by the U.S. Court of Appeals for the Seventh Circuit in *Yuhas v. Libby-Owens-Ford Co.* (CA 7, 1977, 16 FEP Cases 891, cert den., 1978, 17 FEP Cases 87). There, an employer's no-spouse rule prohibited the hiring of spouses of hourly employees. The rule had no effect on employees who married other employees, or on applicants for non-hourly positions. The plaintiff, who had been denied employment as an hourly worker because her husband held an hourly job at the company, established that 71 of the last 74 individuals who had been disqualified under the gender-neutral no-spouse rule were women.

The appeals court agreed with a U.S. district court that the rule had a substantial discriminatory impact on women and that the plaintiff had made a *prima facie* case of discrimination. However, the court ultimately approved of the no-spouse rule, finding that the rule was job-related.

The appeals court agreed with the district court's finding that the employer had failed to demonstrate that the rule was necessary to prevent excessive absenteeism or tardiness or that it would be more difficult to schedule vacation and work assignments without the rule. However, even though the employer could not prove that the rule enhanced its production, the court found that the rule plausibly improved the work environment. According to the court, allowing spouses to work together could interfere with the spouses' work performance, result in spouses' banding together for their personal benefit, subject the workplace to the jealousies of spousal rivalry, or interfere with the job promotion process if one spouse acted on behalf of the other.

Despite the statistics submitted by the plaintiff, the court found that the employer had not discriminated intentionally against women. A different result may have been required had the employer intentionally discriminated against women, the court said.

The U.S. Court of Appeals for the Eighth Circuit, however, found that an employer had engaged in intentional sexual discrimination and struck down the employer's rule prohibiting the hiring of spouses. In *EEOC v. Rath Packing Co.* (1986, 40 FEP Cases 580), the appeals court considered a U.S. district court finding that although facially neutral, the rule had a discriminatory impact on women in light of the fact that the employer's subjective hiring practices had resulted in a male-dominated workforce. However, the district court concluded that the policy was proper, since it was adopted to achieve the employer's interrelated business objectives of maximizing production and employee performance, and since the plaintiff had not shown that a less-restrictive rule would function more effectively in the employer's work environment. *(EEOC v. Rath Packing Co.,* DC SIowa, 1984, 40 FEP Cases 559)

The Eighth Circuit reversed, finding that the employer's no-spouse policy had not been justified by business necessity. According to the appeals court, the district court had used the wrong legal standard to gauge the business necessity of the rule. The proper standard was whether a compelling need existed for the policy, not merely whether it was reasonable or designed to improve conditions. Applying this proper standard, the court went on to find that:

(1) Management's perception that absenteeism by both spouses had a disruptive effect on plant operation was not rationally predicated on sound business interests, since the lower court found that spouses had lower absentee rates than non-spouses and that daily production was not reduced by the minimal dual-spouse absenteeism.

(2) The employer's rule prohibiting the trading of vacation leave in combination with its requirement that all employees indicate their vacation preference in order of seniority already had eliminated any ill effects caused by the vacation conflicts resulting from the employment of spouses.

(3) The district court failed to require the employer to demonstrate how the lower staff morale caused by the employment of spouses had affected the safety or efficiency of its operations.

Furthermore, the court noted, any problems associated with an employee's supervision of a spouse could be dealt with by a less-severe rule.

The appeals court also refused to find that the hiring of spouses would result in the employer being pressured to hire the spouses of employees. The employer failed to show how this alleged pressure would lower production or decrease safety, the court pointed out. In addition, the court placed on the employer the burden of showing that such pressure could not have been alleviated by a rule that did not have a discriminatory impact. This was a burden that the employer could not meet.

The Eighth Circuit in *Rath Packing* went on to distinguish its ruling from that in *Yuhas*. In *Yuhas*, the Seventh Circuit had found the employer's claim of business necessity sufficient to justify a no-spouse rule that resulted statistically in significant discrimination against women. The *Yuhas* court had not required the employer to demonstrate that the employment of spouses posed harm to its efficiency or safety. However, the Eighth Circuit pointed out that in *Yuhas* the court had indicated that its decision might have been different had intentional discrimination been established. In *Rath Packing*, the Eighth Circuit stressed, the district court had found intentional discrimination against women. Therefore, the appeals court said, the standard articulated in *Yuhas* would not be applicable to the facts in *Rath Packing*.

Sample Size

Plaintiffs who charge that a no-spouse rule has a disparate impact on female employees must show that the rule has harmed a significant number of such employees. In *Harper v. Trans World Airlines, Inc.* (CA 8, 1975, 11 FEP Cases 1074), a female spouse was discharged under a rule forbidding the employment of spouses in the same department. Under the policy, if two employees married they had to decide which one would transfer to another department, take a leave of absence, or resign. If the spouses failed to decide, the company was to discharge the least-senior employee.

A female airline employee had less seniority than the male employee she married, and she was discharged after she and her husband failed to select one of the alternative employment options offered under the company's policy. Alleging discriminatory impact, the female employee showed that in four of the five instances in which the rule had been invoked the wife was dismissed. The Eighth Circuit, however, refused to find this evidence sufficient to establish a disparate impact of discrimination. It noted that there was "little predictive value" to be derived from such an "extremely small" sample universe.

In upholding a policy similar to the one upheld in *Harper*, the U.S. Court of Appeals for the Tenth Circuit ruled that one previous discharge under a no-spouse rule was not sufficient to show disparate impact. Although it came to this conclusion because the evidence was insufficient, the court said it did so "reluctantly," observing that in practice no-spouse rules often result in discrimination against women, and they are generally unjustified. *(Thomas v. Metroflight,* CA 10, 1987, 43 FEP Cases 703)

Court Rulings & Constitutional Challenges

Public employees have challenged anti-nepotism rules on constitutional grounds. Plaintiffs who have alleged that such rules are unconstitutional usually have argued that these rules violate an individual's right to marry, which is protected by the due process clause of the Fifth and Fourteenth amendments to the U.S. Constitution. Pointing to this interference with a fundamental right, these plaintiffs have urged the courts to apply the "strict scrutiny" standard in determining the constitutionality of these rules. Under strict scrutiny, anti-nepotism rules can be upheld only if the court finds that a compelling state interest for them exists and that no less-intrusive rule will satisfy this compelling need.

The courts have been unwilling to conclude that anti-nepotism rules interfere with the right to marry. No-spouse rules have been found to be designed primarily to reduce conflict of interest and favoritism in the workplace, and therefore to impose only an indirect burden on the right to marry. The courts have refused to apply the strict scrutiny analysis to anti-nepotism rules, and they have required only that such rules have a rational basis.

In *Keckeisen v. Independent School District* (CA 8, 1975, 509 F.2d 1062, cert. den. 423 U.S. 833), the Eighth Circuit considered a constitutional challenge brought under the Ninth Amendment's right to privacy and the Fourteenth Amendment's equal protection clause. The case was filed by a dismissed male high school principal who challenged the school board's policy of prohibiting the employment of a husband and wife in an administrator-teacher relationship.

The court found that the policy did not deny anyone "the right to marriage," but only prohibited "the employment of married couples in administrator-teacher positions." The court explained that the purpose of the rule was to prevent conflicts of interest and favoritism so as to further the state's interest in providing a good education for its children. The court indicated that had the "right to marriage" claim been more directly involved in the school board's policy, the court may have reached "a different result."

The court, noting that the policy was designed to prevent apparently prejudicial arrangements that could harm the morale of other teachers, concluded that the rule was not "irrational, arbitrary or capricious." However, the court said if the plaintiff had shown that reasonable alternatives to accomplishing the school district's goals were available, it may have found the incidental burden on the right to marriage to have been less than the burden on the state.

In another case, a woman was forced to accept a transfer after her husband had been appointed as the head of her division. She alleged infringement of her right to freedom of marriage under the Fifth Amendment. The U.S. Court of Appeals for the District of Columbia Circuit agreed with the Eighth Circuit's analysis in *Keckeisen*, finding that the policy represented a reasonable regulation that did not interfere significantly with an individual's freedom to marry.

The court said anti-nepotism rules serve a "legitimate and laudatory role" in preventing conflicts of interest and favoritism in the workplace. According to the court, the rule placed only an "attenuated and indirect" burden on the right to marry. The court pointed out that the regulation did not prohibit the plaintiff's marriage, but only prevented her employment in a situation where she would necessarily have been subject to supervision by her husband. In addition, the court said the employer should not have the constitutional burden of waiting until a conflict of interest becomes a problem before it adopts a rule designed to prevent the problem. (*Cutts v. Fowler*, CA DC, 1982, 34 FEP Cases 698)

The U.S. Court of Appeals for the Ninth Circuit also has refused to find that a county's no-nepotism rule interfered with a fundamental right. In *Parsons v. County of Del Norte* (1984, 34 FEP Cases 571, 115 LRRM 3591, cert. den., 35 FEP Cases 1608, 117 LRRM 2552), an anti-nepotism rule prohibited the employment of a husband and wife in the sheriff's department. After her husband was hired as a deputy sheriff, a matron-dispatcher resigned rather than have her husband dismissed. She filed suit claiming the rule violated the due process and equal protection clauses of the Fourteenth Amendment, because it interfered with "her fundamental right in the marital status."

The court found that the plaintiff's right to marry was not threatened or unduly burdened by the rule. Citing *Cutts* and *Keckeisen*, it said the rule was rationally related to the county's goal of avoiding conflict of interest and favoritism in hiring, supervision, and allocation of duties.

The South Carolina Court of Appeals, applying an analysis similar to that used in *Parsons*, upheld a rule forbidding the employment of individuals who were related by blood or marriage to any member of the county school board. The court determined that a woman discharged under the rule had failed to show that it interfered with her right to marry. It pointed out that she had not demonstrated how the rule directly infringed on her rights to cohabitate, engage in sexual intercourse, or procreate. According to the court, the application of strict scrutiny analysis would be appropriate only where a rule "operates to preclude marriage entirely for a class of people." (*Hamilton v. Board of Trustees of Oconee County School District*, SC CtApps, 1984, 319 S.E.2d 717)

The U.S. Supreme Court recently silently affirmed the cases cited above when it decided not to review a constitutional challenge to a county's no-spouse rule that had prevented a female applicant from being considered for a sheriff dispatcher job. The plaintiff, who was the wife of a sheriff's deputy, had argued at trial that the rule raised an unreasonable classification in violation of her rights under the Fourteenth Amendment's equal protection clause. She pointed out that the rule did not apply to the spouses of county firefighters or to close family relatives other than spouses, and that it did not disqualify spouses from jobs other than dispatcher.

The U.S. District Court for the Eastern District of Wisconsin ruled that the county was required only to demonstrate a rational basis for its no-spouse rule to avoid violating the equal protection clause. In addition, the court found that the county reasonably believed that denying spouses of sheriff's deputies access to dispatcher jobs would "reduce the incidents of dangerous accidents and mishaps which can occur where the dispatcher's spouse is a police officer or sheriff's deputy." Furthermore, the court rejected the woman's argument that the rule violated her fundamental right to marry, finding that the policy was a reasonable public safety measure with minimal residual impact on the decision to marry. The court also noted that the policy had not deterred the plaintiffs from getting married. (*Sebetic v. Hagerty*, DC EWis, 1986, 41 FEP Cases 817)

The plaintiff petitioned the Supreme Court after the district court decision was affirmed by the U.S. Court of Appeals for the Seventh Circuit. She renewed her arguments that the no-spouse rule violated the Fourteenth Amendment and that the county could have used less drastic alternatives, such as varying shift assignments to ensure that a spouse would not have to dispatch her husband in an emergency situation. The Court declined to review the case. (*Heyden v. Schoenfeld*, No. 87-387)

A challenge to an anti-nepotism rule based on the First Amendment's right to freedom of association was brought successfully in the supreme court of Minnesota. A teacher alleged that she was not hired by a school district because of the political views of her husband, who was a member of a neighboring school board. The court held that if the teacher could establish that she was not hired due to her husband's memberships and opinions, she would establish a violation of her right to freedom of association and freedom of choice in marriage under the First and Fourteenth amendments. The right to associate with another person in marriage is a basic right, the court said. However, the court noted that "a teacher's associated freedom can be compromised at the school setting if outweighed by an appropriate concern of the public employer." (*Cybyske v. Independent School District No. 196*, Minn SupCt, 1987, 347 N.W.2d 256, cert den. 469 US. 933)

A public transit employer's no-spouse rule as applied to unmarried couples living together was upheld by the U.S. Court of Appeals for the Eighth Circuit, which rejected the contention that the policy under which the rule was adopted violated the individual's equal protection rights under the Fourteenth Amendment. The court found that the rule was a rational classification that was substantially related to the policy's objective of preventing employees from bringing their marital conflicts to the job, and thereby causing unsafe conditions on the streets. The court also found that the word "spouse" included individuals not legally married but living together with all the "attendant responsibilities and commitments of marriage." The court explained that application of the policy to such couples satisfied the underlying purpose of the rule. (*Espinoza v. Thoma*, CA 8, 1978, 17 FEP Cases 1362).

In a New Jersey case, a school board's anti-nepotism policy, which prevented the hiring of a second member of an immediate family, was attacked as a violation of the state's anti-discrimination law. An individual who was not hired because his father also worked in the school district claimed relief under the statute, which made unlawful any discrimination on the basis of "ancestry." The court rejected the claim, holding that the intent of the law was not to prevent discrimination based on specific family relationships, but to prohibit discrimination resulting from racial, religious, ethnic, or national ancestry shared by numerically significant segments of the population that historically have been the objects of discrimination. (*Whateley v. Leonia Board of Education*, NJ AppCt, 1976, 141 NJ Super. 476, 358 A.2d 826)

Marital Status Arguments

No-spouse rules have been attacked successfully under state employment discrimination laws. These laws prohibit discrimination on the basis of several classifications, including race, sex, religion, age, handicap, and national origin. In 23 states, discrimination on the basis of "marital status" also has been outlawed. (8A FEP Manual 451:102-104)

Some state courts have interpreted these laws narrowly when they were asked to apply them to no-spouse rules, whereas others have interpreted them broadly.

The Narrow Reading

Under the narrow interpretation, courts have refused to strike down no-spouse rules as being discrimination against "marital status." These courts have found that the statutes' purpose is to prevent employers from discriminating against individuals on the basis of whether they are married or not married, and does not extend protection to rules regarding to whom the individuals are married.

These states have reached this conclusion:

Michigan — The state supreme court has found that an employer's rule which prohibited the hiring of employees' spouses does not violate the Michigan Civil Rights Act. The court found no discrimination based on marital status, but simply different treatment based on the fact that the applicant's spouse worked in the same place as the applicant. The fact that the law forbade employers from inquiring about the marital status of an applicant was not dispositive, the court pointed out, because the no-spouse rule sought to uncover whether employees were married to other employees and not simply whether they were married. (*Whirlpool Corporation v. Michigan Civil Rights Commission*, Mich SupCt, 1986, 425 Mich. 527, 390 N.W. 2d. 625)

New Jersey — The state appellate court held that the state's anti-discrimination law was not violated when an employer used its anti-nepotism rule to dismiss a woman who worked in the same department as her husband. The court concluded that the woman was discharged due to her relationship to another employee and not because of her marital status. It noted that the company policy was directed to all employees, not just married ones, and the mere fact that the relative here happened to be a spouse did not violate the state's anti-discrimination law. (*Thompson v. Sanborn's Motor Express, Inc.*, 1977, NJ SuperCt, 30 FEP Cases 33)

New York — The state's highest court found that New York's anti-discrimination law referred only to an individual's status —whether married, separated, divorced, widowed, or single. It was not intended to forbid employment discrimination based on the marital relationship, only on the marital status. The policy promulgated by the plaintiff discriminated against those who were married to their supervisor, but not against those who were married, the court said. The law forbade employment discrimination based only on general marital status — either people who are not married or people who are married. The court found, however, that the state law would not prohibit employers from discriminating against employees who were married to supervisors. (*Manhattan Pizza Hut v. New York State Human Rights Appeal Board*, NY CtApp, 1980, 51 N.Y.2d 506, 415 N.E.2d 950, 434 N.Y.S.2d 961)

Hawaii — A U.S. district court applying Hawaii's Employment Practices Act adopted a narrow interpretation of the term "marital status," concluding that the law prohibits discrimination based on whether one is a married person, but does not protect relationships that "may have been coincidentally created by marriage." (*Moore v. Honeywell Information Systems*, Inc., DC Hawaii, 1983, 558 F. Supp. 1229)

The Broad Reading

Courts that have given their state's anti-discrimination statute a broad reading have extended the meaning of "marital status" to include the identity, situation, or occupation of the spouse. Under this broad interpretation, no-spouse rules, which by their nature discriminate against individuals by inquiring into the identity of their spouses, are implicated directly by these laws. For most courts, however, the inquiry does not end there. Unwilling to preclude entirely the validity of no-spouse rules, these courts have upheld rules if the employer can provide a *bona fide* occupational qualification for the rule, or prove that the rule is justified by business necessity.

This interpretation had been accepted in the following states:

Minnesota — The state supreme court held that a company's rule prohibiting the full-time hiring of more than one member of an immediate family was unlawful marital status discrimination under the state's Human Rights Act. The court said the term "marital status" includes the "identity or situation" of one's spouse. Although employers have the opportunity to justify their discriminatory policies, such justification requires that they demonstrate a "compelling and overriding" business necessity. To meet this burden, an employer "must advance a bona fide occupational qualification," the court said. (*Kraft, Inc. v. Minnesota Department of Human Rights*, Minn SupCt, 1979, 30 FEP Cases 31)

Washington — The state supreme court upheld a rule promulgated by the state's Human Rights Commission that made unlawful any employment discrimination based on an individual's marital status, who the individual's spouse is, or what the individual's spouse does for a living. The commission's rule had been issued under a state law that outlawed employment discrimination based on marital status. The court indicated that the commission had complied with the statute by establishing examples of what constituted a *bona fide* occupational qualification that could be asserted by an employer to uphold its anti-nepotism rule. Such examples included situations where a spouse supervises his or her spouse or audits the spouse's work, or where the spouses are in direct or potential competition with each other. (*Washington Water Power Co. v. Washington State Human Rights Commission*, Wash SupCt, 1978, 27 FEP Cases 1499)

Montana — The state supreme court ruled that the term marital status, as used in the state's Human Rights Act, includes the "identity and occupation of one's spouse." Montana is the only state to deny its employers an opportunity to justify their marital status discrimination. Even though a section of the law prohibits discrimination based on marital status unless "reasonable grounds" have been established, the court found that the section was not applicable to employment discrimination. (*Thompson v. Board of Trustees, School District No. 12*, Mont SupCt, 1981, 627 P.2d 1229)

Employers' Uses of Nepotism

Restrictions or bans on nepotism in employment usually are immune from attack. However, if such practices infringe upon a class of people that is protected because of its race, religion, age, or sex, a claim of direct discrimination or of disparate impact discrimination may be upheld. In addition, employers that violate their own anti-nepotism policies may be subject to lawsuits brought by their employees.

In *Kraszewski v. State Farm Insurance Co.* (DC NCal, 1985, 38 FEP Cases 197), an insurance company hired its agents' male relatives. The U.S. District Court for the District of Northern California held that the company's hiring practices discriminated against women, and that its male nepotism policy had "ensured that women were grossly underrepresented" in the company's sales force. Between 1970 and 1981, 383 of the company's agents had relatives also employed at the company. Of these relatives, 370 were male and only 13 were female.

Another court found that a union violated Title VII when it gave preference for work referrals to people who were related to permanent employees, because most of the relatives being referred were white. (*Gibson v. ILGWU*, Local 40, CA 9, 1976, 13 FEP Cases 997). However, a union local that gave preference in work referrals to people who were related to or sponsored by union members did not violate Title VII, because the alleged discrimination was not against a protected class (*Sogluizzo v. Local 817, Teamsters*, DC SNY, 1981, 28 FEP Cases 534).

In another case, the Supreme Court of South Carolina allowed a county employee to bring a lawsuit which asserted that a county nursing home administrator's hiring of his own wife as the home's assistant administrator violated the county's anti-nepotism ordinance. In holding that the employee had standing under the ordinance, the court recognized the employee's personal interest in the enforcement of the county law. *(Blandon v. Coleman,* SC SupCt, 1985, 285 SC 472, 330 S.E.2d. 298)

* * *

Romance in the Office

The workplace is not designed to accommodate people falling in love. Love is an irrational emotion; the workplace is supposedly built on a foundation of rationality. When co-workers — and particularly superiors and subordinates — fall in love or enter into sexual liaisons, the results can have far-reaching consequences. Love affairs definitely affect perceptions of co-workers, can affect productivity, and can have legal consequences. Most companies do not have formal policies forbidding dating, although the issue is sure to continue.

Background

ITEM: The romance between William Agee, chief executive officer of the Bendix Corp., Southfield, Mich., and his executive assistant, Mary Cunningham, generated headlines nationwide. Cunningham thereafter was promoted to vice president for corporate and public affairs and then to vice president for strategic planning. Eventually both Agee and Cunningham left the firm. They married, and currently have their own consulting business.

While most romantic relationships between co-workers seldom make news, such romances on any level in a corporate structure can create a groundswell of unease among co-workers and/or subordinates. According to experts interviewed for this report, romances between high-level executives cause nervousness among subordinates, who worry about:

- *Whether the liaison means unequal treatment for the other workers in the office.* This is especially the case if one member of the pair is a supervisor at a particular workplace, but it also may surface in situations where co-workers are dating, according to some experts. If other employees feel that the pair are looking for excuses to spend time together during work hours and are not pulling their fair share of the workload, resentment can build.

- *Whether the executives' thinking and decision-making abilities are clouded because they are in love.* Eliza G.C. Collins, a senior consulting editor at the Harvard Business School who has written extensively on the subject of office romances, told BNA that Agee, for example, lost his credibility when the romance with Cunningham became public. The view of others at Bendix, she said, was that "just because he fell in love, he's out of control."

- *If the balance of power in the corporation will be upset because of the personal alliance between the executive lovers.*

- *Whether the channels of communication will be scrambled both horizontally within departments and vertically within the corporate hierarchy.* Employees are concerned, said one expert, that if the romance ends, the workers will be left with divided loyalties — "like children in a divorce."

Romances between high-level executives, however, are only the tip of the iceberg. While such high-profile liaisons can have highly visible consequences at the workplace, analysis of survey research, as well as wide-ranging interviews conducted for this report, indicate that not every romance is disruptive. Several experts and corporate officials said if a romance between co-workers is handled well by the parties involved, it can improve rather than disrupt the work environment.

Most people still are not comfortable talking about the issue of office romance and how it affects the office atmosphere, according to Marcy Crary, an associate professor of management at Bentley College in Waltham, Mass.

Crary said the prevailing view seems to be that the issue is "personal, it's private." Romance in the office is a taboo subject, much like sexual harassment used to be, she said. For that reason, she indicated, many strong feelings remain suppressed and issues remain unresolved.

This may explain why executives interviewed for this report often said that as long as productivity is not affected, they usually view an office romance as being "none of my business." Ronald C. Pilenzo, president of the American Society for Personnel Administration, said if a romance does not affect a company's reputation or productivity, "Who cares?"

James Liddell, vice president for personnel at Rainier National Bank, Seattle, Wash., and Bev Pavlick, district manager, corporate policy and guidelines for AT&T, echoed this view. Said Liddell, "We do not try to get involved" unless "it gets to be a work problem." AT&T, Pavlick explained, does not have a formal policy on the matter. Any problems that arise affecting the work, she said, are treated as being another area to be dealt with by effective management.

Such relationships, however, are likely to occur more often — and more visibly — than in the past, with the influx of women into the workforce over the past 15 years into jobs of authority.

As noted by Mortimer R. Feinberg and Aaron Levinstein, who conducted a survey of 112 top executives in 1982, "The influx of women into management ranks has multiplied contacts between the sexes."

Corporate Trends

BNA's research and interviews found the following trends in this area:

- Most corporations do not have formal policies discouraging romances between employees of the same firm, even those companies that have formal policies against married couples working together *(see chapter on nepotism)*. Only a few, such as United Parcel Service *(see case study)*, actively discourage dating between employees.

This may be because a romance, unlike a marriage, is not a legal contract. One corporate human resources officer said "I'm not smart enough to know all the relationships we're trying to prevent." Several academic experts and corporate executives interviewed for this report said the same thing: "You can't stop it."

- The type of romance considered to be most disruptive of office routine and most negative in its consequences is an affair between a supervisor and a subordinate, especially when one or both of the lovers is married. These romances cause jealousy and suspicion among co-workers and can result in lowered productivity. Such involvements can lead to charges of favoritism, when the two parties to the romance are not of equal rank. Co-workers of the romantically linked pair, said one expert, can have feelings of "jealousy, anger and abandonment."

Rainier Bank's Liddell said that a superior/subordinate affair "definitely creates a problem in the office."

Collins observed, "There's no way a man who's a subordinate can compete with a female subordinate who's sleeping with the boss."

- Most romances between co-workers of equal rank are not disruptive to the workplace routine, unless the lovers spend too much time romancing, thus leading co-workers to believe they are not doing their fair share of the work.

The executives, researchers, and other experts interviewed for this report had wide-ranging views as to what should be done when an office romance is affecting the workplace negatively. Suggestions ranged from "do nothing and hope for the best," to having group counseling sessions with a psychologist on the subject as a preventive measure, to transferring and sometimes even terminating one of the lovers. Very few thought that one solution could be applied to all situations.

- Broken love affairs differ from sexual liaisons that end. In the latter case, the co-workers sometimes can resume their former roles as working colleagues. In the former case, often one of the partners in the broken love affair ends up leaving because of the discomfort involved in seeing the other person each day. Also, when a romance ends unhappily, an atmosphere of stress can result, not only for the couple, but also for their co-workers.

- When only one of the parties to the romance no longer is interested in continuing the relationship, what once was romance can become sexual harassment.

- Romantically involved co-workers can adversely affect other employees' productivity, when time is taken up in gossip, and in watching the lovers.

- An office romance that is known to others can have a strong and negative influence on the careers of those involved. Natasha Josefowitz, a management consultant who has written extensively on the subject of male-female interactions at work, counseled that when the lovers are of unequal rank, to avoid co-worker charges of favored treatment, the lower-ranked partner should be passed over for promotions and choice assignments — even when such advancements are deserved.

Logical Systems and Love

Some authorities have attempted to devise logical systems for dealing with relationships when — or even before — they occur. For example, Lois B. Hart and J. David Dalke, in their 1983 book *The Sexes at Work: Improving Work Relationships Between Men & Women*, recommended that people who are romantically involved with a co-worker ask themselves:

— How much do I really like this person with whom I am involved?

— Have I been seduced into a relationship because it is the thing *not* to do?

— What am I going to gain from this relationship?

— Is my work production suffering as a result of my involvement?

— Am I creating a situation at work that I may later regret?

— Is my willingness to be diverted caused by my low commitment to my job?

— Is there a lack of purpose and excitement in my life, which causes me to be susceptible and vulnerable?

Most experts interviewed by BNA, however, said that love is an irrational emotion that is difficult to deal with logically.

Different Approaches

Opinions vary widely on what corporations should do regarding intra-office romances.

Nancy Woodhull, president of Gannett New Media, the research and development section of Gannett Co., Inc., said problems associated with office romances are due largely to misperceptions by the pair's co-workers. Woodhull has presented seminars on dealing with intra-office romances, and has been interviewed extensively on the subject.

The co-workers of a romantically linked pair, she said, may feel that the relationship is causing an unfair advantage at the workplace for one of the parties, particularly if it is a superior/subordinate relationship. The reality, she said, is often that two co-workers (or superior and subordinate) who are dating "will stand on their heads sometimes to be fair" to others in the office.

Perhaps because of this, several experts said, supervisors should try to get their employees to express their concerns when an affair between two co-workers exists.

Like Woodhull, Crary said the other employees' negative perceptions will generate a new situation in the office that may result in one of the parties to the romance having to leave that office environment.

Woodhull nevertheless recommended that employers not "outlaw such relationships" because they will continue to occur, at least in part because of the large number of women who have entered the workforce in recent years.

Both Woodhull and Crary said two co-workers (or even superiors and subordinates) of the opposite sex dating has about the same effect on an office as two male co-workers (or superiors and subordinates) being close friends or having what Crary termed a "mentor/golden boy" relationship. In all such situations, they said, the two people share confidences, spend time together outside of work, and sometimes help each other at work. The only difference, said Woodhull, is that the male friends have no sexual relationship. But both Woodhull and Crary said co-workers get more upset and jealous when two co-workers are dating than when two male co-workers are close friends.

Because of the growing incidence of intra-corporate romance, even "no policy is a policy on this issue," according to an article in the October 1987 issue of the American Society for Personnel Administration's magazine, *Personnel Administrator*, entitled "Should Cupid Come to the Workplace?"

Authors Frank McLaughlin and Robert C. Ford noted that institutional involvement in love or sex in the work environment is not an easily resolved issue: "The extent that Cupid is allowed to operate in the workplace reflects an important dimension of the tradeoff between employee and organizational rights."

Channeling Energy

The late Kaleel Jamison, a consultant who advised corporations on such issues, felt that — when properly managed — sexual attraction in the office "can be not disruptive but actually energizing and productive within the organization." Several experts interviewed by BNA for this report pointed out that when sexual attraction is channeled into putting more energy into the work at hand, rather than into the liaison itself, work productivity improves.

Feinberg and Levenstein said the "legitimate" type of relationship — which they defined as courtship between two single persons — becomes a problem "only if the romance ends unhappily, creating an atmosphere of stress not only for the couple but for their co-workers."

Barry McCarthy, a Washington, D.C., psychologist who specializes in sexual and relationship problems, agreed, noting that he has had five clients in the past year who sought counseling to deal with the aftermath of a broken romance with a co-worker or fellow employee from another department. In these cases, McCarthy said, "it becomes an untenable situation" to try to re-establish a working colleague relationship, and one of the former lovers leaves for another job.

Collins thinks it is very difficult to work with someone with whom one has been in love — as opposed to someone with whom one has had a sexual liaison. She recommended that victims of broken love affairs with a co-worker should seek new jobs.

Two workers as cohabitants and illicit affairs involving one or more married partners were seen as being more of a problem by several experts, particularly when they involved superiors and subordinates.

Surveys, Studies, and Reports

Following is a review of surveys, studies, and reports on romance in the office:

Feinberg/Levenstein Survey (1982) — Mortimer Feinberg and Aaron Levenstein found in an informal survey of 112 executives that office-plant romances leading to marriage usually do not create problems. The executives expressed concern, however, about unmarried-couple relationships, particularly illicit affairs between married employees — especially when such affairs are between superiors and subordinates.

Fifty-seven of the 112 survey respondents said they "believe in a policy of absolute hands-off in cases of simple romance," while 39 said they do not believe in such a policy, and 16 did not answer. The authors added, however, that only 32 advised against intervening in "more complex relationships," while 62 supported intervention and 19 gave no answer.

Regarding illicit affairs and unmarried employees who are living together, 76 respondents said people in their organizations had been admonished by their superiors to "observe caution" and 50 said warnings were issued to discontinue the relationship. Twelve said the relationship was penalized by a denial of promotion; 20 indicated that other action, including discharge, had been taken. Thirty-two said sexual involvements had led to charges of favoritism, while 52 reported no such experience.

On two other possible negative effects of office romances, 44 said "scandal mongering" had resulted, while 41 said it had not. Forty-five said morale had been undermined, and 43 said it had not.

Feinberg and Levenstein noted that companies often will tolerate such relationships if they do not impinge on workplace productivity:

> Many companies will tolerate a relationship between superior and subordinate if it: is not conducted on company premises; does not utilize company facilities, such as a company-rented apartment; involves no company funds, for example, use of business credit cards or expense accounts to entertain a sex partner; does not divert energy from effective work performance; is not furthered on company time; does not damage the company's public image; and is not deliberately flaunted in a way that offends the sensibilities of others in the organization.

Hart and Dalke (1983) — In their 1983 book, *The Sexes at Work: Improving Work Relationships Between Men & Women,* Lois B. Hart and J. David Dalke concluded that men "see sexual attractiveness on the job as a bigger problem than women do — it is the one area where men experience a lessening of power."

Hart and Dalke distributed questionnaires in August 1981 to 300 women professionals and 200 men professionals. They received 55 responses from men and 92 from women.

In response to the question, "Is one excessively distracted when sexually attracted to someone of the opposite gender at work?," 32 percent of the men said yes, compared to only 17 percent of the women.

Fortune 500 Survey (1985) — A survey sent by researcher Rose Ann Swartz to human resources managers at 220 *Fortune* 500 companies (industrial and non-industrial) yielded 37 responses. Ninety-four percent of the respondents said they had not developed formal policies regarding personal/romantic relationships. A plurality of 36 percent said their companies tried to overlook such relationships, and 18 percent said they felt that any problems would resolve themselves. Only 6 percent said they gave any orientation or instruction to new employees about such relationships. Fifty-two percent said when lovers marry, the company alters its approach to the situation. Human resources managers at the 37 participating firms annually dealt with an average of five romantic/personal relationships among employees.

Business Horizons Survey (1986) — *Business Horizons* magazine surveyed 249 undergraduate students in an introductory management course and 102 part-time evening students in masters of business administration courses at a large state university. The findings were contained in an article in the July/August 1986 issue of the magazine, entitled "What Do Tomorrow's Managers Think About Sexual Intimacy in the Workplace?"

The students were asked to rate on a seven-point scale the extent of their agreement with 18 statements, ranging from "strongly disagree" (1) to "strongly agree" (7). According to the author of the survey, Gary N. Powell, a professor of management and organization at the University of Connecticut, the survey results reveal "an uneasy coexistence between sexual intimacy and work."

The survey found some differences between the views of men and women on beliefs concerning sexual intimacy in the workplace.

For example, the men surveyed averaged 3.58 on the statement "Some sexual intimacy among coworkers can create a more harmonious work environment," while women averaged 2.95 on that question. On the statement, "A person's personal life is not the business of management," women scored 5.77 and men scored 5.18. Women felt more strongly (5.64) than men (4.97) that "Management should take strong steps to discourage sexual propositions toward coworkers."

However, both men (5.53) and women (5.95) felt strongly that "Supervisors who direct sexual attention toward their subordinates should be reprimanded."

Those surveyed found less wrong with getting "intimately involved" with a co-worker than with a supervisor. The composite rating to the question regarding a co-worker was 3.51 and for a supervisor was 4.43.

Both men and women agreed fairly strongly (5.15) with the statement, "It is all right for someone to look for a marriage partner at work."

American Society For Personnel Administration Survey (1987) — The ASPA survey indicated that personnel managers perceive affairs between superiors and subordinates to be more of a problem for the organization than affairs between co-workers. For example, only 9.8 percent of respondents said they believed that eventually an affair between two equal co-workers will evolve into a claim of sexual harassment, but the percentage rose to 30.3 percent for affairs between a manager and a subordinate.

This survey of 1,100 ASPA members — human resource professionals in a wide range of organizations — yielded 245 usable responses. Nearly one-third of those surveyed agreed with the statement that "when co-workers become romantically involved, their job performance suffers." A plurality of 42.8 percent agreed with the statement, "A known office romance has a strong and negative influence on the careers of those involved."

Slightly more than half of those surveyed agreed that "With so many men and women working together, it is common to see professional interest turn into romantic attraction." Nearly 70 percent agreed that "There is really nothing the organization can do to stop romantic attractions between men and women working together." Yet, 42.4 percent said that "It is part of a supervisor's job to recognize and counsel subordinates who are romantically involved."

The study's authors concluded the survey showed that "personnel managers are concerned and are looking for some help in developing workable, defensible guidelines for dealing with Cupid when he comes to the workplace."

Men's Health Magazine Readership Survey (1987) — Surveys filled out by 444 readers of *Men's Health*, with results tabulated in the fall 1987 issue, focused on the degree of sexuality the respondents perceived to be present in the workplace. The magazine stressed that the study was not a scientific random sample, since it was the result of a mail-in survey from a previous issue of the magazine, and thus was self-selecting.

Among the findings:

— Fifty-seven percent of respondents said they had been sexually propositioned by someone at work.

— Eighteen percent said they had had sex with a co-worker during working hours, and 26.1 percent said they had had sex in their place of work.

— About one-third of the sample said men should report for sexual harassment women who act or dress in a sexually provocative way in the workplace. However, 60.4 percent agreed with a statement that all other things being equal, they would hire someone of the opposite sex who was sexy over someone who was not.

BNA Panel (1987) — As part of this report, BNA asked a group of nine academicians, authors, and corporate officials knowledgeable about office romances:
— Are office romances a negative force in the workplace?
— When they are a negative force, what is the major reason?
— What is the best way to ensure that office romances are not a negative force in the workplace?
The experts included Eliza G.C. Collins, senior consulting editor at the Harvard Business School and author of a widely discussed article on the subject; Marcy Crary, associate professor, Department of Management, Bentley College, Waltham, Mass.; Natasha Josefowitz, management consultant and author; and James Liddell, vice president, personnel administration, Rainier National Bank.

Also, Bev Pavlick, district manager, corporate policy and guidelines, AT&T; Ronald C. Pilenzo, president, American Society for Personnel Administration; Leslie Westoff, author of the book *Corporate Romance*; Joan Wexler, associate dean and professor of law, Brooklyn Law School; and Nancy Woodhull, president, Gannett New Media, and organizer of corporate seminars on the topic.

Although much has been written about the potential problems that can arise when co-workers become involved romantically, none of the panel members said such romances always have a negative impact on the workplace. Panel members said the effect of office romances on the workplace could be positive, neutral, or negative only in certain specific cases.

Westoff said office romances, "if they're handled properly [are] extremely positive." She noted that people who are in love are happy to come to work, are willing to work longer hours, and are not rushing out the door to get ready for a date.

Collins said romances between co-workers are "humanizing" to the office environment. They are, she said, "quite natural."

Nearly all panel members agreed that office romances have negative effects on the workplace when two people are in the same office and one is higher-ranking than the other, a view that is reflected in survey research. They said, however, that negative consequences often arise not so much out of the actions of the couple themselves, but from negative perceptions and jealousy on the part of their co-workers.

Panel members differed considerably on the best course of action to take to ensure that office romances are not a negative force in the workplace. All agreed that forbidding employees to date each other is not a feasible solution, because the employees will do it, anyway.

Collins said in most instances the best course of action is to do nothing and hope for the best. Westoff recommended that companies hold psychologist-led "awareness sessions" on the issue, in which employees discuss their fears. Josefowitz advocated a preventive approach. She said couples who are dating should be very discreet, so as not to engender jealousy among their co-workers.

Woodhull and Pilenzo emphasized the role of the supervisor in diffusing tension caused by an office romance. Woodhull said good management and open communication on the issue improve such situations. Pilenzo said supervisors must sit down and talk with the couple, if their behavior toward each other is disrupting the office. Crary and Wexler advocated that situations be treated on a case-by-case basis; they said sometimes a transfer of one of the parties is necessary. Pavlick also advocated a case-by-case approach, with the supervisor playing an active role in trying to resolve any problems.

Legal Developments

Problems caused by the "boss" demanding sexual favors from his or her employees may be as old as the employment relationship itself (see chapter on sexual harassment). However, in the modern workplace, dating between bosses and their employees, between co-workers, and between employees and workers at competing firms, as well as bans or limits on such dating, may spawn lawsuits based on one of several possible causes of action.

In one, a derivative of the traditional sexual harassment suit, individuals allege that they lost promotions or other work benefits because their employer gave special consideration to another employee with whom their supervisor was having a sexual relationship.

Another cause of action arises when an employer prohibits its employees from dating each other. No-dating policies have been attacked by public employees as an unlawful infringement on their right to privacy, and by private employees who, when fired for disobeying them, claim that their dismissals were unjust and exceeded the legal limits of the employment-at-will doctrine.

Where employers have disciplined the female member of a dating co-worker couple and not the male, sexual discrimination charges have been filed. Employees fired for dating co-workers also have cited state laws prohibiting employment discrimination based on "marital status."

A review of current law and the most significant court rulings on workplace romance reveals that:

- Employers usually may prohibit dating in their work environment. As with anti-nepotism rules, employers have justified their no-romance policies by asserting that dating and romantic relationships interfere with company morale, risk creating favoritism or the appearance of it in hiring, assignment, and promotion decisions, and may result in reduced work productivity by the couples involved. However, several employee challenges to dating bans have been upheld.

- Thus far, no court has found that discrimination based on a dating relationship is equivalent to discrimination based on marital status. However, some courts recognize that dating relationships spur the same arguments employers use to justify rules prohibiting married couples from being employed in the same workplace: harm to employee morale, favoritism, and reduced productivity. But these courts have ruled that marital status discrimination laws only protect and further the sanctity of marriage, and they do not apply to dating.

- Romantic relationship prohibitions on public workers may infringe on their right to privacy and, therefore, be subject to court decisions on employees' constitutional claims under a strict scrutiny standard. Rules prohibiting dating among employees probably will be upheld, although three current U.S. Supreme Court justices have opposed them. However, in cases involving romantic relationships between public employees and non-employees, where no harm to the employer or the employee's work performance is established, a constitutional challenge probably would succeed. A ban on activity not protected by the right to privacy will be upheld if it has a rational basis.

- Where an employee submits to the sexual advances of a supervisor and is granted a promotion or some other employment benefit because of that submission, another employee who is harmed by the favoritism has a right of action under Title VII of the Civil Rights Act of 1964, which bars discrimination on the basis of sex. However, it is not clear whether such a right of action exists if the favored employee has entered into the sexual relationship willingly and without coercion. Title VII can be invoked only if the affair in question involves a sexual relationship, although the plaintiff is required only to present circumstantial evidence, not direct evidence, of such a relationship.

Romance and Employment-at-Will

Under the employment-at-will doctrine, an employer has, absent a collective bargaining agreement or an individual employment contract, the right to discharge an employee for good reason or no reason. In recent years, state courts have recognized certain exceptions to this judicial doctrine, and have permitted recovery based on wrongful discharge. These exceptions have included discharges that violated a state law or a municipal ordinance, public policy, an implied employment contract, or an implied covenant of good faith and fair dealing.

Some employees have used this "erosion" of the employment-at-will doctrine to challenge discharges based on their romantic relationships. In 1984, the California Court of Appeals cited the covenant of good faith and fair dealing exception in upholding a $200,000 jury award in favor of a woman discharged for dating an employee of a competing firm. The court found that the employer, through the actions of one of its managers, had breached this covenant when it failed to apply equally its written policy requiring that its supervisors respect the privacy rights of its employees unless clear evidence exists that the employee's off-duty conduct was harming the company.

Under California law, implicit in any contract of indefinite duration is an underlying principle requiring an employer to deal openly and fairly with its employees, the court said. The company's written policy of protecting the private affairs of its employees had created just such an employment contract.

The jury's findings were supported by substantial evidence, according to the court. The company had no rule against socializing with competitors, the court noted, and although the policy did permit discharge for conflict of interest, the jury found no such conflict. (*Rulon-Miller v. IBM*, Calif CtApp, 1984, 117 LRRM 3309).

Other suits asserting exceptions to the employment-at-will doctrine have not been successful, however. In *Crozier v. UPS* (Calif CtApp, 1983, 115 LRRM 3585) a manager was discharged for dating a non-manager in violation of the company's policy prohibiting fraternization between management and non-management employees. The California Court of Appeals found no grounds for an exception to the doctrine. The company's policy legitimately was concerned with the appearance of favoritism and possible claims of sexual harassment, as well as employee dissension created by romantic relationships between management and non-management employees, the court found.

In articulating whether good cause existed for dismissal, the court explained that it was necessary to balance the employer's interest in operating its business efficiently and profitably with the interest of an employee in maintaining his employment, and that it also must consider the public's interest in maintaining a proper balance between the two. In balancing these factors, the court noted that the plaintiff had been warned to stop the relationship and that the company had been consistent in applying the policy. The court also noted that the public had an interest in preventing sexual harassment and favoritism in the workplace.

In addition, the court rejected the claim that the employer did not act in good faith toward the plaintiff. The court noted that the plaintiff had promoted the women he was dating. It was clear to the court that the company's morale had been harmed, since co-workers had complained of favoritism and were considering bringing claims of sexual harassment.

The Wisconsin Court of Appeals also rejected an action by an unmarried employee who was discharged for living with another unmarried employee. The relationship disrupted the workplace, the court found. In addition, it said the employee had not been discharged for attempting to exercise any guaranteed statutory or constitutional right or for performing a public duty. The court would not second-guess the employer's business judgment absent an allegation that it violated some clearly defined and well-established public policy (*Ward v. Frito-Lay, Inc.*, Wis CtApp, 1980, 115 LRRM 4320).

In another case, the Wisconsin Supreme Court ruled that an employer did not violate public policy by discharging an employee for, among other things, engaging in an open affair with his secretary (*Brockmeyer v. Dun & Bradstreet* Wis SupCt, 1983, 115 LRRM 4484). The employee had alleged that the discharge violated the state's public policy of encouraging the prevention of injury to business or the pursuit of work. At worst, the employee was discharged in bad faith, which was unprotected by the state's narrow public policy exception to the employment-at-will doctrine, the court said.

In a third case, a manager filed an action in U.S. District Court for Western Pennsylvania after he was discharged following complaints from co-workers about his personal relationship with a subordinate worker (*Rodgers v. IBM*, DC WPa, 1980, 115 LRRM 4608). The manager alleged that his right to privacy had been infringed, but the court held that no public policy was violated by the discharge. The employer had a legitimate interest in preserving harmony among its employees and in avoiding the disruption of its normal operating procedures, the court said.

The court explained that under the employment-at-will doctrine an employee may be discharged for good reason or for no reason, but not for illegitimate reasons. However, the employee had presented no illegal reason for his discharge, and, therefore, no exception to the employment-at-will doctrine existed. Similarly, an employer's discharge of two management employees for dating was upheld by the Alaska Supreme Court, because the relationship disrupted and lowered employee morale (*Somers v. Westours, Inc.*, Alaska SupCt, 1986, 1 Individual Employment Rights Cases 1479).

A wrongful discharge action based on a dating rule violation also was rejected by the Oregon Supreme Court in *Patton v. J.C. Penney Co.* (Ore SupCt, 1986, 122 LRRM 2445). In finding no exception to the employment-at-will doctrine, the court noted that the manager, who had been discharged for dating a co-worker, had not alleged that his discharge was related to his pursuit of any statutory rights related to his employment status, and had not alleged "interference with an interest of public importance equal or analogous to serving on a jury or avoiding false, defamatory remarks." In addition, the court rejected the manager's claim that his right to privacy had been violated, saying that such an assertion "blurs 'rights' against governmental infringement with 'rights' against a private employer." The manager's activity was voluntary, and he was subject to discharge at the whim of his employer, the court added.

In *Patton*, the discharge was upheld even though the company had no written policy prohibiting employee dating and it did not show that the dating had interfered with the manager's work performance. However, the employer had asked the manager to discontinue the relationship.

In *Schuermann v. American KA-RO Corp.* (SC SupCt, 1986, 1 Individual Employment Rights Cases 1360) such a warning became the crucial defense against a wrongful discharge claim. The employer appealed a jury's award of damages to an executive whom it found had been wrongfully discharged for having an adulterous affair with the wife of another employee. The South Carolina Supreme Court remanded the case to the appeals court, instructing the lower court to determine whether the executive had been warned not to engage in such "affairs inside the company." According to the supreme court, if such a warning had been issued, the discharge would be for just cause, based on the executive's disloyalty and disobedience.

In a recent Oregon case, the state supreme court heard a claim involving sexual harassment committed by the son of the company's owner against a female employee. The court upheld a jury's finding that the son intentionally had interfered with the employee's contractual employment relationship. (*Lewis v. Oregon Beauty Supply Co.*, Ore SupCt, 1987, 733 P. 2d. 430, 302 Or. 616).

The plaintiff had been dating the owner's son. When she informed the son that she planned to date other men in addition to him, he became jealous and hostile toward her. He physically and verbally intimidated her, threatened her, defamed her to other employees, and purposefully interfered with her job performance. Despite her efforts to have the owner stop his son's misconduct, the harassment continued. Finally, she quit her job and filed a state court action alleging intentional interference with her employment relationship.

The court found that the employment-at-will relationship that existed between the company and the worker created an employment contract with which the son intentionally had interfered. However, it found that the owner did not know of the specific acts engaged in by his son and, therefore, was not liable. Furthermore, the court found the company was not liable under this cause of action, since it was not possible for the firm to interfere with an employment contract to which it was a party.

Marital Status Discrimination

In Michigan, a female employee brought suit under the state's fair employment practices law, which prohibits discrimination on the basis of marital status. She alleged that she had been discharged as a result of her romantic relationship with a fellow employee, whereas he was not fired. The court found no sexual discrimination and noted that the employer had been put into a difficult situation. The wife of the male employee informed the employer's owner that her husband and the plaintiff had previously engaged in an affair, and that she did not want her husband working in the same building with the plaintiff. When the owner confronted the male employee he decided to resign to save his marriage. Because the male employee was valuable to the firm and had key skills, the owner decided to discharge the plaintiff rather than accept her former lover's resignation.

The employer was in an "irremediable dilemma" in that whatever it did it would lose one of the employees, the court said. It concluded that the employer chose to discharge the female employee not because of her sex but because she was less skilled and less trained. The plaintiff was unable to cite any other similarly situated male employee who was treated differently than she (*C. Thorrez Industries v. Mich Dept. of Civil Rights*, Mich CtApp, 1979, 24 FEP Cases 113).

In another case, a city ordinance that prohibited employment discrimination on the basis of marital status was cited when an employee was discharged for having an affair with his married secretary.

The employer had a long-established work rule forbidding any "romantic association" between any employee with a married employee of the opposite sex. The court held that the rule did not affect one's marital status. The rule applied equally to married and unmarried employees, since either would violate it by being involved in an extramarital affair with another employee. The rule prohibited a course of conduct rather than a status, the court concluded.

The employee argued that the rule did not prohibit associations outside of work between single employees and, therefore, placed a greater restriction on the conduct of married employees than single employees. However, the court was satisfied that the work rule was justified, since it compelled conformity with the public policy of prohibiting extramarital affairs (*Federated Rural Electric Ins. Co. v. Kessler*, Wis SupCt, 1986, 388 N.W.2d. 553, 131 Wis.2d 189).

Where a female employee and a male employee were advised to end their dating relationship or one would be discharged, the female, who held a lower-paid island attendant position, resigned to protect her male companion, a district manager. Subsequently, she filed an action under Michigan's fair employment practice statute claiming that her dating relationship was akin to a marital relationship and therefore protected under the law's prohibition against employment discrimination based on marital status. The court, however, refused to extend the act's protection to non-spousal relationships. (*Sears v. Ryder Truck Rental*, DC Mich, 1984, 41 FEP Cases 1347)

Public Employees' Rights

Rules promulgated by public employers prohibiting dating among employees have been attacked as an infringement of constitutional rights. In *Shawgo v. Spradlin* (CA 5, 1983, 1 IER Cases 164, cert den., 1 IER Cases 174) two police officers were suspended and demoted for cohabiting. The U.S. Court of Appeals for the Fifth Circuit found that the police department's disciplinary action did not infringe upon the couple's right to privacy. The court said the right to privacy is not unqualified, adding that the state had significant interest in regulating the activities of its employees. Furthermore, it found a rational connection between the department's punishment here and its interest in forbidding "members of a quasi-military unit, especially those different in rank, from sharing an apartment or from cohabiting." No evidence was presented that the officers had not performed their jobs while dating, that the public had been aware of their relationship, or that the officers had violated any state law.

Although the U.S. Supreme Court refused to hear the case (*Whisenhunt v. Spradlin*, US SupCt, 1 IER Cases 174), Justice Brennan, along with Justices Marshall and Blackmun, filed a dissent to the Court's decision not to grant certiorari. According to Brennan, the officers' relationship raised questions of fundamental rights, since the conduct involved "intensely personal decisions." Because the petitioners' conduct involved such rights, it could be abridged only to the extent necessary to achieve strong, clearly articulated state interests, he said. Although Brennan noted that "public employers in general and police departments in particular, may well deserve considerable latitude in enforcing codes of conduct," here, where the officers had never been warned that their cohabitation could result in discipline, it was not possible for the police department to apply its rule effectively or fairly.

Right to Privacy

In *Hollenbaugh v. Carnegie* (DC WPa, 1977, 436 F.Supp. 1328, aff'g , CA 3, 1978, 578 F.2d 1374, cert den., US SupCt, 1978, 439 U.S. 1052) a claim alleging violation of the right to privacy under the First, Fourth, Ninth, and Fourteenth Amendments to the U.S. Constitution was rejected in an action brought by two library employees who were discharged for engaging in "open adultery" with each other. According to the trial court, personal rights encompassing and protecting personal intimacies of the home, the family, motherhood, procreation, and child rearing were included in the Constitution's guarantee of personal privacy. Any right that the two had in living together was to be balanced against the library's interest in being able to perform its function properly in the community. Since evidence showed that members of the community were aware of and objected to the librarians' living arrangement, the court found the discharge was not arbitrary, unreasonable, or capricious and, therefore, did not violate their equal protection rights under the Fourteenth Amendment.

Similarly, in *Suddarth v. Slane* (DC WesternVa, 1982, 539 F.Supp. 612), a police officer's adultery was held not protected by the First Amendment's right to privacy or freedom of association.

The U.S. Court of Appeals for the Sixth Circuit has, however, upheld a trial court's finding that a married police officer's right to privacy was violated when he was discharged for cohabiting with a woman other than his wife (*Briggs v. Northern Muskegon Police Department*, DC WMich, 1983, 563 F.Supp. 585, aff'g, CA 6, 1984, 746 F.2d 1475, cert den., US SupCt, 1985, 473 U.S. 909). The trial court held that without persuasive evidence that the cohabitation had an adverse impact on the police officer's work performance, the relationship was beyond the department's regulation.

In *Thorne v. City of El Segundo* (CA 9, 1983, 726 F.2d 459, cert den., US SupCt, 1984, 469 U.S. 979) the U.S. Court of Appeals for the Ninth Circuit held that private, off-duty personal activities were protected by the constitutional guarantees of privacy and association unless it was shown that such activity affected job performance. The court found a police department's interrogation of a female applicant concerning her sexual conduct, including her affair with a married member of the force, to be a violation of her right to privacy.

When a private employee alleged that his constitutional right to privacy and freedom of association had been violated due to his discharge for attending a business convention with a woman other than his wife, a U.S. district court was not sympathetic. The court held that although freedom of association is an important social right and one that ordinarily should not dictate employment decisions, here the discharge was not a threat to "some recognized facet of public policy." (*Staats v. Ohio National Life Inc. Co.*, DC WPa, 1985, 118 LRRM 3242).

Title VII Cases

According to regulations issued by the U.S. Equal Employment Opportunity Commission:

> Where employment opportunities or benefits are granted
> because of an individual's submission to the employer's
> sexual advances or requests for sexual favors the employer
> may be held liable for unlawful sex discrimination against
> other persons who were qualified for but denied that
> employment opportunity or benefit." (*EEOC Guidelines*, 29
> C.F.R. 0061604.11(g)).

Following these guidelines, a U.S. district court in Delaware held
that a Veterans Administration hospital had violated Title VII when
the chief of the hospital's administrative division conditioned his
selection of a chief medical administration assistant on the receipt of
sexual favors and selected for the promotion a woman who had
engaged in an affair with him. The plaintiff, a female who was not
selected for the job, earlier had refused the sexual advances of the
supervisor.

In her pleading, she alleged that her discrimination was based on
"sex" within the scope of Title VII. She argued that to get the
promotion, a woman was required to grant sexual favors, while this
condition was not imposed on males who sought the promotion. The
court rejected the supervisor's claim that he hired the most qualified
employee, finding that the qualifications of the woman promoted
were not superior to those of the plaintiff (*Toscano v. Nimmo*, DC
Del, 1983, 32 FEP Cases 1401).

A sexual relationship between a supervisor and another employee,
however, does not automatically provide co-workers with grounds
for a sex discrimination lawsuit, since it must be shown that the
sexual relationship resulted in some favoritism, promotion, or the
replacement of another worker (*Anderson v. Univ. Health Center*,
DC WPa, 41 FEP Cases 1197).

Although sexual favoritism may provide an avenue for judicial
redress via a Title VII discrimination action, the scope of such actions remains in conflict.

Under one view, supported by the U.S. Court of Appeals for the
District of Columbia, the mere fact that a sexual relationship was a
substantial reason for an individual receiving an employment benefit
is sufficient to support a discrimination action by another individual
who is harmed by this favoritism. In *King v. Palmer* (CA DC, 1985,
39 FEP Cases 877) a nurse employed by the District of Columbia jail
brought suit under Title VII after she failed to obtain a promotion to
a supervisory position. She alleged that the individual who received

the promotion had been so rewarded because of her sexual involvement with the hiring supervisor.

The U.S. district court concluded that the nurse had made out a
prima facie case of discrimination, since the sexual relationship had
been a substantial factor in the promotion decision (DC DC, 35 FEP
Cases 1302). It also found that the defendant's explanation for its
hiring decision was clearly a pretext. Nevertheless, the court ruled in
favor of the defendant, saying that the woman had failed to submit
direct proof that the sexual relationship between the successful applicant and the hiring supervisor had been consummated.

The District of Columbia Circuit reversed, ruling that the plaintiff
was not required to show direct proof of the sexual consummation.
It was sufficient, the court said, that the plaintiff had presented
evidence to enable the court to infer that some form of sexual
relationship between the woman who was promoted and the supervisor had been a substantial factor in the promotion.

The court pointed out that an action under Title VII lies whenever
discrimination is based on "sex." Here, the court found that the
plaintiff had been the victim of sexual discrimination, even though
no allegations were made that the plaintiff had been required to
submit to the supervisor's advances, or that the sexual relationship
in question had been entered into involuntarily. Thus, the court implied that when favoritism is the result of a sexual relationship, such
discrimination has been based on "sex."

Consistent with the notion that favoritism based solely on a sexual
relationship may establish a cause of action under Title VII is the
decision in *Kersul v. Skulls Angels, Inc.* (DC SNY, 1985, 42 FEP
Cases 987). There the U.S. district court held that an employee had
stated a claim under Title VII by alleging that she was denied
favorable benefits and terms and conditions of employment because
her supervisor favored another employee with whom he had a sexual
relationship. However, the court noted that the plaintiff's complaint,
which alleged that the favoritism was due to a "close personal
relationship," was insufficient, and allowed her to amend her complaint to allege that the favoritism was the result of a "sexual
relationship." Neither the plaintiff in *King* or *Kersul* alleged that they
were propositioned by their supervisors, nor was it shown that the
individuals promoted had entered into the relationship involuntarily.

However, the U.S. Court of Appeals for the Second Circuit has expressed a conflicting view, ruling that an employment preference for
a particular individual, as opposed to a class of individuals, does not
violate Title VII. In *Decinto v. Westchester County Medical Center*

(CA 2, 1986, 42 FEP Cases 921), seven male respiratory therapists were denied a promotion to a newly created supervisory position. They alleged sexual discrimination because the requirements of the position were created specifically for a male officer's female companion, and each of them lacked the required qualifications.

The court found that the officer had discriminated against the staff therapists by preferring his sexual partner for the position. However, the court refused to find that a cause of action under Title VII had been established. The officer's discrimination was due to his preference for the woman he selected for the job and was not discrimination because of the plaintiffs' gender, the court explained. The court pointed out that all individuals who might have wanted the job, both male and female, had been discriminated against. Mere favoritism based on a sexual relationship would not trigger relief under Title VII, the court found. Only where the individual promoted is forced to submit to a sexual relationship to obtain a benefit or promotion would the statute be implicated. In situations such as the one before the court, where the relationship was consensual, the court said it would not find sexual harassment discrimination.

Prima Facie Case Rebuttal

A plaintiff's *prima facie* case of discrimination may be rebutted by an employer. In one case, a woman charged that she had been the victim of sexual discrimination when she was discharged for dating a general manager at her company. The Kansas Supreme Court found that she had established a *prima facie* case of discrimination by showing that she and not the general manager had been discharged. However, the employer presented valid business reasons for her discharge, claiming that the woman had been discourteous and unreliable. Since she was unable to show that the employer's rebuttal was a mere pretext, the court found no sex discrimination (*Reber v. Mel Falley, Inc.*, Kan SupCt, 1984, 683 P.2d 1229, 235 Kan. 562).

* * *

Sexual Harassment

The legal treatment of sexual harassment of employees — once considered either an unmentionable topic or a humorous one — has been revolutionized by the enactment of Title VII of the Civil Rights Act of 1964. Before this statute was adopted, sexual harassment was something that a female employee endured or tried to escape, because she had virtually no legal weapons to stop it. Title VII provided the legal weapons, but the statute, in fact, was in place for a decade before women began to think that its ban on sex discrimination might be broad enough to encompass sexual harassment.

Enactment of the statute had a two-fold effect: It provided a basis for the development of legal principles to fight sexual harassment at the same time that it invalidated barriers to greater female participation in the labor market, thereby increasing the opportunities to apply the principles. By making it easier for women to enter jobs formerly held only by men, the statute expanded the opportunities for conflict between the sexes.

Sexual harassment cases take up a larger percentage of the cases reported in *Fair Employment Practice Cases* than ever before. Volume 44 of FEP Cases — which covered a four-month period in 1987 — carries the text of 19 decisions concerned with some facet of the subject. In contrast, the first 20 volumes of the reporting service, covering from 1938 until mid-1979, contain a total of only 25 sexual harassment decisions.

Although sexual harassment has existed in the workplace ever since persons of opposite sexes came into contact there, it did not become a subject of judicial interest until women began to realize that Title VII might provide a remedy. Twenty years ago the subject was barely discussed; 14 years ago the first reported decision was handed down (and it treated on-the-job sexual harassment by a supervisor as not involving the employer. Today, courts everywhere are discussing the fine points of liability, and conferences across the country put the subject on their brochures as a selling point.

There are two generally recognized ways of analyzing sexual harassment claims. One is hostile work environment harassment in which an employee is subjected to unpleasant treatment of a sexual nature by a supervisor, a co-worker, or a customer. The other is known as *quid pro quo* harassment and involves retaliation in the form of a job action by a supervisor against an employee for refusing to acquiesce to harassment. There is little dispute at this time about the *quid pro quo* form of sexual harassment. Courts generally agree that an employer is automatically liable for the untoward acts of its supervisors — even if higher management does not know about them — when the consequences are denial of a promotion or salary increase, an unwanted transfer, or a discharge.

The subject of hostile environment harassment is more controversial. It is unsettled whether actual knowledge by higher management of the supervisor's conduct is necessary to establish employer liability. Furthermore, there is no judicial consensus on how much harassment there has to be before the requisite pattern of harassment can be said to exist; hostile environment harassment is one of the rare forms of illegal conduct for which liability does not attach on the basis of a single act that could be regarded as unlawful. Once is not enough. Furthermore, much of the time that the courts spend on the subject involves the issue of whether the conduct in question was actually unwelcomed.

Sexual harassment is difficult to analyze — and to devise preventive measures for — because it is often subjective in nature, dealing as it does with emotions, words, and gestures, all of which can have overtones and undertones very different from a neutral report of the conduct at issue. Frequently, the legal issue begins when the target employee's reactions do not match the initiating employee's expectations. When a supervisor puts his arms around a subordinate, she may not necessarily be pleased.

The law can tell employers and employees, after the fact, that certain conduct was illegal. But a workplace rule against sexual harassment is not like one against a practice such as smoking. A smoking rule can tell employees what they may not do and where they may not do it, since the conduct is well defined. But sexual harassment arises out of a relationship between people — frequently a flawed relationship — and the conduct the law seeks to prohibit is not well defined. Conduct that one employee may object to may not be unwelcome to another employee; behavior that may be acceptable under some circumstances may be regarded as improper under others. Thus, a rule simply forbidding sexual harassment could work only if it also prohibits any fraternizing among employees. A rule that prohibits objectionable conduct but not all social interaction would need to be pocketed with nuances and definitions because it would have to provide for all types of contingencies. Because it cannot always be predicted what behavior will be regarded as an unwelcome sexual advance, such a rule would be difficult to apply.

The law of sexual harassment involves drawing lines on a sea of human emotion. This analysis will discuss the lines drawn, examine the types of situations in which questions of possible harassment have come up, and attempt to answer the questions left open by the courts.

Background

The First Decisions (1974-1979)

The first reported decisions on sexual harassment refused to recognize this conduct as actionable sex discrimination. In *Barnes v. Train,* 13 FEP Cases 123 (D. D.C. 1974), reversed sub nom. *Barnes v. Costle,* 561 F.2d 983, 15 FEP Cases 345 (1977), the district court ruled that alleged retaliatory actions taken by a supervisor because an employee refused his request for an "after hours affair" were not the type of discriminatory conduct that Title VII was intended to prohibit, since they did not involve an arbitrary barrier to continued employment based on the employee's sex.

In *Corne v. Bausch & Lomb, Inc.,* 390 F.Supp. 161, 10 FEP Cases 289 (D. Ariz. 1975), vacated and remanded on other grounds without discussion of this issue, 562 F.2d 55, 15 FEP Cases 1370 (9th Cir. 1977), the district court rejected the very idea that sexual harassment by a supervisor could impose liability on an employer. The supervisor's alleged conduct, the court said, was nothing more than a "personal proclivity, peculiarity or mannerism." He was satisfying a personal urge, not carrying out a company policy, the court said. The consequence of a contrary holding, it prophesied, would be "a potential federal lawsuit every time any employee, made amour or sexually oriented advances toward another."

With few exceptions, the pattern of the early cases was for the district courts to find no employer liability and for the courts of appeals to reverse. See, in addition to *Barnes v. Costle,* the following cases:

- *Garber v. Saxon Business Products, Inc.,* 552 F.2d 1032, 15 FEP Cases 344 (4th Cir. 1977) (reversing a decision that a female former employee had not stated a claim under Title VII by al-

leging that she had been discharged for rebuffing her
supervisor's sexual advances).

- *Tomkins v. Public Service Electric & Gas Co.,* 422 F.Supp. 553,
  13 FEP Cases 1574 (D. N.J. 1976), reversed and remanded,
  568 F.2d 1044, 16 FEP Cases 22 (3d Cir. 1977). The district
  court stated that Title VII was not intended to provide a
  federal tort remedy for what amounts to a physical attack
  motivated by supervisor's sexual desire, but the court of appeals found that the supervisor's alleged demand that the
  employee submit to his advances was a condition of employment covered by the Act and ruled that the statute is violated
  if the supervisor, with the actual or constructive knowledge of
  the employer, conditions an employee's job status on a
  favorable response to sexual advances or demands and if the
  employer does not take prompt and appropriate remedial action).

- *Miller v. Bank of America,* 418 F.Supp. 233, 13 FEP Cases 439
  (N.D. Calif. 1976), reversed and remanded, 600 F.2d 211, 20
  FEP Cases 462 (1979). The district court found no violation in
  woman's discharge, allegedly for refusal to cooperate sexually
  with her supervisor, because she failed to complain to the
  employer, which had a policy of discouraging sexual advances
  and disciplining violators; the court of appeals held that the
  employer would be liable anyway under the doctrine of *respondeat superior.*

The First Circuit, however, upheld a lower court's rejection of a
lawsuit against a college by a female professor who alleged only that
the college conditioned her continued employment on her acquiescence to the alleged sexual advances of her department chairman
(*Fisher v. Flynn,* 598 F.2d 663, 19 FEP Cases 932 (1st Cir. 1979).

The first decision finding liability was issued in 1976. A male supervisor made sexual advances to a female employee, she declined
them, and he then terminated her. The court said that the conduct of
the supervisor "created an artificial barrier to employment which
was placed before one gender and not the other." *Williams v. Saxbe,*
413 F.Supp. 654, 12 FEP Cases 1093 (D.D.C. 1976), subsequent
decisions, 13 FEP Cases 969 and 17 FEP Cases 1657 (D.D.C. 1976),
reversed in part and remanded on other grounds sub nom. *Williams
v. Bell,* 587 F.2d 140, 17 FEP Cases 1662 (D.C. Cir. 1978), liability on

remand found sub nom. *Williams v. Civiletti,* 487 F.Supp. 1387, 22 FEP Cases 1311 (D.D.C. 1980).

Other early decisions set the stage for the debates of the present day. Courts that found no liability ruled:

- There had to be a tie-in between the sexual advance and a term or condition of employment for the advance to be actionable, *Smith v. Rust Engineering Co.,* 20 FEP Cases 1172 (N.D. Ala. 1978)

- An employee who was not reappointed to her position by a new county attorney because she had rebuffed his sexual advances before he became the county attorney had no Title VII claim, *Cordes v. County of Yavapai,* 17 FEP Cases 1224 (D. Ariz. 1978.

- There could not be liability for a vice president's sexual acts and statements because the employer was unaware of them and had a policy against sexual advances, *Neely v. American Fidelity Assurance Co.,* 17 FEP Cases 482 (W.D. Okla. 1978.

- Sexual harassment by itself is not sex discrimination affecting the terms and conditions of employment, *Bundy v. Jackson,* 19 FEP Cases 828 (D. D.C. 1979).

- Verbal passes made by a foreman to an employee failed to rise to a level that would violate the Act, *Smith v. Amoco Chemicals Corp.,* 20 FEP Cases 724 (S.D. Tex. 1979).

- The employer was not alleged to have sanctioned the conduct of its supervisory employees, *Ludington v. Sambo's Restaurants, Inc.,* 474 F.Supp. 480, 20 FEP Cases 1002 (E.D. Wis. 1979).

- An employer with a firm rule against sexual fraternization among employees could not be liable for alleged sexual harassment of which it was unaware *Price v. John F. Lawhorn Furniture Co.,* 24 FEP Cases 1506 (N.D. Ala. 1978).

- A Supervisor who allegedly made sexual advances did not condition the complainant's job status on a favorable response to his advances *Robinson v. E. I. duPont de Nemours & Co.,* 33 FEP Cases 880 (D. Del. 1979).

Decisions favoring the imposition of liability, on the other hand, held that sexual harassment was actionable if submission to unwelcome sexual advances of a supervisor was a *de facto* term or condition of employment but not if the alleged conduct was an isolated incident or mere flirtation, and that an employer could not avoid liability by arguing that the employee did not take advantage of a non-existent internal grievance procedure (*Heelan v. Johns-Manville Corp.*, 451 F.Supp. 1382, 20 FEP Cases 251 (D. Colo. 1978); at an employer could be liable for the acts of its agents or supervisors if it failed to investigate complaints of sexual harassment (*Munford v. James T. Barnes & Co.*, 441 F.Supp. 459 (E.D. Mich. 1977); and that an employee was subjected to unjustified criticism, harassment, and eventual discharge because she refused her supervisor's sexual advances (*Stringer v. Commonwealth of Pennsylvania*, 446 F.Supp. 704, 17 FEP Cases 605 (M.D. Pa. 1978)).

Sexual Harassment Comes of Age (1980-1982)

Rulings by two courts of appeals gave the emerging body of sexual-harassment law an analytical definition that it previously had lacked. First, the District of Columbia Circuit laid down a principle — later adopted by courts everywhere — that sexual harassment was actionable even if it did not result in tangible economic harm to the employee. Then, the Eleventh Circuit developed the concepts of *quid pro quo* and hostile environment sexual harassment, laid out the elements of a *prima facie* case of each, and set forth the rules for determining liability.

In the District of Columbia case, *Bundy v. Jackson*, 641 F.2d 934, 24 FEP Cases 1155 (1981), the court relied on the principle that sex discrimination occurs whenever sex is a substantial, but not legitimate, factor in the employment decision. Holding that sexual harassment is sex discrimination in the "terms, conditions, or privileges of employment," the court viewed "conditions of employment" as including the psychological and emotional work environment. Thus, it held, the employer would be liable even if the employee could not prove that she resisted the advances and, as a result, suffered a loss or denial of tangible job benefits.

The Eleventh Circuit decision was *Henson v. City of Dundee*, 682 F.2d 897, 29 FEP Cases 787 (1982). It agreed with *Bundy* that a hostile or offensive atmosphere created by sexual harassment can, standing alone, constitute a violation of Title VII. But the court went beyond *Bundy* — even though it cited *Bundy* as authority — in holding that an employer could not be liable for a hostile work environment unless it knew of the supervisor's behavior and failed to take prompt corrective action. The court said that there were two ways to show knowledge. One was a demonstration by the employee that she complained to higher management about the harassment, and the other was a showing that the harassment was pervasive, which would give rise to an inference of knowledge or constructive knowledge.

At the same time, the court acknowledged that an employer would be liable automatically if the sexual harassment were to cause a tangible job detriment. In such a situation, it explained, a supervisor relies on his apparent or actual authority to extort sexual consideration from the employee. But in the hostile environment situation, the court stated, the capacity of any person — supervisor, co-employee, or stranger to the workplace — to create a hostile or offensive environment is not necessarily enhanced or diminished by any degree of authority that the employer confers on that individual. A supervisor who gratuitously insults an employee generally does so for reasons of his own and, consequently, acts outside the actual or apparent authority that he possesses as a supervisor, the court observed. As a result, it declared, his conduct cannot automatically be imputed to the employer any more than can the conduct of an ordinary employee.

The district courts during the 1980-1982 period disagreed on whether there had to be a showing that sexual harassment affected a condition of employment to be actionable. Among the cases so holding were *Clark v. World Airways, Inc.*, 24 FEP Cases 305 (D.D.C. 1980), *Hall v. F.O. Thacker Contracting Co.*, 24 FEP Cases 1499 (N.D. Ga. 1980), *Walter v. KFGO Radio*, 518 F.Supp. 1309, 26 FEP Cases 982 (D.N.D. 1981), *Hill v. BASF Wyandotte Corp.*, 27 FEP Cases 66 (E.D. Mich. 1981) and *Reichman v. Bureau of Affirmative Action*, 536 F.Supp. 1149, 30 FEP Cases 1644 (M.D. Pa. 1982).

But *Hayden v. Cox Enterprises, Inc.*, 534 F.Supp. 1166, 8 FEP Cases 1315 (N.D. Ga. 1982) and *Robson v. Eva's Super Market, Inc.*, 538 F.Supp. 857, 30 FEP Cases 1212 (N.D. Ohio 1982) refused to impose such a requirement. The district courts generally held that employer knowledge was required. See *Meyers v. I.T.T. Diversified Credit Corp.*, 527 F.Supp. 1064, 27 FEP Cases 995 (E.D. Mo. 1981) and *Martin v. Norbar, Inc.*, 537 F.Supp. 1260, 30 FEP Cases 103 (S.D. Ohio 1982).

Another issue that the district courts explored during this period was whether the conduct at issue should be regarded as sexual harassment. Some courts, in refusing to impose liability, found that the employee either actually encouraged the alleged sexually harassing conduct, *Gan v. Kepro Circuit System, Inc.*, 28 FEP Cases 639 (E.D. Mo. 1982), or participated in the conduct at issue, *Halpert v. Wertheim & Co.*, 27 FEP Cases 21 (S.D. N.Y. 1980). Others refused to impose liability on the ground that the employee had an unusual sensitivity to actions that she perceived as sexual in nature. *Sand v. George P. Johnson Co.*, 33 FEP Cases 716 (E.D. Mich. 1982).

The EEOC Guidelines

In 1980, long after the courts had substantially developed the law of sexual harassment, the EEOC adopted guidelines on the subject. The guidelines attempted to codify the law while, at the same time, encouraging the courts to take a liberal attitude in finding liability. Most notably, the guidelines took a position favoring the finding of liability on an issue that, at the time, had not been the subject of any published judicial decision.

The EEOC said that unwelcome sexual advances, requests for sexual favors, or other verbal or physical conduct of a sexual nature can constitute sexual harassment in three situations: when submission to such conduct is, explicitly or implicitly, a term or condition of employment; when submission to rejection of such conduct is used as the basis for employment decisions; and when such conduct has the purpose or effect of unreasonably interfering with work performance or creating an intimidating, hostile, or offensive work environment. The Commission rejected the position that an employer could not be liable for an incident of sexual harassment unless it knew, independently of the supervisor committing the harassment, about the incident. Instead, it declared that the employer is responsible for its acts and those of its agents and supervisory employees "regardless of whether the specific acts complained of were authorized or even forbidden by the employer and regardless of whether the employer knew or should have known of their occurrence." The EEOC did not distinguish between hostile environmental harassment and *quid pro quo* harassment.

However, the Commission imposed an actual or constructive knowledge requirement with respect to conduct between fellow employees, as well as to conduct of non-employees. It said that the employer would be liable in these situations only if it knew or should have known of the conduct and failed to take immediate and appropriate corrective action. Moreover, the EEOC created a new offense: giving a job-related benefit to an employee who acquiesces in sexual misconduct instead of to a more job-worthy one who refuses to do so. The Commission did not indicate whether there would be a violation even if the two employees were of the same sex.

The Road to Vinson (1983-1986)

This period saw an increasing number of cases and the growing willingness of the courts of appeals to find liability. For example:

- The Third Circuit, while continuing to require that an employer know of the supervisor's sexual harassment, said that such knowledge could be imputed when the supervisor has complete authority over employment decisions affecting the employee, so long as a distinction is maintained between purely personal conduct and conduct having direct employment consequences. *Craig v. Y & Y Snacks, Inc.,* 721 F.2d 77, 33 FEP Cases 187 (3d Cir. 1983).

- The Fourth Circuit found liability for the use of sexually related epithets; it held that an official policy against harassment did not absolve the employer of liability, since it was required in fact to end the harassment. *Katz v. Dole,* 709 F.2d 251, 31 FEP Cases 1521 (4th Cir. 1983).

- The Fifth Circuit, joining the other circuits in holding that sexual harassment constitutes employment discrimination because of the victimized individual's sex, went on to hold that Title VII reaches a public officeholder's refusal to rehire an employee because of her rejection of his sexual advances before he took office. *Simmons v. Lyons,* 746 F.2d 265, 36 FEP Cases 410 (1984).

- The Seventh Circuit held that an employer was liable for a supervisor's sexual harassment without having actual or constructive knowledge of the supervisor's conduct; it said that strict liability was appropriate because the tort was caused by the exercise of supervisory power given to the supervisor. *Horn v. Duke Homes,* 755 F.2d 599, 37 FEP Cases 228 (7th Cir. 1985).

- The Eighth Circuit adopted the prevailing view that a sexually hostile work environment violates Title VII, and it also agreed with *Henson* that knowledge is a requisite for employer liability. *Moylan v. Maries County,* 792 F.2d 746, 40 FEP Cases 1788 (9th Cir. 1986).

- The Eleventh Circuit imposed liability on an employer for terminating an employee after she refused to have sex with the employer's owner. *Phillips v. Smalley Maintenance Services, Inc.,* 711 F.2d 1524, 32 FEP Cases 975 (11th Cir. 1983).

- The District of Columbia Circuit said that an assault and battery of an employee that occurred allegedly because of her rejection of sexual advances could amount to sexual harassment, even though the use of force was not overtly sexual; the court also suggested that any conduct that would not occur but for the sex of the victims may violate Title VII if it is sufficiently pervasive. *McKinney v. Dole,* 765 F.2d 1129, 38 FEP Cases 364 (D.C. Cir. 1985). The same court held an employer liable for giving a promotion to an employee who entered into a sexual relationship with a supervisor instead of to a better qualified employee. *King v. Palmer,* 778 F.2d 878, 39 FEP Cases 877 (D.C. Cir. 1985).

District courts also confronted new issues. They refused to permit an employer to discover a sexual-harassment complainant's past sexual behavior, *Priest v. Rotary,* 98 F.R.D. 755, 32 FEP Cases 1064 (ND. Calif. 1983), or to discover the records of her psychotherapist, *Jennings v. D.H.L. Airlines,* 101 F.R.D. 549, 34 FEP Cases 1423 (N.D. Ill. 1984). One court found an employer liable when a supervisor gave a promotion to a woman who had an affair with him instead of to another woman who refused his advances, *Toscanno v. Nimmo,* 570 F.Supp. 1197, 32 FEP Cases 1401 (D. Del. 1983), although another court refused relief because of the lack of direct evidence of an explicit sexual relationship between the supervisor and the favored employee, *King v. Palmer,* 598 F.Supp. 65, 35 FEP Cases 1302 (D.D.C. 1984), reversed on this ground, 778 F.2d 878, 39 FEP Cases 877 (D.C. Cir. 1985). Liability was found for resistance to unwelcome homosexual advances, *Joyner v. AAA Cooper Transportation,* 597 F.Supp. 537, 36 FEP Cases 1644 (M.D. Ala. 1983).

An increasing number of district courts held that employers could be liable for supervisory sexual harassment of which they were not notified. *Jeppsen v. Wunnicke,* 611 F.Supp. 78, 37 FEP Cases 994 (D. Alas. 1985); *Ambrose v. United States Steel Corp.,* 39 FEP Cases 30 (N.D. Calif. 1985); *Bohen v. City of East Chicago,* 622 F.Sup. 1234, 39 FEP Cases 917 (N.D. Ind. 1985); *Horbaczewsky v. Spider Staging Sales Co.,* 621 F.Supp. 749, 41 FEP Cases 1008 (N.D. Ill. 1985); and *Mitchell v. OsAir, Inc.,* 629 F.Supp. 636, 45 FEP Cases 580 (N.D.

Ohio 1986); but see *Wimberly v. Shoney's, Inc.,* 39 FEP Cases 444 (S.D. Ga. 1985). On the other hand, courts refused to hold employers liable for *quid pro quo* harassment if the adverse job decision was made by an official other than the supervisor accused of harassment. *Kwiatkowski v. Bolger,* 39 FEP Cases 1740 (N.D. Ill. 1985); *Anderson v. University Health Center of Pittsburgh,* 623 F.Supp. 795, 41 FEP Cases 1197 (W.D. Pa. 1985).

Up to this point, the federal courts had acted without guidance from the U.S. Supreme Court. There were disputes as to whether sexual harassment had to involve a specific term or condition of employment to be actionable, whether an employee who engaged in voluntary conduct could thereafter sue, and whether an employer could be held liable for the unreported misconduct of its supervisors. Now it was the turn of the Supreme Court to explore the subject.

Supreme Court's Vinson Decision

Background

The *Vinson* case involved a bank teller who claimed that she had engaged in sexual relations with her branch manager at his insistence and that she did so for fear that refusal would lead to discharge. She never complained to any officer or representative of the bank.

A federal district court ruled that the bank could not be liable unless it had received notice of the harassment. It rejected the teller's argument that notice to her supervisor, who was an assistant vice president, was notice to the bank. The court said that "it seems reasonable that an employer should not be liable in these unusual cases of sexual harassment where notice to the employer must depend upon the actual perpetrator and when there is nothing else to place the employer on notice." The court said the sexual relationship was a voluntary one, having nothing to do with her continued employment at the bank or her advancement or promotion there. *Vinson v. Taylor,* 23 FEP Cases 37 (D.D.C. 1980).

In a sweeping opinion, the U.S. Court of Appeals for the District of Columbia Circuit reversed. It held that Title VII outlawed a discriminatory work environment regardless of whether tangible job benefits were lost. The court rejected the district court's assertion that liability could not be imposed for "voluntary" behavior; instead, it asserted, the proper question was whether the supervisor made the employee's toleration of sexual harassment a condition of her employment. In this regard, it added, the female employee could have other women testify to being harassed by the same supervisor. Moreover, the court held, an employer is responsible for a supervisor's sexual harassment even if it has no specific notice of this form of discrimination, since the supervisor is the agent of the employer. The court held that an employer could be held accountable for sexual harassment by any supervisory employee with authority to hire, promote, or discharge. The court explained:

> An employer's delegation of this much authority vests in the supervisor such extreme power over the victimized employee that the supervisor's stature as an 'agent' of the employer cannot be doubted. We do not believe, however, that vicarious responsibility is limited to discrimination by supervisors so richly endowed. The mere existence − or even the appearance − of a significant degree of influence in vital job decisions gives any supervisor the opportunity to impose upon employees. That opportunity is not dependent solely upon the supervisor's authority to make personnel decisions; the ability to direct employees in their work, to evaluate their performances and to recommend personnel actions carries attendant power to coerce, intimidate and harass. For this reason, we think employers must answer for sexual harassment of any subordinate by any supervising superior.

The court refused to apply the common-law doctrine of *respondeat superior*. Under this doctrine, an employer is liable for the acts of an agent that are committed within the scope of his authority. This doctrine is not altogether suitable for resolutions of question of Title VII liability, the court reasoned, since it would lead to situations in which employers would become accountable only if they explicitly require or consciously allow their supervisors to molest female employees. *Vinson v. Taylor*, 753 F.2d 141, 36 FEP Cases 1423, rehearing denied, 760 F.2d 1330, 37 FEP Cases 1266 (1985).

Supreme Court Ruling

In *Vinson*, the Court was unanimous on all questions except that of employer liability. *Meritor Savings Bank v. Vinson*, 477 US. 57, 40 FEP Cases 1822 (1986). It ratified the position taken by many of the courts of appeals that a supervisor who sexually harasses a subordinate discriminates on the basis of sex and that Title VII forbids sexual harassment even if the injury is not economic in nature. However, the Court added, the harassment, to be actionable, must be sufficiently severe or pervasive to alter the conditions of the victim's employment and to create an abusive working environment. The fact that sex-related conduct was "voluntary" in the sense that the complainant was not forced to participate against her will is not a defense, the Court said, since the correct inquiry is whether the complainant by her conduct indicated that alleged sexual advances were unwelcome. Her sexually provocative speech or dress is relevant in determining whether she found particular sexual advances unwelcome, the Court added.

But the Court refused to decide what requirements are necessary to hold an employer liable for hostile environment sexual harassment. Noting that Title VII defines "employer" to include any "agent" of an employer, the Court said that Congress intended the courts to look to agency principles for guidance in assessing employer liability (although it noted that such common-law principles "may not be transferable in all their particulars to Title VII"). While holding that the court of appeals erred in concluding that employers are always automatically liable for sexual harassment by their supervisors, the Court enigmatically warned that absence of notice to an employer does not necessarily absolve it of liability.

The Court noted that while the EEOC guidelines hold an employer liable for the acts of its agents without regard to notice, the solicitor general, speaking for the Justice Department and the EEOC, took the position that an employer should not be held liable for hostile environment harassment — though it would continue to be liable for *quid pro quo* harassment — if it has a grievance procedure and a policy against harassment and if the complainant failed to invoke the procedure. But the Court refused to insulate the bank from liability based on its policy against discrimination and the employee's failure to invoke its grievance procedure. The Court pointed out that the bank's general non-discrimination policy did not address sexual harassment in particular and that its grievance procedure apparently required an employee to complain first to her supervisor, who was the alleged perpetrator. The bank's contention might be substantially stronger, the Court declared, if its procedures were better calculated to encourage victims of harassment to come forward.

Justice Marshall, joined by Justices Brennan, Blackmun, and Stevens, would have held that sexual harassment by a supervisor of an employee under his supervision, leading to a discriminatory work

environment, should be imputed to the employer for Title VII purposes regardless of whether the employee gave notice to the
employer. Justice Marshall said that he would have applied the
standard applicable to all other situations of discrimination. Rejecting the solicitor general's distinction between sexual harassment that
affects tangible job benefits and sexual harassment that creates a discriminatory work environment, he noted that in both cases it is the
authority vested in the supervisor by the employer that enables him
to commit the wrong. Thus, he concluded, there is no justification
for a rule that sexual harassment does not create employer liability
unless the employee notifies other supervisors.

Justice Marshall agreed with the majority that agency principles
and the goals of Title VII make appropriate some limitation on the
liability of employers for the acts of their supervisors. He suggested
that if the supervisor has no authority over an employee, it may be
improper to find strict employer liability. He also suggested that an
effective complaint procedure could, in the case of hostile work environment, warrant denial of relief to an employee who failed to
take advantage of it. A court might be reluctant to find that a former
employee who bypassed a complaint procedure known to be effective was constructively discharged, he said, and, thus, she could be
denied reinstatement or back pay.

Observations

Although the Court settled the question of whether sexual harassment was discrimination, its decision raised new issues:

- Its statement that an employer was not always automatically liable for a supervisor-created sexually hostile environment
  opened the door for every employer to argue that its case was
  one in which actual notice could properly be required. The
  Court's countervailing statement that actual notice was not always necessary did not clarify matters.

- The Court said agency principles apply to the question of
  employer liability, but its suggestion that these principles
  might not be transferable in all their particulars to Title VII
  created an issue as to the extent to which an employer can be
  held liable on an agency theory for the unreported acts of its
  supervisors.

- The Court, in suggesting that the existence of a publicized, effective mechanism for dealing with complaints of sexual harass-

ment could preclude the finding of a violation, may have created an issue as to whether this concept would apply to all forms of sexual harassment or just to hostile environment harassment.

- The Court's holding that provocative speech or dress can be relevant in determining whether particular sexual advances were unwelcome raised the question of whether an employer could also inquire into the employee's sexual history.

Developments Since Vinson

Vinson established that sexual harassment by supervisors could subject an employer to liability. But the Supreme Court left open other questions, such as: What is harassment? When is it actionable? When is the employer liable? Lacking the Supreme Court's guidance, the lower courts have been required to fashion their own answers.

In the first year after the *Vinson* decision, the appeals courts ruled for employers in four of the five Title VII sexual-harassment cases that they decided.

Circuit Court Rulings

The Fifth Circuit held, in a case involving alleged sexual advances by one of the employer's vice presidents and the sculpting of bare-breasted mermaids by the employer's executive chef as table decorations for an office Christmas party, that when harassment occurs without tangible job consequences, a commensurately higher showing that the sexually harassing conduct was pervasive and destructive of the working environment is required. Here, the court decided, the conduct complained of was not sufficiently pervasive to constitute a hostile work environment. Because the case was not a class action, the court said, evidence of sexually harassing incidents reported by other women did not bear on the complainant's claim absent evidence that these incidents affected her psychological well-being. *Jones v. Flagship International,* 793 F.2d 714, 41 FEP Cases 358 (5th Cir. 1986).

The Sixth Circuit said that a complainant seeking to hold an employer responsible for a hostile work environment is required to show that the employer had actual or constructive knowledge of the offending conduct. The complainant is also required to prove that she was offended by the employer's conduct and that she suffered injury, the court ruled. Furthermore, it held, she has to demonstrate that the injury-causing incidents, comments, or conduct occurred frequently. *Rabidue v. Osceola Refining Co.*, 805 F.2d 611, 42 FEP Cases 631 (6th Cir. 1986).

The Sixth Circuit subsequently rejected a claim of sexual harassment by a woman who complained of one alleged incident that, it noted, she had induced by her suggestion that she meet her supervisor in a bar. The court observed that she regarded the alleged incident at the time as not "that big of a deal," that she did not report another incident that involved her supervisor for a period of three months, and that her husband had characterized that incident as having been made in jest. *Highlander v. K.F.C. National Management Co.*, 805 F.2d 644, 42 FEP Cases 654 (6th Cir. 1986).

But the court upheld a finding of employer liability in another case involving a supervisor's harassment of subordinate employees, even though the employer had a published procedure for dealing with sexual-harassment complaints. The court noted that this policy, which assumed that the supervisor was not the harasser, was vague on paper and in implementation. The employer knew or should have known of the supervisor's conduct, it added, since he harassed women on a daily basis in the course of his supervision of them. Traditional agency principles were applicable, the court said, since the harassment took place at the office during working hours by someone with the authority to hire, fire, promote, and discipline employees, and the harassment was foreseeable in that the employer had a policy attempting to deal with it. *Yates v. Avco Corp.*, 819 F.2d 630, 43 FEP Cases 1595 (6th Cir. 1987).

The Seventh Circuit took the position that the threshold issue in hostile environment cases is whether the instances of alleged harassment rise to a level of "hostility" offensive enough to be actionable. It decided that the harassment that a female employee was subjected to by fellow employees was not severe enough to support a hostile environment claim. While she complained of being offensively propositioned, the court noted that her only example was a co-employee's request that she join him at a restaurant after work. It said that his winks and suggestions that he be allowed to give her a rub-down were not so pervasitve or psychologially debilitating that they affected her ability to perform on the job. *Scott v. Sears, Roebuck & Co.*, 798 F.2d 210, 41 FEP Cases 805 (7th Cir. 1986).

District Court Rulings

Similar to the appeals courts, the federal district courts ruled for employers or for supervisors in 20 of the 31 reported cases that were decided in the first year after *Vinson* was handed down. In some cases, complainants lost because they were not believed, but, generally, their problems were that the conduct they complained of was not regarded as actionable harassment or that the employer was not held liable for the harassment.

Courts refused to find liability on the following grounds:

- The complained-of conduct was not sexual in nature but was the sort of teasing treatment that might have occurred to any other co-employee, *Vermett v. Hough,* 627 F.Supp. 587, 42 FEP Cases 1432 (W.D. Mich. 1986);

- The conduct of fellow employees, which included sending a birthday card containing an obscenity, assigning of a menial task, and reacting coolly after rejection of a sexual solicitation, did not create a hostile environment and was not brought to the employer's attention, *Freedman v. American Standard, Inc.,* 41 FEP Cases 471 (D. N.J. 1986);

- The supervisor's sexual harassment did not subject the employee to an offensive work environment remediable under Title VII, *Neville v. Taft Broadcasting Co.,* 42 FEP Cases 1314 (W.D. N.Y. 1987);

- A police captain's single effort to get a female police officer to go out with him was insufficient to affect her psychological well-being, *Sapp v. City of Warner Robins,* 655 F.Supp. 1043, 43 FEP Cases 486 (M.D. Ga. 1987);

- The complainant lied, *Grier v. Casey,* 643 F.Supp. 298, 41 FEP Cases 1259 (W.D. N.C. 1986), and *Jackson-Colley v. Department of the Army Corps of Engineers,* 655 F.Supp. 122, 43 FEP Cases 617 (E.D. Mich. 1987);

- A supervisor's occasional impropriety does not establish actionable sexual harassment, *Volk v. Coler,* 638 F.Supp. 1555, 44 FEP Cases 1111 (C.D. Ill. 1986).

Courts ruling in favor of complainants in the first year after *Vinson* held that:

- An employer would be strictly liable if a terminated employee proved that her discharge was the result of her failure to submit to her supervisor's advances, even though the first alleged advance occurred in a restaurant parking lot well after working hours, *Schroeder v. Schrock*, 42 FEP Cases 1112 (D. Kan. 1986);

- Title VII's ban on sexual harassment applied to unions as well as to employers, *Egger v. Local 276, Plumbers & Pipe Fitters*, 644 F.Supp. 795, 41 FEP Cases 1465 (D. Mass. 1986);

- The Navy was responsible for a sexually hostile working environment created and maintained by the head of an equal employment opportunity office, *Delgado v. Lehman*, 665 F.Supp. 460, 43 FEP Cases 593 (E.D. Va. 1987);

- The improper treatment of a female employee was due to her resistance to her supervisor's sexual advances, *Boyd v. James S. Hayes Living Health Care Agency, Inc.*, 671 F.Supp. 1155, 44 FEP Cases 332 (W.D. Tenn. 1987);

- An employer could be liable for an assistant manager's alleged sexual harassment of an employee despite the employee's failure to complain to the manager, who was the assistant manager's roommate, *Salazar v. Church's Fried Chicken, Inc.*, 44 FEP Cases 472 (S.D. Tex. 1987);

- A woman who was discharged at the insistence of the employer's wife after the employer drugged the woman and had sexual relations with her while the wife was in the same bed could recover from the employer, *Gilardi v. Schroeder*, 672 F.Supp. 1043, 45 FEP Cases 283 (N.D. Ill. 1986);

- An employer was liable for sexual harassment that was frequent and increasingly offensive, although it lasted only a short time because the victims were discharged, (*Ross v. Double Diamond, Inc.*, 672 F.Supp. 261, 45 FEP Cases 313).

Latest Circuit Court Decisions

In the second post-*Vinson* year, there have been four appeals court decisions. The Fourth Circuit gave a literal interpretation to the concept of unwelcomed conduct. While rejecting on their merits most of the claims of a stewardess who asserted that she had been harassed by a pilot, the court held that the use of foul language of sexual innuendo in a consensual setting does not waive an employee's protection against unwelcome harassment. It said that, apart from its content, harassment is "unwelcome" if it simply is not welcomed. *Swentek v. USAir, Inc.,* 830 F.2d 552, 44 FEP Cases 1808 (4th Cir. 1987).

The Fifth Circuit reversed a finding of liability to a female employee who was harassed on a business trip by a co-employee. It found that the employer took prompt remedial action and that the employee did not give the employer a fair opportunity to demonstrate that it could curb the co-employee's behavior. The court observed that the manner and promptness of an employer's response to a harassment complaint may be assessed proportionally to the seriousness of the offense. *Dornhecker v. Malibu Grand Prix Corp.,* 828 F.2d 307, 44 FEP Cases 1604 (5th Cir. 1987).

The Tenth Circuit took the position that forbidden sexual harassment includes not only overt sexual acts but also any unequal treatment that would not occur but for an employee's sex. Thus, it decided, threats of physical violence and incidents of verbal abuse should be considered along with sexual conduct to determine whether a hostile environment existed. The court ruled that evidence of racial hostility can be combined with evidence of sexual hostility in making this determination. The employer can be liable even if it lacks actual or constructive knowledge of a supervisor's harassment, the court held. Liability can be based on negligence or recklessness, it said. It added that liability also could be based on a supervisor's representation that he was acting or speaking on the employer's behalf if either the employee relied on this apparent authority or if the existence of the employment relationship aided the supervisor in harassing the employee. *Hicks v. Gates Rubber Co.,* 833 F.2d 1406, 45 FEP Cases 608 (10th Cir. 1987).

The Eleventh Circuit adopted the EEOC regulation that a supervisor acts as the agent of an employer — rendering the employer directly liable for his actions — when he exercises authority that the employer actually delegated to him or by making or threatening to make decisions affecting the employment status of subordinates. It reversed a summary judgment against a former employee on the ground that she had presented evidence that her supervisor used his actual and apparent authority to assist him in harassing her. (*Sparks v. Pilot Freight Carriers, Inc.,* 830 F.2d 1554, 45 FEP Cases 160 (11th Cir. 1987).

Latest District Court Rulings

There have been few district court decisions handed down in *Vinson*'s second year. Employers have prevailed in five of the eight reported decisions.

Women have obtained favorable district court decisions in cases involving intolerable conditions that continued even after the employer's lawyer investigated the situation and the offending supervisor was made to apologize to the employee, *Brooms v. Regal Tube Co.*, 44 FEP Cases 1119 (N.D. Ill. 1987); and the posting of sexually oriented posters and the use of anti-female language, *Barbetta v. Chemlawn Services Corp.*, 669 F.Supp. 565, 44 FEP Cases 1563 (W.D. N.Y. 1987). But one district court refused to find liable an employer that conducted a good-faith investigation of sexual harassment claims and erroneously decided that the claims were not substantiated, *Carrero v. New York City Housing Authority*, 668 F.Supp. 196, 44 FEP Cases 1772 (S.D. N.Y. 1987), and another court, while rejecting a claim of sexual harassment on the ground that the alleged advance did not occur, ruled that, in light of the employee's character, she would have welcomed rather than rejected any advance. *McLean v. Satellite Technology Services, Inc.*, 673 F.Supp. 1458, 45 FEP Cases 523 (E.D. Mo. 1987).

Roundup of the Circuits

The federal courts of appeals have issued numerous published decisions on the subject of sexual harassment and sexual favoritism. For ease of reference, they are listed below by circuit:

District of Columbia Circuit (Washington, D.C.): *Barnes v. Costle*, 561 F.2d 983, 15 FEP Cases 345 (1977); *Bundy v. Jackson*, 641 F.2d 934, 24 FEP Cases 1155; *Bouchet v. National Urban League, Inc.*, 730 F.2d 799, 34 FEP Cases 545 (1984); *Vinson v. Taylor*, 753 F.2d 141, 36 FEP Cases 1423 (1985), rehearing en banc denied, 760 F.2d 1330, 37 FEP Cases 1266 (1985), affirmed in part and remanded in part, 477 U.S. 57, 40 FEP Cases 1822 (1986); *McKinney v. Dole*, 765 F.2d 1129, 38 FEP Cases 364 (1985); *King v. Palmer*, 778 F.2d 878, 39 FEP Cases 877 (1985), rehearing en banc denied, 778 F.2d 878 at 883, 40 FEP Cases 190 (1986).

First Circuit (Maine, Massachusetts, New Hampshire, Puerto Rico, and Rhode Island): *Fisher v. Flynn*, 598 F.2d 663, 19 FEP Cases 932 (1979).

Second Circuit (Connecticut, New York, and Vermont): *DeCintio v. Westchester County Medical Center,* 807 F.2d 304, 42 FEP Cases 921 (1986).

Third Circuit (Delaware, New Jersey, Pennsylvania, and Virgin Islands): *Tomkins v. Public Service Electric & Gas Co.,* 568 F.2d 1044, 16 FEP Cases 22 (1977); *Craig v. Y & Y Snacks, Inc.,* 721 F.2d 77, 33 FEP Cases 187 (1983); *Wolk v. Saks Fifth Avenue, Inc.,* 728 F.2d 221, 34 FEP Cases 193 (1984); *Owens v. United States,* 822 F.2d 408, 44 FEP Cases 247 (1987).

Fourth Circuit (Maryland, North Carolina, South Carolina, Virginia, and West Virginia): *Garber v. Saxon Business Products, Inc.,* 552 F.2d 1032, 15 FEP Cases 344 (1977); *Sipes v. U.S. Postal Service,* 677 F.2d 375, 30 FEP Cases 1257 (1982); *Katz v. Dole,* 709 F.2d 251, 31 FEP Cases 1521 (1983); *Hostetter v. U.S.,* 739 F.2d 983, 35 FEP Cases 693 (1984); *Davis v. United States Steel Corp.,* 779 U.S. 209, 39 FEP Cases 955 (1985); *Davis v. USX Corp.,* 819 F.2d 1270, 43 FEP Cases 1685 (1987); *Swentek v. USAir, Inc.,* 830 F.2d 552, 44 FEP Cases 1808 (1987).

Fifth Circuit (Louisiana, Mississippi, and Texas): *Simmons v. Lyons,* 746 F.2d 265, 36 FEP Cases 410 (1984); *Whitaker v. Carney,* 778 F.2d 216, 39 FEP Cases 987 (1985); *Jones v. Flagship International,* 793 F.2d 714, 41 FEP Cases 358 (1986); *Garziano v. E.I. duPont de Nemours & Co.,* 818 F.2d 380, 43 FEP Cases 1790 (1987); *Dornhecker v. Malibu Grand Prix Corp.,* 828 F.2d 307, 44 FEP Cases 1604 (1987).

Sixth Circuit (Kentucky, Michigan, Ohio, and Tennessee): *Polk v. Yellow Freight System, Inc.,* 801 F.2d 190, 41 FEP Cases 1279 (1986); *Rabidue v. Osceola Refining Co.,* 805 F.2d 611, 42 FEP Cases 631 (1986); *Highlander v. K.F.C. National Management Co.,* 805 F.2d 644, 42 FEP Cases 654 (1986); *Yates v. AVCO Corp.,* 819 F.2d 630, 43 FEP Cases 1595 (1987).

Seventh Circuit (Illinois, Indiana, and Wisconsin): *Huebschen v. Department of Health and Human Services,* 716 F.2d 1167, 32 FEP Cases 1582 (1983); *Horn v. Duke Homes, Inc.,* 755 F.2d 599, 37 FEP Cases 228 (1985); *Zabkowicz v. West Bend Co.,* 789 F.2d 540, 40 FEP Cases 1171 (1986); *Scott v. Sears, Roebuck & Co.,* 798 F.2d 210, 41 FEP Cases 805 (1986); *Bohen v. City of East Chicago,* 799 F.2d 1180, 41 FEP Cases 1108 (1986); *Callaway v. Hafeman,* 832 F.2d 414, 45 FEP Cases 154 (1987).

Eighth Circuit (Arkansas, Iowa, Minnesota, Missouri, Nebraska, North Dakota, and South Dakota): *Barrett v. Omaha National Bank,* 726 F.2d 424, 35 FEP Cases 593 (1984); *Stubbs v. U.S.,* 744 F.2d 58,

35 FEP Cases 1521 (1984); *Crimm v. Missouri Pacific Railroad Co.,* 750 F.2d 703, 36 FEP Cases 883 (1984); *Moylan v. Maries County,* 792 F.2d 746, 40 FEP Cases 1788 (1986); *Johnson v. Perkins Restaurants, Inc.,* 815 F.2d 1220, 43 FEP Cases 830 (1987).

Ninth Circuit (Alaska, Arizona, California, Hawaii, Idaho, Montana, Nevada, Oregon, and Washington): *Miller v. Bank of America,* 600 F.2d 211, 20 FEP Cases 462 (1979); *Otto v. Heckler,* 781 F.2d 754, 39 FEP Cases 1754 (1986); *Arnold v. United States,* 816 F.2d 1306, 43 FEP Cases 1256 (1987).

Tenth Circuit (Colorado, Kansas, New Mexico, Oklahoma, Utah, and Wyoming): *Jones v. Intermountain Power Project,* 794 F.2d 546, 41 FEP Cases 1 (1986); *Hicks v. Gates Rubber Co.,* 833 F.2d 1406, 45 FEP Cases 608 (1987)

Eleventh Circuit (Alabama, Florida, and Georgia): *Henson v. City of Dundee,* 682 F.2d 897, 29 FEP Cases 787 (1982); *Phillips v. Smalley Maintenance Services, Inc.,* 711 F.2d 1524, 32 FEP Cases 975 (1983); *Sparks v. Pilot Freight Carriers, Inc.,* 830 F.2d 1554, 45 FEP Cases 160 (1987).

Federal Circuit: *Downes v. Federal Aviation Administration,* 775 F.2d 288, 39 FEP Cases 70 (1985); *Jackson v. Veterans Administration,* 768 F.2d 1325, 39 FEP Cases 100 (1985); *Carosella v. U.S. Postal Service,* 816 F.2d 638, 43 FEP Cases 845 (1987); *Hanley v. General Services Administration,* 829 F.2d 23, 44 FEP Cases 1241 (1987).

Legal Principles

General Standards

1. *Scope:* Title VII forbids sexual harassment without regard to whether the resulting injury is economic or non-economic. *Meritor Savings Bank v. Vinson,* 477 U.S. 57, 40 FEP Cases 1822 (1986). Thus, it covers such matters as a female former employee's allegation that her supervisor embarked on a campaign of abusive behavior after she terminated a sexual relationship with him, *Koster v. Chase Manhattan Bank,* 554 F.Supp. 285, 36 FEP Cases 941 (S.D. N.Y. 1983); an employer's requirement that a female employee cheerfully accept suggestive remarks by a non-employee who provided a substantial amount of business to the employer, *Crockwell v. Blackmon-Mooring Steamatic, Inc.,* 627 F.Supp. 800, 43 FEP Cases 1451 (W.D. Tenn. 1985); and a human resources manager's constant sexual remarks and pranks directed at an employee whom

he did not directly supervise, *Brooms v. Regal Tube Co.*, 44 FEP Cases 1119 (N.D. Ill. 1987).

2. *Types of harassment:* There are two types of sexual harassment: *quid pro quo* and hostile working environment. The first occurs when an employee suffers economic detriment due to resistance to a supervisor's sexual advances or other misconduct; the employer is automatically liable regardless of whether it knew of the supervisor's conduct. The second occurs when conduct by supervisors, fellow employees, or outside customers is such as to create an abusive working environment on the basis of sex. Many courts require that an employer have actual or constructive knowledge to be held liable for this type of harassment. *Henson v. City of Dundee*, 682 F.2d 897, 29 FEP Cases 787 (11th Cir. 1982). The Supreme Court has not decided this issue. See *Meritor Savings Bank v. Vinson*, 477 U.S. 57, 40 FEP Cases 1822 (1986).

3. *Hostile environment:* A hostile environment is one in which the harassment is sufficiently severe or pervasive to alter the conditions of employment and create an abusive working environment. *Meritor Savings Bank v. Vinson*, 477 U.S. 57, 40 FEP Cases 1822 (1986). But hostile environment is merely one position on the continuum of sexual harassment; the threat of job detriment is no less real for being implied rather than explicit. *Mitchell v. OsAir, Inc.*, 629 F.Supp. 636, 45 FEP Cases 580 (N.D. Ohio 1986). A hostile environment situation turns into a *quid pro quo* one when an employee is terminated for rejecting sexual advances. See, for example, *Boyd v. James S. Hayes Living Health Care Agency, Inc.*, 671 F.Supp. 1155, 44 FEP Cases 332 (W.D. Tenn. 1987). Thus, a probationary assistant superintendent who was required to meet every morning and work closely with the superintendent who harassed her and who was responsible for her training was subjected to a hostile environment. *Carrero v. New York City Housing Authority*, 668 F.Supp. 196, 44 FEP Cases 1772 (S.D. N.Y. 1987). Another employee proved that the constant sexual remarks and pranks of a manager poisoned the workplace through psychological evidence that her problems with him made her phobic about the employer and that she suffered a severe and debilitating depression requiring psychiatric treatment when she quit after a final incident. *Brooms v. Regal Tube Co.*, 44 FEP Cases 1119 (N.D. Ill. 1987). But complete psychological debilitation need not be shown to establish liability. *Ross v. Double Diamond, Inc.*, 672 F.Supp. 261, 45 FEP Cases 313 (N.D. Tex. 1987).

4. *Pervasiveness:* The harassing conduct has to be pervasive for a hostile work environment claim to be made out. *Jones v. Flagship In-*

ternational, 793 F.2d 714, 41 FEP Cases 358 (5th Cir. 1986). Proof of occasional, isolated, and /or trivial remarks are insufficient to satisfy the requirement of pervasiveness. *Downes v. Federal Aviation Administration,* 775 F.2d 288, 39 FEP Cases 100 (Fed. Cir. 1985). The working conditions have to become "poisoned." *Scott v. Sears, Roebuck & Co.,* 798 F.2d 210, 41 FEP Cases 805 (7th Cir. 1986). Evidence of racial and sexual harassment can be aggregated to establish a pervasive pattern of discriminatory harassment. *Hicks v. Gates Rubber Co.,* 833 F.2d 1406, 45 FEP Cases 608 (10th Cir. 1987).

5. *Severity:* The sexual harassing conduct has to be sufficiently severe to affect seriously the employee's psychological well-being. *Sparks v. Pilot Freight Carriers, Inc.,* 830 F.2d 554, 45 FEP Cases 160 (11th Cir. 1987). Even if the period of harassment is short, it is actionable if sufficiently intense. *Ross v. Double Diamond, Inc.,* 672 F.Supp. 261, 45 FEP Cases 313 (N.D. Tex. 1987). But a single incident of harassment is not regarded as sufficient to warrant liability. *Sardigal v. St. Louis National Stockyards Co.,* 42 FEP Cases 497 (S.D. Ill. 1986); *Sapp v. City of Warner Robins,* 655 F.Supp. 1043, 43 FEP Cases 486 *(M.D. Ga. 1987).* Occasional foul language or gestures by a supervisor also are insufficient. *Volk v. Coler,* 638 F.Supp. 1155, 44 FEP Cases 1111 (C.D. Ill. 1986).

6. *Nexus:* A sexual harassment complainant has to show a causal nexus between a supervisor's alleged sexual advances and the subsequent tangible adverse treatment to make out a *quid pro quo* claim. *Fisher v. Flynn,* 598 F.2d 663, 19 FEP Cases 932 (1st Cir. 1979); *Henson v. City of Dundee,* 682 F.2d 897, 29 FEP Cases 787 (11th Cir. 1982); *Sand v. George P. Johnson Co.,* 33 FEP Cases 716 (E.D. Mich. 1982); *Potenec v. Morgan Guaranty Trust Co.,* 44 FEP Cases 1256 (S.D. N.Y. 1985). But one court said that a female former part-time employee's failure to allege a causal connection between her employment opportunities and a desk officer's alleged refusal to forward her application for full-time employment because she refused his sexual advances went to the issue of damages rather than liability, since the mishandling of a job application based on the applicant's sex itself violates Title VII. *Brown v. Town of Allenstown,* 648 F.Supp. 831, 42 FEP Cases 611 (D. N.H. 1986).

7. *Factors:* Factors that should be considered in determining whether an abusive work environment exists are the nature of the unwelcome sexual acts or words, the frequency of the offensive encounters, the total number of days over which all of the offensive meetings occur, and the context in which the sexually harassing conduct occurred. A short duration can be enough if there is a pattern,

and a pattern can be established if harassment is frequent and/or intentionally offensive. *Ross v. Double Diamond, Inc.,* 672 F.Supp. 261, 45 FEP Cases 313 (N.D. Tex. 1987). The Sixth Circuit provided a somewhat different formulation. It said that a proper assessment of a hostile environment claim would include consideration of such objective and subjective factors as the nature of the alleged harassment, the background and experience of the employee, her co-workers, and her supervisors, the totality of the physical environment of her work area, the lexicon of obscenity that pervaded the environment of the workplace both before and after her introduction into its environs, and her reasonable expectation on voluntarily entering that environment. *Rabidue v. Osceola Refining Co.,* 805 F.2d 611, 42 FEP Cases 631 (6th Cir. 1986).

8. *Differential treatment:* Severe sexual harassment becomes discriminatory because it deprives the victim of the right to participate in the workplace on an equal footing with others similarly situated. *Scott v. Sears, Roebuck & Co.,* 798 F.2d 210, 41 FEP Cases 805 (7th Cir. 1986). Thus, a sexual harassment claim is not made out when the complained-of conduct proves equally offensive to male and female employees. *Rabidue v. Osceola Refining Co.,* 805 F.2d 611, 42 FEP Cases 631 (6th Cir. 1986).

9. *Welcomeness:* Conduct that otherwise would constitute sexual harassment will not be actionable if the complaining employee welcomed it. *Gan v. Kepro Circuit Systems,* 28 FEP Cases 639 (E.D. Mo. 1982); *Evans v. National Post Office Mail Handlers Union,* 32 FEP Cases 634 (D. D.C. 1982). An employee cannot later complain that the conduct was unwelcomed if she did not so indicate at the time. *Ukarish v. Magnesium Elektron,* 31 FEP Cases 1315 (D. N.J. 1983); *Loftin-Boggs v. City of Meridian,* 633 F.Supp. 1323, 41 FEP Cases 532 (S.D. Miss. 1986). The EEOC takes the position that an employee who participates in activity of a sexual nature has an affirmative duty, once she decides that such activity is unwelcome, to notify the alleged harasser of her change in feelings; this notification will overcome the presumption that the continuing activity was not unwelcome to the employee after her participation in the activity ceased. *EEOC Decision No. 84-1,* 33 FEP Cases 1887 (November 28, 1983). While one court said, on the basis of its review of a female employee's character, that she would have welcomed rather than rejected what she claimed was a supervisor's sexual advance, *McLean v. Satellite Technology Services, Inc.,* 673 F.Supp. 1458, 45 FEP Cases 523 (E.D. Mo. 1987), another court ruled that the mere fact that a complaining employee may have engaged in certain behavior

in the past does not mean that she cannot assert that the complained-of conduct was unwelcome. *Swentek v. USAir, Inc.,* 830 F.2d 552, 44 FEP Cases 1808 (1987).

10. *Voluntariness:* Voluntariness should not be confused with welcomeness. The voluntariness of an employee's conduct does not determine whether the supervisor's conduct was unwelcome. *Meritor Savings Bank v. Vinson,* 477 U.S. 57, 40 FEP Cases 1822 (1986). Thus, the fact that an employee was voluntarily in a supervisor's hotel room and rode home with him voluntarily did not make the supervisor's sexual advances welcome, where she did not solicit or incite the supervisor's conduct in any way and, in fact, resisted his advances. *Boyd v. James S. Hayes Living Health Care Agency, Inc.,* 671 F.Supp. 1155, 44 FEP Cases 332 (W.D. Tenn. 1987).

11. *Applicable perspective:* Courts measure offensiveness on the basis of an objective standard — keyed to a reasonable person, a reasonable employee, or a reasonable victim — rather than by the plaintiff's actual reaction. The Sixth Circuit took the position that the trier of fact is to adopt the perspective of a reasonable person's reaction to a similar environment under essentially like or similar circumstances. A complainant who actually was offended by the conduct in question may not make out a claim of hostile environment, it said, unless the conduct would interfere with a hypothetical reasonable individual's work performance and affect seriously the psychological well-being of that reasonable person under like circumstances. But, according to the court, even a complainant who makes this showing cannot recover unless she also demonstrates that she was actually offended by the conduct and that she suffered some degree of injury as a result of the abusive and hostile work environment. *Rabidue v. Osceola Refining Co.,* 805 F.2d 611, 42 FEP Cases 631 (6th Cir. 1986). Thus, an employee who had an unusual sensitivity to actions that she perceived as sexual in nature was not a victim of sexual harassment, even though her supervisor may have attempted a flirtatious relationship with her during her first year of employment, since this conduct did not rise to the level of sexual harassment, one court found. *Sand v. George P. Johnson Co.,* 33 FEP Cases 716 (E.D. Mich. 1982). Courts appear to focus on the employer's conduct rather than on the employee's perception of that conduct. *Jennings v. D.H.L. Airlines,* 101 F.R.D. 549, 34 FEP Cases 1423 (N.D. Ill. 1984). Thus, an employer may not conduct discovery into the sexual proclivities of the complaining employee. *Mitchell v. Hutchings,* 116 F.R.D. 481, 44 FEP Cases 615 (D. Utah 1987). Furthermore, the fact that some employees did not object to an owner's

conduct does not establish that the complained-of conduct was objectively inoffensive. *Priest v. Rotary,* 634 F.Supp. 571, 40 FEP Cases 208 (N.D. Calif. 1986).

12. *Burden of proof:* Most courts that have considered the question of how to prove and defend a hostile-environment case have decided that the three-step disparate treatment model of proof adopted by the Supreme Court in *McDonnell Douglas Corp. v. Green,* 411 U.S. 792, 5 FEP Cases 965 (1973) cannot be applied in full force. *McDonnell Douglas* requires the plaintiff to present enough evidence at the *prima facie* case stage to create an inference of discrimination, but the hostile-environment cases have required the plaintiff to shoulder a heavier burden. The Eleventh Circuit noted that a hostile-environment claim does not present an elusive question of intentional discrimination. *Henson v. City of Dundee,* 682 F.2d 897 (11th Cir. 1982). Thus, the Fourth Circuit said that a complainant is required to show that sexually harassing actions took place; the employer can then attempt to demonstrate either that the events did not take place or that they were isolated or genuinely trivial. The court also required the complainant to prove that the employer knew or should have known of the harassment and did not correct the situation. *Katz v. Dole,* 709 F.2d 251, 31 FEP Cases 1521 (4th Cir 1983). The Sixth Circuit decided that the most efficient procedural format was to require the complainant to prove that she was subjected to a sexually hostile work environment. The employer could then present a defense, which the complainant could challenge as pretextual. *Rabidue v. Osceola Refining Co.,* 805 F.2d 611, 42 FEP Cases 631 (6th Cir. 1986). One district court placed on the complainant the burden of proving that she was subjected to unwelcome harassment, that the harassment was based on sex, that it affected a term, condition, or privilege of employment, that the employer failed to take prompt remedial action despite its actual or constructive knowledge of the harassment, and that she acted reasonably under the circumstances. *Volk v. Coler,* 638 F.Supp. 1555, 44 FEP Cases 1111 (C.D. Ill. 1986).

Specific Types of Situations:

1. *Verbal abuse:* Verbal abuse is enough to find liability if it constitutes a pattern of conduct. *Katz v. Dole,* 709 F.2d 251, 31 FEP Cases 1521 (4th Cir. 1983); *Owens v. United States,* 822 F.2d 408, 44 FEP Cases 247 (3d Cir. 1987); *Swentek v. USAir, Inc.,* 830 F.2d 552, 44 FEP Cases 1808 (1987); *Delgado v. Lehman,* 665 F.Supp. 460, 43 FEP Cases 593 (E.D. Va. 1987); *Barbetta v. Chemlawn Services*

Corp., 669 F.Supp. 569, 44 FEP Cases 1563 (W.D. N.Y. 1987). But verbal abuse will not create liability if the complaining employee never indicated that it was unwelcomed. *Ukarish v. Magnesium Elektron,* 31 FEP Cases 1315 (D. N.J. 1983). Occasional foul language or gestures by a supervisor toward an employee do not establish sexual harassment. *Volk v. Coler,* 638 F.Supp. 1555, 44 FEP Cases 1111 (C.D. Ill. 1986); *Seep v. Commercial Motor Freight, Inc.,* 575 F.Supp. 1097, 45 FEP Cases 203 (S.D. Ohio 1983). The fact that a female employee was the subject of gender-related jokes and occasional teasing is not enough to establish a hostile work environment, since the remarks were not obvious and intrusive. *Hallquist v. Max Fish Plumbing and Heating Co.,* No. 85-1965-C (D. Mass. August 14, 1987).

2. *Pictures and photographs:* A work atmosphere can be abusive to female employees if the walls are laden with sexually explicit pictures and photographs, several courts have said. *Arnold v. City of Seminole,* 614 F.Supp. 853, 40 FEP Cases 1539 (E.D. Okla. 1985); *Barbetta v. Chemlawn Services Corp.,* 669 F.Supp. 569, 44 FEP Cases 1563 (W.D. N.Y. 1987). But the Sixth Circuit apparently has decided that exposure to sexually oriented posters does not result in intimidating, hostile, or offensive working environment. *Rabidue v. Osceola Refining Co.,* 805 F.2d 611, 42 FEP Cases 631 (1986).

3. *Sexually suggestive uniforms:* A sexually provocative dress code that is imposed as a condition of employment and that subjects employees to sexual harassment can violate Title VII. *Marentette v. Michigan Host, Inc.,* 506 F.Supp. 909, 24 FEP Cases 1665 (E.D. Mich. 1980). Thus, an employer was found liable for requiring a female lobby attendant to wear a sexually revealing "Bicentennial uniform" that resulted in harassment by the public. *EEOC v. Sage Realty Corp.,* 507 F.Supp. 599, 24 FEP Cases 1521 (S.D. N.Y. 1981). But one court rejected an employee's claim that she was required to wear "skimpy costumes." It noted that she wore costumes of her own choice that belonged to her, that were furnished to her, and that were not forced on her. *Sardigal v. St. Louis National Stockyards Co.,* 42 FEP Cases 497 (S.D. Ill. 1986).

4. *Homosexual advances:* Unwelcome homosexual harassment is a violation of Title VII. *Wright v. Methodist Youth Services, Inc.,* 511 F.Supp. 307, 25 FEP Cases 563 (N.D. Ill. 1981); *Joyner v. AAA Cooper Transportation,* 597 F.Supp. 537, 36 FEP Cases 1644 (1983), affirmed, 749 F.2d 732, 41 FEP Cases 496 (11th Cir. 1984); *EEOC Decision No. 81-16,* 27 FEP Cases 1789 (January 26, 1981). But the Sixth Circuit rejected a claim of intentional infliction of emotional

distress as a result of a supervisor's conduct, which included homosexual advances. The court said that the employee's reactions were consistent with those of any employee faced with a unhappy or unpleasant situation. *Polk v. Yellow Freight System, Inc.,* 801 F.2d 190, 41 FEP Cases 1279 (6th Cir. 1986).

5. *Preferences for acquiescing employees:* Courts, following the EEOC guidelines, have found Title VII violations when employers promote employees who give sexual favors to supervisors rather than other, better-qualified employees. *King v. Palmer,* 778 F.2d 878, 39 FEP Cases 877 (D.C. Cir. 1985), rehearing denied, 778 F.2d 878. 883, 40 FEP Cases 190 (D.C. Cir. 1986); *Toscanno v. Nimmo,* 570 F.Supp. 1197, 32 FEP Cases 1401 (D. Del. 1983); *Priest v. Rotary,* 634 F.Supp. 571, 40 FEP Cases 208 (N.D. Calif. 1986). But there can be no liability when a supervisor has a sexual relationship with another employee if that employee does not obtain the promotion in question. *Anderson v. University Health Center of Pittsburgh,* 623 F.Supp. 795, 41 FEP Cases 1197 (W.D. Pa. 1985). Moreover, the Second Circuit refused to find an employer guilty of sex discrimination for hiring a supervisor's paramour, saying that the men who were rejected for the position were in precisely the same situation as ay woman other than the paramour. *DeCintio v. Westchester County Medical Center,* 807 F.2d 304, 42 FEP Cases 921 (2d Cir. 1986).

Liability Issues:

1. *Agency:* Employers that are not put on notice of a supervisor's sexual harassment can be held directly liable when the supervisor is an agent of the employer, since Title VII's definition of an employer includes an agent of the employer. *Sparks v. Pilot Freight Carriers, Inc.,* 830 F.2d 1554, 45 FEP Cases 160 (11th Cir. 1987); *Hicks v. Gates Rubber Co.,* 833 F.2d 1406, 45 FEP Cases 608 (10th Cir. 1987); *Boyd v. James S. Hayes Living Health Care Agency, Inc.,* 671 F.Supp. 1155, 44 FEP Cases 332 (W.D. Tenn. 1987). But some courts require, for liability to attach, that there be some benefit to or acquiescence by the employer arising from the agent's behavior. *Ferguson v. E.I. duPont de Nemours and Co.,* 560 F.Supp. 1172, 31 FEP Cases 795 (D. Del. 1983); *Brown v. Town of Allenstown,* 648 F.Supp. 831, 42 FEP Cases 611 (D. N.H. 1986); *Carrero v. New York City Housing Authority,* 668 F.Supp. 196, 44 FEP Cases 1772 (S.D. N.Y. 1987).

2. *Liability for co-employees:* The EEOC takes the position that an employer is not liable for sexual harassment perpetrated by co-employees if it does not have knowledge of their activity or if, when it learns of the harassment, takes effective action to end it. The

courts have agreed with this position. *Swentek v. USAir, Inc.,* 830 F.2d 552, 44 FEP Cases 1808 (4th Cir. 1987); *Durant v. Owens-Illinois Glass Co.,* 517 F.Supp. 710, 31 FEP Cases 215 (E.D. La. 1980), affirmed, 656 F.2d 89, 31 FEP Cases 228 (5th Cir. 1981); *Ross v. Communications Satellite Corp.,* 34 FEP Cases 260 (D. Md. 1984); *Zabkowicz v. West Bend Co.,* 589 F.Supp. 780, 35 FEP Cases 610 (E.D. Wis. 1984); *Collins v. Pfizer, Inc.,* 39 FEP Cases 1316 (D. Conn. 1985); *Miller v. Lindenwood Female College,* 616 F.Supp. 860, 40 FEP Cases 510 (E.D. Mo. 1985); *Freedman v. American Standard, Inc.,* 41 FEP Cases 471 (D. N.J. 1986). But the employer can be liable if the employer's officials disregarded the complaints of harassment. *Estate of Scott v. deLeon,* 603 F.Supp. 1328, 37 FEP Cases 563 (E.D. Mich. 1985). Conversely, the employer will not be liable if the complaining employee refuses to cooperate in an investigation of her claims, thereby preventing the employer from learning the facts of the alleged harassment. *Hollis v. Fleetguard, Inc.,* 668 F.Supp. 631, 44 FEP Cases 1527 (M.D. Tenn. 1987).

3. *Sexual harassment by non-employees:* An employee is liable for sexual harassment by non-employees — such as customers and clients — only if it had adequate notice of the harassment. Thus, one employer was found liable for requiring a female lobby attendant, despite her complaints, to wear a sexually revealing "Bicentennial uniform" that resulted in harassment by the public. *EEOC v. Sage Realty Corp.,* 507 F.Supp. 599, 24 FEP Cases 1521 (S.D. N.Y. 1981). Another employer was found to have acted unlawfully by requiring a female employee cheerfully to accept suggestive remarks by a non-employee who provided a substantial amount of business to the employer. *Crockwell v. Blackmon-Mooring Steamatic, Inc.,* 627 F.Supp. 800, 43 FEP Cases 1451 (W.D. Tenn. 1985). The EEOC ruled that a restaurant owner was liable to a waitress for his failure to take corrective action when she complained that a male customer subjected her to unwelcome physical, as well as verbal, conduct of a sexual nature that interfered with her work performance. *EEOC Decision No. 84-3,* 34 FEP Cases 1887 (February 16, 1984).

4. *Constructive knowledge:* Knowledge of the alleged harassment can be imputed to the employer under certain circumstances. One court said that constructive knowledge could be inferred if, as alleged, sexual harassment was widespread and common among the employer's supervisory personnel. *Cummings v. Walsh Construction Co.,* 561 F.Supp. 872, 31 FEP Cases 930 (S.D. Ga. 1983). Another court said that constructive knowledge could be found from the fact that the alleged sexual incidents took place over a period of two

years despite protests from female employees. *Barbetta v. Chemlawn Services Corp.,* 669 F.Supp. 569, 44 FEP Cases 1563 (W.D. N.Y. 1987). But evidence of three isolated incidents of alleged harassment by a supervisor extending over three years was found insufficient to justify imputing constructive knowledge to the employer of the supervisor's conduct. *Smith v. Acme Spinning Co.,* 40 FEP Cases 1104 (W.D. N.C. 1986).

5. *Individual liability of supervisors:* One court held that a supervisor who engages in sexual harassment can be held individually liable under Title VII for back pay, though not for reinstatement or other equitable relief, *Salazar v. Church's Fried Chicken, Inc.,* 44 FEP Cases 472 (S.D. Tex. 1987), but another court, following Ninth Circuit precedent, decided that a supervisor cannot be liable for back pay under Title VII. *Seib v. Elko Motor Inn,* 648 F.Supp. 272, 42 FEP Cases 1708 (D.Nev. 1986). Courts disagree as to whether supervisors who allegedly either knew or should have known about a non-supervisory employee's rude remarks and sexual advances but did nothing to stop his conduct can be found liable under Title VII. Compare *Hendrix v. Fleming Companies,* 650 F.Supp. 301, 42 FEP Cases 461 (W.D. Okla. 1986) (no liability because actual misfeasance is necessary for liability) with *Robson v. Eva's Super Market,* 538 F.Supp. 857, 30 FEP Cases 1212 (N.D. Ohio 1982) (supervisor can be liable in capacity as employer's agent). Supervisors who refuse to act can be held liable under 42 U.S.C. Sec.1983. *Wymer v. N.Y. State Division for Youth,* 671 F.Supp. 210, 44 FEP Cases 1785 (W.D. N.Y. 1987).

6. *Union liability:* Unions as well as employers are forbidden to engage in sexual harassment. The EEOC's sexual harassment guidelines apply to a union's relationship to its members and employers with which it has agreements. *Egger v. Local 276, Plumbers and Pipefitters Union,* 644 F.Supp. 795, 41 FEP Cases 1465 (D. Mass. 1986). Union officials who sexually harass a female union member can be sued under the Racketeer Influenced and Corrupt Organizations Act. *Hunt v. Weatherbee,* 626 F.Supp. 1097, 39 FEP Cases 1469 (D. Mass. 1986).

7. *Constructive discharge:* A sexually harassed employee who leaves her job to escape the harassment may be able to recover back pay even after she stops working if she shows that the harassment was intolerable and that a reasonable person would have felt compelled to resign. See *Coley v. Consolidated Rail Corp.,* 561 F.Supp. 645, 34 FEP Cases 129 (E.D. Mich. 1982); *Brooms v. Regal Tube Co.,* 44 FEP Cases 1119 (N.D. Ill. 1987). A constructive-discharge claim can be made out even if the employee does not immediately leave her

employment. *Barbetta v. Chemlawn Services Corp.,* 669 F.Supp. 569, 44 FEP Cases 1563 (W.D. N.Y. 1987). But because the standard is that of a reasonable employee, an employee who leaves her employment without giving the employer a sufficient opportunity to stop the harassment may be denied relief. *Yates v. Avco Corp.,* 819 F.2d 630, 43 FEP Cases 1595 (6th Cir. 1987); *Dornhecker v. Malibu Grand Prix Corp.,* 828 F.2d 307, 44 FEP Cases 1604 (5th Cir. 1987).

8. *Retaliation:* It is a separate violation of Title VII for an employer to retaliate against an employee because she complained of alleged sexual harassment. *Crockwell v. Blackmon-Mooring Steamatic, Inc.,* 627 F.Supp. 800, 43 FEP Cases 1451 (W.D. Tenn. 1985); *Boyd v. James S. Hayes Living Care Agency, Inc.,* 671 F.Supp. 1155, 44 FEP Cases 332 (W.D. Tenn. 1987). But the employee has to show a causal connection between her complaints and her discharge. *Hollis v. Fleetguard, Inc.,* 668 F.Supp. 631, 44 FEP Cases 1527 (M.D. Tenn. 1987). Thus, terminated employees made out a case of retaliatory discharge by showing that the employer was highly agitated by the fact that they had complained to its management and to the county sheriff about sexual harassment. *Ross v. Double Diamond, Inc.,* 672 F.Supp. 261, 45 FEP Cases 313 (N.D. Tex. 1987).

9. *Adverse treatment by non-harasser:* Courts have rejected claims of *quid pro quo* harassment where the supervisor who makes the decision to deny a merit increase or to discharge an employee is not the person who engaged in the harassment. *Barrett v. Florida Power & Light Co.,* 42 FEP Cases 1816 (S.D. Fla. 1987); *Sapp v. City of Warner Robins,* 655 F.Supp. 1043, 43 FEP Cases 486 (M.D. Ga. 1987); *Potenec v. Morgan Guaranty Trust Co.,* 44 FEP Cases 1256 (S.D. N.Y. 1985). But liability may attach if the discharging supervisor had consulted with the harassing supervisor. *Sparks v. Pilot Freight Carriers, Inc.,* 830 F.2d 1554, 45 FEP Cases 160 (11th Cir. 1987).

Treatment of Supervisors Accused of Harassment:

1. *Age and state-law claims:* Supervisors who are discharged or otherwise punished for allegedly engaging in sexual harassment usually have obtained no judicial relief. Courts have rejected age discrimination claims, *Crimm v. Missouri Pacific Railroad Co.,* 750 F.2d 703, 36 FEP Cases 883 (8th Cir. 1984; *Johnson v. Perkins Restaurants, Inc.,* 815 F.2d 1220, 43 FEP Cases 830 (8th Cir. 1987). They have rejected claims of breach of contract and other state-law claims, *Johnson v. International Minerals and Chemical Corp.,* 40

FEP Cases 1651 (D. S.D. 1986), but see *Jones v. Intermountain Power Project,* 794 F.2d 546, 41 FEP Cases 1 (10th Cir. 1986).

2. *Reverse discrimination:* Reverse sexual-harassment actions have been uniformly unsuccessful. In rejecting a discharged male supervisor's claim, the Tenth Circuit noted that he was replaced by another man. This indicated, it said, that, under the same circumstances, a woman would not have been treated any differently. *Jones v. Intermountain Power Project,* 794 F.2d 546, 41 FEP Cases 1 (10th Cir. 1986). A district court ruled that a male supervisor who was discharged following complaints that he was sexually harassing employees did not establish a *prima facie* case, inasmuch as he was replaced by another man. The court further held that the employer was justified in discharging him by showing that it reasonably believed that he had made unwelcome sexual overtures that had an adverse effect on the employees' work environment. It said that the employer was not barred from discharging him by its failure ever to have adopted an official policy with regard to sexual harassment. *Fench v. Mead Corp.,* 33 FEP Cases 635 (S.D. Ohio 1983). Another district court upheld the discipline of a black male teacher's aide on the ground that he failed to show that the disciplinary measures enforced against him were more severe than those enforced against another person of a different race or sex. *Crawford v. Charlotte-Mecklenberg Board of Education,* 576 F.Supp. 812, 41 FEP Cases 1100 (W.D. N.C. 1986).

3. *Libel:* The Fifth Circuit overturned a judgment in favor of a former employee who brought a defamation action after he was discharged following a complaint that he had engaged in sexual harassment. The employer had sent a memorandum to all supervisors and employees following his discharge in which it referred to the reasons for discharge, although the memorandum did not mention the former employee by name. The court said that the employer had a qualified privilege to inform employees about harassment, but it allowed the former employee to pursue a claim that the employer abused its privilege by excessive publication. *Garziano v. E.I. duPont de Nemours & Co.,* 818 F.2d 380, 43 FEP Cases 1790 (5th Cir. 1987). But a former county official stated a claim for violation of due process by alleging that, after he was forced to resign without a hearing because of allegations that he had sexually harassed two employees, the county published sordid tales of his "immoral" activities, thereby spreading them throughout the community and tarnishing his reputation. *Huff v. County of Butler,* 524 F.Supp. 751, 27 FEP Cases 63 (W.D. Pa. 1981).

4. *Race:* A black supervisor who was discharged because he had kissed a white female employee while off duty and because it was believed that he had engaged in unacceptable off-duty behavior with another white female employee established a Title VII violation. The supervisor showed that no superior had ever suggested to him that touching people was improper, that none of the employer's policies applied to off-duty actions, and that he was not given the names of the complaining parties even though three white male employees, who were accused of misconduct considerably more suggestive than his, had been given the names of the complainants, and two of these employees had been told specifically what the complaints against them were. *Marsh v. Digital Equipment Corp.,* 44 FEP Cases 1192 (D. Ariz. 1987).

5. *Federal supervisors:* The courts have rejected most of the claims filed by discharged or demoted U.S. government supervisors. *Sipes v. U.S. Postal Service,* 677 F.2d 375, 30 FEP Cases 1257 (4th Cir. 1982); *Hostettler v. United States,* 739 F.2d 983, 35 FEP Cases 693 (4th Cir. 1984); *Hanley v. General Services Administration,* 829 F.2d 23, 44 FEP Cases 1241 (Fed. Cir. 1987). The supervisor can be removed even if no discrimination complaint is filed. *Carosella v. U.S. Postal Service,* 816 F.2d 638, 43 FEP Cases 845 (Fed. Cir. 1987). But when an agency charges a supervisor with sexual harassment, the agency is to be held to the same standard as an employee who might bring the charge. *Downes v. Federal Aviation Administration,* 775 F.2d 288, 39 FEP Cases 70 (Fed. Cir. 1985). The Federal Circuit decided that the removal of a supervisor for one incident of harassment was too severe a penalty; it said that he should be placed in a non-supervisory position and given counseling. *Jackson v. Veterans Administration,* 768 F.2d 1325, 39 FEP Cases 100 (Fed. Cir. 1985).

Defenses Against Liability

1. *Inadequate work performance:* An employer that sexually harasses an employee, whose work performance then suffers, cannot justify its discharge of the employee on the ground that her work performance is inadequate. *Lamb v. Drillco Division,* 32 FEP Cases 105 (S.D. Tex. 1983); *Delgado v. Lehman,* 665 F.Supp. 460, 43 FEP Cases 593 (E.D. Va. 1987). But inadequate work performance is otherwise a valid justification for discharge of an employee who had been sexually harassed. *Neville v. Taft Broadcasting Co.,* 42 FEP Cases 1314 (W.D. N.Y. 1987).

2. *Investigation:* An employer that engages in a prompt and good-faith investigation of a claim of sexual harassment will not be found

liable for hostile-environment discrimination, even though it erroneously concludes that harassment did not occur. *Sapp v. City of Warner Robins,* 655 F.Supp. 1043, 43 FEP Cases 486 (M.D. Ga. 1987); *Carrero v. New York City Housing Authority,* 668 F.Supp. 196, 44 FEP Cases 1772 (S.D. N.Y. 1987). The employer is not required, when it conducts an investigation, to credit all of an employee's allegations of harassment in order to escape liability. *Swentek v. USAir, Inc.,* 830 F.2d 552, 44 FEP Cases 1808 (4th Cir. 1987). Documents relating to such an investigation are discoverable to the extent that they were generated for the purpose of determining whether the alleged harasser should be continued in his job and not in anticipation of a lawsuit. *Foore v. Crumpton,* 43 FEP Cases 638 (D. Ore. 1987).

3. *Believability:* Some sexual-harassment cases turn on credibility, and employers have won when they have demonstrated that the complainants simply made up their stories. See *Grier v. Casey,* 643 F.Supp. 298, 41 FEP Cases 1259 (W.D. N.C. 1986); *Sardigal v. St. Louis National Stockyards Co.,* 42 FEP Cases 497 (S.D. Ill. 1986); *Jackson-Coley v. U.S. Army Corps of Engineers,* 655 F.Supp. 122, 43 FEP Cases 617 (E.D. Mich. 1987); *Swentek v. USAir, Inc.,* 830 F.2d 552, 44 FEP Cases 1808 (4th Cir. 1987).

4. *Non-seriousness of conduct:* Employers also have prevailed by showing that the complainant herself did not think that the complained-of conduct was serious at the time it occurred. *Highlander v. K.F.C. National Management Co.,* 805 F.2d 644, 42 FEP Cases 654 (6th Cir. 1986); *Smith v. Acme Spinning Co.,* 40 FEP Cases 1104 (W.D. N.C. 1986); *Neville v. Taft Broadcasting Co.,* 42 FEP Cases 1314 (W.D. N.Y. 1986).

5. *Proper response:* Employers have prevailed in hostile environment cases by showing that they took appropriate measures as soon as feasible. Thus, the Fifth Circuit overturned an award in favor of a female employee, who was sexually harassed by a co-worker, on the ground that the employer's president personally assured her about 12 hours after she complained that she would not have to work with the co-worker after the current project ended in just one and one-half days. *Dornhecker v. Malibu Grand Prix Corp.,* 828 F.2d 307, 44 FEP Cases 1604 (5th Cir. 1987). Another employer was exonerated by showing that it promptly investigated the allegations of harassment, that it assumed the truth of the allegations and took prompt remedial measures, and that the incidents indisputably stopped. *Ferguson v. E.I. duPont de Nemours and Co.,* 560 F.Supp. 1172, 31 FEP Cases 795 (D. Del. 1983). But an employer that offered comparable

employment in a nearby location to a female employee who complained of sexual harassment by a co-worker was denied summary judgment on the ground that the evidence was ambiguous as to whether it took "immediate and appropriate corrective action" within the meaning of the EEOC's sexual-harassment guidelines. *Taylor v. Faculty-Student Assn. of State University College at Fredonia, Inc.*, 40 FEP Cases 1292 (W.D. N.Y. 1986).

6. *Mere admonitions:* Employers that have been put on notice of the existence of sexual harassment cannot avoid liability merely by indicating the existence of an official policy against such harassment; it cannot limit its preventive measures to mere admonitions against sexual harassment if the harassment continues. *Katz v. Dole,* 709 F.2d 251, 31 FEP Cases 1521 (4th Cir. 1983); *Delgado v. Lehman,* 665 F.Supp. 460, 43 FEP Cases 593 (E.D. Va. 1987).

7. *Policy against harassment:* The fact that an employer has a policy against sexual harassment does not, by itself, insulate it from liability for a supervisor's harassment of an employee who does not come forward to complain to the employer. While the Supreme Court in *Meritor Savings Bank v. Vinson,* 477 U.S. 57, 40 FEP Cases 1822 (1986), suggested that a properly designed policy might provide a defense, the Sixth Circuit found an employer's policy vague on paper, vague and ad hoc in its implementation, and ineffective. *Yates v. Avco Corp.,* 819 F.2d 630, 43 FEP Cases 1595 (6th Cir. 1987). Another court held a parent corporation liable for the sexual harassment of an employee of its wholly owned subsidiary on grounds that the subsidiary's sexual-harassment policy was distributed under the parent's letterhead and that the parent's management actively participated in determining how to handle the employee's allegations. *Brooms v. Regal Tube Co.,* 44 FEP Cases 1119 (N.D. Ill. 1987).

Evidence

1. *Other employees:* It is appropriate, in determining whether the alleged harassment is part of a pattern, to look at the treatment of other employees of the same gender. *Phillips v. Smalley Maintenance Services, Inc.,* 711 F.2d 1524, 32 FEP Cases 975 (11th Cir. 1983); *Vinson v. Taylor,* 753 F.2d 141, 36 FEP Cases 1423 (D.C. Cir. 1985); *Hicks v. Gates Rubber Co.,* 833 F.2d 1406, 45 FEP Cases 608 (10th Cir. 1987); *Goodall v. Sedgwick County,* 43 FEP Cases 1683 (D. Kan. 1985). But the Fifth Circuit held that testimony of sexually harassing incidents reported by other women were not relevant to a lone female employee's own claim absent evidence that such incidents affected her psychological well-being. *Jones v. Flagship International,*

793 F.2d 784, 41 FEP Cases 358 (5th Cir. 1986). Furthermore, the fact that some employees did not complain of harassment does not, by itself, serve as a defense to a harassment claim by other employees. *Priest v. Rotary,* 634 F.Supp. 571, 40 FEP Cases 208 (N.D. Calif. 1986).

2. *Character evidence:* One court, while rejecting a claim of sexual harassment on the ground that the alleged advance did not occur, ruled that, in light of the employee's character, she would have welcomed rather than rejected any advance. *McLean v. Satellite Technology Services, Inc.,* 673 F.Supp. 1458, 45 FEP Cases 523 (E.D. Mo. 1987). But other courts have forbidden pretrial discovery seeking evidence as to the complainant's character on the ground that such evidence is irrelevant. *Priest v. Rotary,* 98 F.R.D. 755, 32 FEP Cases 1064 (N.D. Calif. 1983); *Mitchell v. Hutchings,* 116 F.R.D. 481, 44 FEP Cases 615 (D. Utah 1987).

3. *Psychological evidence:* Courts have been reluctant to permit employers, in pretrial discovery, to probe too closely into the personal lives of sexual-harassment complainants. Thus, one court refused to permit an employer, which claimed that a former employee's complaints of sexual harassment were caused by her emotional problems, to subpoena the records of her psychologist. The court explained that the focus of her sexual-harassment claim was on the employer's conduct rather than on her perception of and reaction to that conduct. *Jennings v. D.H.L. Airlines,* 101 F.R.D. 549, 34 FEP Cases 1423 (N.D. Ill. 1984). Another court refused to permit an employer to explore a complainant's sexual history. *Priest v. Rotary,* 98 F.R.D. 755, 32 FEP Cases 1064 (N.D. Calif. 1983). A third court said that the employer could discover evidence concerning the complainants' work environment and their work-place behavior, but not evidence as to their past sexual conduct. The court also allowed the employer to question a psychologist who treated one of the employees for emotional trauma, even though he could be asked to discuss matters that would otherwise be inadmissible. *Mitchell v. Hutchings,* 116 F.R.D. 481, 44 FEP Cases 615 (D. Utah 1987).

Non-Title VII Remedies

1. *Civil Rights Act of 1871:* Most courts agree that a public employer can be sued under 42 U.S.C. Sec. 1983 for subjecting a female employee to sexual harassment. This conduct is viewed as a violation of the Equal Protection Clause of the Fourteenth Amendment. *Bohen v. City of East Chicago,* 799 F.2d 1180, 41 FEP Cases

1108 (7th Cir. 1986); *Woerner v. Brzeczek,* 519 F.Supp. 517, 26 FEP Cases 897 (N.D. Ill. 1981); *Skadegaard v. Farrell,* 578 F.Supp. 1209, 33 FEP Cases 1528 (D. N.J. 1984); *Scott v. City of Overland Park,* 595 F.Supp. 520, 41 FEP Cases 1211 (D. Kan. 1984); *Gobla v. Crestwood School District,* 609 F.Supp. 972, 38 FEP Cases 977 (M.D. Pa. 1985); *Saldivar v. Cadena,* 622 F.Supp. 949, 39 FEP Cases 836 (W.D. Wis. 1985). One court went so far as to hold that it was clearly established by 1979 that sexual harassment could violate equal protection, even though no case had yet considered the issue, since common sense as well as relevant Title VII case law indicated that such harassment involved the sort of invidious gender discrimination that the Equal Protection Clause forbade. *Estate of Scott v. deLeon,* 603 F.Supp. 1328, 37 FEP Cases 563 (E.D. Mich. 1985).

2. *Intentional infliction of emotional distress:* Title VII does not authorize the recovery of compensatory or punitive damages. The only relief, other than attorneys' fees, that is available for hostile-environment discrimination is a declaratory judgment and an injunction. Thus, complainants have sought to bring claims under state law. The most common claim is for intentional infliction of emotional distress. The cases are mixed on the availability and success of this claim. Cases allowing it include *Davis v. U.S. Steel Corp.,* 779 F.2d 209, 39 FEP Cases 955 (4th Cir. 1985); *Vegh v. General Electric Co.,* 34 FEP Cases 135 (E.D. Pa. 1983); *Shaffer v. National Can Co.,* 565 F.Supp. 909, 34 FEP Cases 172 (E.D. Pa. 1983); *Coleman v. American Broadcasting Companies, Inc.,* 38 FEP Cases 65 (D. D.C. 1985); *Fawcett v. IDS Financial Services, Inc.,* 41 FEP Cases 589 (W.D. Pa. 1986); *Clay v. Quartet Manufacturing Co.,* 644 F.Supp. 56, 45 FEP Cases 51 (N.D. Ill. 1986); and *Egger v. Local 276, Plumbers and Pipefitters Union,* 644 F.Supp. 795 (D. Mass. 1986). Cases rejecting this remedy include *Forde v. Royal's, Inc.,* 537 F.Supp. 1137, 31 FEP Cases 213 (S.D. Fla. 1982); and *Hooten v. Pennsylvania College of Optometry,* 601 F.Supp. 1151, 36 FEP Cases 1826 (E.D. Pa. 1984). The Sixth Circuit, in rejecting a discharged employee's contention that she should be able to recover for intentional infliction of emotional distress because of a supervisor's unwanted touching, sexual suggestions, and homosexual advances, declared that her reactions to the supervisor's conduct were "consistent with those of any employee faced with an unhappy or unpleasant work situation." *Polk v. Yellow Freight System, Inc.,* 801 F.2d 190, 41 FEP Cases 1279 (6th Cir. 1986).

3. *Other claims:* The Eleventh Circuit upheld a damage award of battery and invasion of privacy. *Phillips v. Smalley Maintenance Ser-*

vices, Inc., 711 F.2d 1524, 32 FEP Cases 975 (11th Cir. 1983). The Seventh Circuit recently upheld an award of compensatory and punitive damages for an employer's rape of an employee. *Gilardi v. Schroeder,* 45 FEP Cases 346 (7th Cir. 1987), affirming 672 F.Supp. 1043, 45 FEP Cases 283 (N.D. Ill. 1986). Employees have also been allowed to sue for intrusion and assault and battery, in addition to intentional infliction of emotional distress (*Rogers v. Loews L'Enfant Plaza Hotel,* 526 F.Supp. 523, 29 FEP Cases 828 (D. D.C. 1981).

4. *Federal employees:* Title VII is the exclusive remedy for U.S. government employees with claims of sex discrimination. *Brown v. General Services Administration,* 425 U.S. 820, 12 FEP Cases 1361 (1976). But it does not bar them from suing their supervisors under state tort law for acting outside their authority. See *Otto v. Heckler,* 781 F.2d 754, 39 FEP Cases 1754 (9th Cir. 1986); *Arnold v. United States,* 816 F.2d 1306, 43 FEP Cases 1256 (9th Cir. 1987); *Owens v. United States,* 822 F.2d 408, 44 FEP Cases 247 (3d Cir. 1987); *Stewart v. Thomas,* 538 F.Supp. 891, 30 FEP Cases 1609 (D. D.C. 1982); and *Epps v. Ripley,* 30 FEP Cases 1632 (D. D.C. 1982).

Questions & Answers

1. How meaningful is the difference between quad pro quo sexual harassment and hostile environment sexual harassment? Many courts believe that employers should be strictly liable if employees suffer economic harm as a result of being subjected to sexual advances, but that employers are entitled to notice at the managerial level before they should be held liable for maintaining a discriminatory work atmosphere. The underlying premise for the distinction appears to be this: An employer that has notice can stop the harassment, but actual harm to an employee is simply not redressable by a mere change in the working conditions. Since Title VII provides for recovery of economic losses but does not allow compensatory and punitive damages, the only remedy for an abusive work environment is an injunction. If the employer takes strong measures as soon as it learns of the misconduct, it is providing as much relief as an injunction would give.

In many cases, the only difference between the two types of harassment concerns not what the supervisor does, but how the employee reacts. If she simply puts up with what the supervisor says or does, she suffers from an abusive work environment (assuming that his remarks or actions create a sexually charged atmosphere). If she complains and is discharged as a result, she has a claim of *quid pro quo* discrimination. But suppose she has sex with her supervisor so that she can keep her job. What form of sexual harassment is this? The supervisor is taking advantage of the employee, based on his superior authority and her fear of losing her job, to obtain sexual gratification. But she is suffering no adverse economic consequences, since she has not lost any compensation and is unable, at least under Title VII, to seek damages. If this is regarded as a *quid pro quo* situation, the employer is liable for the supervisor's conduct even if the employee never tells the employer (assuming that the employer does not have an effective complaint system and assuming further that the failure to use such a system has no bearing on liability). But if it is a hostile environment situation, the employer is not liable unless it is told of the harassment by the victim or a co-employee or has a reasonable opportunity to find out. Yet the damage to the employee is the same in either event.

Thus, liability for psychological and other emotional harm to the employee depends on an employer's realization that the misconduct is occurring, but liability for financial harm is automatic. From an employer's perspective, it could be argued that it makes more sense to hold it financially liable only when it knew that harassment was occurring, since the ultimate harm to the employer is greater here than when it is being enjoined from committing or tolerating harassment.

Perhaps the real reason for the distinction between the two types of sexual harassment concerns the problem of proof. Psychological harm is harder to establish — and to rebut — than economic harm. Thus, for example, the Fifth Circuit, while holding that a tangible job detriment is not necessary to establish a *prima face* case of sexual harassment, declared that the absence of such detriment requires a commensurately higher showing that the sexually harassing conduct was pervasive and destructive of the working environment. *Jones v. Flagship International,* 793 F.2d 714, 41 FEP Cases 358 (5th Cir. 1986).

The hostile environment theory seems to treat the supervisor as though he were just a co-worker rather than as an agent of the employer (since the employer is liable for co-worker misdeeds only if it knows of them and fails to take effective action to stop them). But employees tend to be more reluctant to challenge a supervisor than someone who is just another employee; a supervisor can affect the terms and conditions of employment in a way that fellow employees cannot. A supervisor who takes advantage of his position to engage in work-environment harassment is behaving not very differently from one who causes economic detriment to the employee.

The *quid pro quo* theory may or may not depend on there being actual economic consequences (although it is not clear why the employer should be entitled to notice if the employee mitigates the employer's losses by not provoking the supervisor into causing economic harm to the employer). In any event, the courts have not clearly explained why the liability of an employer for the acts of a supervisor should turn on the employee's reaction to those acts rather than on the acts themselves or on the motive behind them.

2. Can the use of the agency theory reach the same results as the now-discredited strict liability approach of the court of appeals in Vinson? Cases handed down since *Vinson's* suggestion that employers may not always be strictly liable for the conduct of their supervisors show that some courts are attempting to develop a theory of agency that would achieve the same results that were obtained when they relied on the doctrine of *respondeat superior*. Under that doctrine, espoused in the EEOC guidelines and adopted by several courts of appeals, employers were strictly liable for the acts of their supervisors without regard to whether the supervisors were acting as employer agents (and, in fact, regardless of whether the supervisors' acts were actually for the benefit of the employer). The Supreme Court rejected this view in *Vinson,* but it did not say what the proper standard for liability was. The Court made a favorable reference to the agency standard, but then noted that "such common-law principles may not be transferable in all their particulars to Title VII."

An employer's liability for the acts of an agent depends on the relationship between the two and not on the extent of the employer's knowledge. The question is complicated by the Court's failure to indicate whether *any* agency relationship is sufficient to hold the employer liable or whether the relationship must take a particular form. In referring to the *Restatement (Second) of Agency,* the Court said merely, "See generally Restatement (Second) of Agency Sec.Sec.219-237 (1958)." But the Restatement offers numerous routes to the finding of an agency relationship. Some of these routes bear a striking resemblance to *respondeat superior*.

The issue is complicated by another fact. The *Vinson* court of appeals rejected the use of respondeat superior and instead looked to an agency theory! Yet that court's approach was rejected by the Supreme Court. Perhaps the court of appeals cast too wide an agen-

cy net: It seemed to hold an employer liable for *anything* the superior did, even if the supervisor had no authority over the employee.
But the Supreme Court did not reveal what it thought was wrong
with the court of appeals' approach. Hence, the matter is unsettled
— and unsettling.

Surprisingly, only five reported post-*Vinson* decisions have discussed the question of agency in the context of hostile work-environment harassment. The Sixth Circuit in *Yates v. Avco Corp.*, 819 F.2d
630, 43 FEP Cases 1595 (1987), upheld a liability finding on the
basis that it was grounded on "traditional agency principles." It said
that the harassment occurred at the office during regular working
hours and was carried out by someone with the authority to hire,
fire, promote, and discipline the employees. There was no question,
the court added, that harassment was foreseeable, since the
employer had a policy attempting to deal with it. The court then observed that because the person who committed the harassment was
both an agent and supervisor of the employer, it was easier to im-
pute his own knowledge to the employer's management than it
would have been had he been merely another employee.

The Eleventh Circuit was much more direct in *Sparks v. Pilot
Freight Carriers, Inc.*, 830 F.2d 1554, 45 FEP Cases 160 (1987). It
held that a company was directly liable for sexual harassment by
someone who could be regarded as an employer, even without
notice. Title VII defines "employer" to include an agent, it pointed
out. Thus, it said, an employer is automatically liable for a
supervisor's misconduct if he was its agent. Agency is not limited to
acts within the scope of employment, the court said. It noted that
Section 219(2)(d) of the Restatement (Second) of Agency makes a
master liable for the torts of his servants acting outside the scope of
their employment even when "the servant purported to act or to
speak on behalf of the principal and there was reliance upon apparent authority, or he was aided in accomplishing the tort by the existence of the agency relationship." Thus, there can be liability here,
the court said, even if the servant was acting entirely for his own
benefit and outside the scope of employment.

The Eleventh Circuit adopted the EEOC's proposal, made in its
Vinson brief, that an employer is directly liable where the supervisor
exercises the authority actually delegated to him by the employer, by
making or threatening to make decisions affecting the employment
status of his subordinates. In so doing, the court explicitly left open
the question of what rule should govern the employer's liability
when the sexual harassment claim rests exclusively on a hostile en-

vironment theory in which the supervisor did not explicitly or implicitly threaten to use his authority against the employee.

A dissenting judge argued that an employer should be automatically liable only when the supervisor's behavior was patently offensive. However, he asserted, when the supervisor's behavior is less than overtly offensive, the complainant should be required to display objection by some objective action at the time of the allegedly offensive conduct. The expression of dissatisfaction may provide notice to the employer, though there is no guarantee that it will, the judge observed, but he said that the objective demonstration of displeasure would clarify and define the otherwise ambiguous actions of the supervisor and would prevent any reinterpretation of the situation in hindsight.

The Tenth Circuit, like the Eleventh Circuit, has taken the position that the Restatement (Second) of Agency suggests that a supervisor's misconduct will bind his employer when he "purported to act or to speak on behalf of the principal and there was reliance on apparent authority, or he was aided in accomplishing the tort by the existence of the agency relation." Thus, it rejected the employer's claimed lack of notice as an absolute defense. *Hicks v. Gates Rubber Co.,* 833 F.2d 1406, 45 FEP Cases 608 (1987).

The district court in *Ross v. Double Diamond, Inc.,* 672 F.Supp. 261, 45 FEP Cases 313 (N.D. Tex. 1987), decided to follow the EEOC guideline that makes the employer automatically liable for the supervisor's acts of sexual harassment. The court noted that the supervisor was the manager of the employer's facility and had the power to hire and fire employees at that facility. It cited the court of appeals decision in *Vinson* as its authority for the proposition that an individual with this authority is considered a supervisory employee or agent for Title VII purposes.

But the fifth court to discuss the concept of agency took a very different approach. It looked at Section 219(1) of the Restatement (Second) of Agency, which says: "A master is subject to liability for the torts of his servants while acting in the scope of their employment." The court noted that the master is generally not liable for the acts of the servant acting outside that scope. The court suggested that the supervisor's conduct was outside the scope of his employment, since the employer had forbidden it. The court explored one of the exceptions to this approach, which is that the master is liable if it is reckless or negligent, and found that the employer failed to act against the supervisor only because it conducted a good-faith investigation of the sexual-harassment complaint and did not find evidence to support it. The court did not discuss any other bases of the Restatement for holding the employer liable for the supervisor's actions. In effect, while discussing the concept of agency, it applied *respondeat superior. Carrero v. New York City Housing Authority,* 668 F.Supp. 196, 44 FEP Cases 1772 (S.D. N.Y. 1987).

Except for the *Carrero* decision, the courts have been using agency theory to find employers liable for supervisory acts that constitute hostile environment discrimination. The supervisors were actually exercising their authority. Would the courts find liability if the supervisors threatened to use their authority? If so, would employer liability also be found if the supervisors merely made sexual advances and the employee-victim fears that complaining would cause the supervisor to take a different form of adverse action against her? The courts have not yet spoken on these questions.

3. If the employer makes a reasonable investigation of an employee's harassment complaint and incorrectly finds no misconduct, can it be liable for a supervisor's behavior? One recent decision, *Carrero v. New York City Housing Authority,* 668 F.Supp. 196, 44 FEP Cases 1772 (S.D. N.Y. 1987), took the position that the employer is not liable, despite the employee's complaint, for the hostile environment created by the supervisor. The court assumed that the supervisor was acting for his own motives and not on behalf of the employer when he harassed the complainant, who was a probationary employee. (See the discussion above concerning the court's theory of agency.) Therefore, it said, the employer could be liable only if it was negligent or reckless. But since the investigation was not negligent, the employer could not be liable, since, in effect, it lacked actual knowledge that the supervisor was harassing the employee.

The apparent assumption behind this result is that an employer's liability for hostile-environment harassment should be based on fault and that there can be no liability for mere errors. However, at the same time, the court noted that the employee failed her probationary period. Without indicating that she was the victim of *quid pro quo* harassment, the court said that she was entitled to a new probationary period under another supervisor.

The court's decision provides an incentive for employers to conduct investigations of sexual harassment complaints, so long as they are prepared to act on what they learn. By learning what their supervisors are doing, the employers can reduce their exposure by stopping the harassment. Under this decision, the cost of a good-faith mistake is borne by the employee rather than by the employer.

4. Should a hostile-environment complainant be required to demonstrate injury when the only Title VII remedy is an injunction? The Sixth Circuit requires female employees who are offended by the behavior of their supervisors and co-workers to show actual injury, even though that injury cannot, at least under Title VII, be recompensed in the form of compensatory damages. In *Rabidue v. Osceola Refining Co.*, 805 F.2d 611, 42 FEP Cases 631 (6th Cir. 1986), the court held that an employee who is actually offended by conduct that would have interfered with a reasonable individual's work performance and would have seriously affected such an individual's psychological well-being is also required to show that she suffered some degree of injury as a result.

Use of the reasonable-individual standard serves to exclude sexual harassment claims based on isolated or trivial remarks or incidents. Since not all women are offended by given remarks or actions, the requirement that a complainant show that she was actually offended is a important tool for ensuring that she is suing because of the remarks or actions and not for ulterior reasons. But the court's decision could lead to a judgment against an employee who brings a valid sexual-harassment claim in good faith. If her only injury is unhappiness at being subjected to such behavior or a sense that she should not have to put up with it, she apparently does not have enough cause to prevail. The court may be suggesting that she has to develop psychological problems before her claim will be recognized. But as one court pointed out, "The EEOC guidelines and the Courts of Appeals decisions in *Bundy* and *Henson*, all of which were relied on by the Supreme Court in *Vinson*, do not mention the need for complete psychological debilitation in order for there to be a successful claim under Title VII. Basically what these sources are saying is that the trial court should look at the totality of the circumstances and determine whether the harassment is so egregious that it will create an abusive work environment." *Ross v. Double Diamond, Inc.*, 672 F.Supp. 261, 45 FEP Cases 313, 319 (N.D. Tex. 1987).

5. How pervasive must offensive conduct be to affect the conditions of employment as a matter of law? Courts seem to have agreed on an "objective" standard — the reasonable employee — for determining whether conditions are abusive enough that liability should attach. They want to avoid the problem of the hypersensitive employee, see *Sand v. George F. Johnson Co.,* 33 FEP Cases 716 (E.D. Mich. 1982), and the employee who fabricates, see *Jackson-Colley v. U.S. Army Corps of Engineers,* 655 F.Supp. 122, 43 FEP Cases 617 (E.D. Mich. 1987). But the courts have also decided that there has to be a threshold of annoyance below which employers should not be held liable. As in *Rabidue v. Osceola Refining Co.,* 805 F.2d 611, 42 FEP Cases 631 (6th Cir. 1986), the courts have sometimes required a very high level of proof before they will find a Title VII violation. They seem not to want to find widespread harassment.

6. Should supervisory conduct that allegedly results in a hostile work environment be analyzed in terms of whether the employee is subjected to different treatment — without regard to whether the technical requirements for meeting the hostile work-environment standard is met — since Title VII forbids an employer to subject an employee to differential working conditions on the basis of sex? It is not clear whether the plaintiffs in the early sexual harassment cases argued that they were treated as they were because they were women and that they would not have been so treated had they been men. But the extensive litigation on the question whether the annoying and threatening conduct is severe enough to impose liability raises a question as to whether the judicial focus is misplaced.

Title VII forbids discrimination in conditions of employment. If a supervisor makes offensive remarks to a female employee that he would not make to a male employee, the employer is normally not held liable, since the courts require a pattern of offensive conduct, and they tend to assume that women who enter the workplace, especially places that historically have had few female employees, should have to put up with a certain amount of harassment. The consequence is that women who do not like sexual remarks and advances have no federal remedy.

The difficulty with the idea that any supervisory remarks or conduct should be forbidden is, of course, that not all women would be offended by the conduct at issue. Sexual harassment is not illegal if it is welcomed. It can be argued that a supervisor should be free to "test the waters" and find out whether the employee would welcome an advance. Under this view, the employee's reaction would put the supervisor on notice of how thereafter to proceed. If he continued the same conduct, then it would be appropriate to impose liability.

7. Should supervisory conduct occurring on the employer's premises during working hours be treated more severely than conduct outside of working hours or off the premises? As an original matter, it is not clear why mistreatment during working hours on the employer's premises is not automatically illegal if it occurs on the basis of sex. Title VII forbids sex discrimination in working conditions, and conduct to which only one sex is subjected because of gender cannot be but on the basis of sex. The problem may be due to the failure of courts and litigants to focus on the fact that the statute forbids unequal treatment (such as requiring only one sex to wear uniforms — see *Carroll v. Talman Federal Savings & Loan,* 604 F.2d 1028, 20 FEP Cases 764 (7th Cir. 1979)), without regard to the economic consequences of the unequal treatment. Discrimination in working conditions is as illegal as discrimination in promotions. A supervisor who, entirely because of personal predilections, sexually harasses an employee while at work is changing that employee's working conditions on the basis of sex. While this seems elementary, this analysis has not always been accepted.

Assume that the above argument is generally accepted. Would the analysis be different if the harassment occurs outside of working hours or if the supervisor expresses displeasure at that time? It can be argued that it is one thing for the employer to be liable for matters that occur on its premises — since it, theoretically at least, has control of those premises — and another thing to hold it responsible for matters that occur elsewhere after working hours. Of course, if the supervisor, off the job, threatens an employee who resists his off-the-job advances with adverse job consequences, it can be argued that this amounts to *quid pro quo* harassment. But if the supervisor refrains from making such threats, it can be argued that the employer should not be liable unless, at least, the employee complains to the employer. But since most employees view supervisors not only in terms of what they have done and are doing but also in terms of what they could do, it can be argued — at least from the subordinate's perspective — that a supervisor's off-the-job behavior always has job implications. Hence, the answer to the question may depend on whose perspective is the proper one — the employer's or the employee's.

8. Since the focus in a hostile-environment case is on whether the allegedly offending conduct was unwelcome, how far can an employer explore the matter? It seems clear, in light of the Supreme

Court's decision in *Vinson,* that the employer can offer evidence of the complainant's own behavior and dress to show that she welcomed the advances. Can the employer also discover the complainant's sexual history? The only court to discuss the subject since *Vinson* said that the employer did not show the relevance of this information. *Mitchell v. Hutchings,* 116 F.R.D. 481, 44 FEP Cases 615 (D. Utah 1987).

To the extent that courts adopt a narrow view of welcomeness, they make unnecessary an employer's discovery into the personal life of a complainant. Thus, the Fourth Circuit said in *Swentek v. USAir, Inc.,* 830 F.2d 552, 44 FEP Cases 1808 (1987), that the mere fact that a complainant may have engaged in certain behavior in the past did not mean that she cannot assert that the complained-of conduct was unwelcome. If this decision becomes generally accepted, employers likely will not be allowed to discover personal matters that are not directly tied to the incidents at issue.

9. What remedy does a discharged or demoted supervisor have if he believes that he was wrongfully punished because he did not in fact commit sexual harassment? Supervisors have not fared well when they have pursued state-law contract claims. At least one has managed to prevail by showing that he was subjected to differential treatment on the basis of race. *Mash v. Digital Equipment Corp.,* 44 FEP Cases 1192 (D. Ariz. 1987). Another was found to have stated a claim under 42 U.S.C. Sec.1983 for overly hasty action by an public employer. *Huff v. County of Butler,* 524 F.Supp. 751, 27 FEP Cases 63 (W.D. Pa. 1981). But suppose a private employer reacts to a claim of sexual harassment by discharging the supervisor named in the complaint without doing a careful investigation. While the supervisor might have a remedy in some states that have recognized exceptions to the employment-at-will doctrine if an exception applies, it does not appear that he has a Title VII remedy.

Title VII can be invoked by a "person claiming to be aggrieved." But the grievance has to be one within the scope of Title VII. The statute forbids discrimination on the basis of race, religion, national origin, and sex. It does not, in terms, forbid discrimination against someone accused of committing sex discrimination by engaging in sexual harassment. If a male supervisor is discharged for allegedly engaging in sexual harassment and if he is replaced by another man, it does not appear that Title VII can protect him, even if the accusation was false. Thus, a supervisor in a state that has not recognized exceptions to the employment-at-will doctrine may have no remedy at all, even though courts throw out a large number of sexual-harassment cases precisely because the claims are unfounded.

As a matter of policy, it can be argued, an employer should not summarily discharge an accused supervisor but should instead conduct an investigation of the claim. It appears that the courts are willing to insulate an employer from liability if it carries out a good-faith investigation, even if the investigation does not reveal the actual facts. It is possible that state courts that are willing to recognize public policy exceptions to the employment-at-will doctrine might fashion a remedy here.

10. Why are so many sexual harassment cases unsuccessful? Many sexual harassment claims are not raised until the employee is threatened with discharge or other adverse job consequence or after the discharge occurs. The employee at this point may bring up conduct that occurred sometime in the past. Frequently, she will argue that her discharge was due to her resistance to the supervisor's advances. The court will then have to determine whether the alleged advances, if they occurred, amounted to actionable harassment and whether the harassment bore any relationship to the discharge. Frequently, a harassment claim is raised by an employee who seeks to stave off her discharge. See, for example, *Jackson-Colley v. U.S. Army Corps of Engineers*, 655 F.Supp. 122, 43 FEP Cases 617 (E.D. Mich. 1987); and *McLean v. Satellite Technology Services, Inc.*, 673 F.Supp. 1458, 45 FEP Cases 523 (E.D. Mo. 1987).

* * *

Case Studies

A. United Parcel Service/Federal Express

B. Quad Graphics

C. Steelcase, Inc.

D. El Paso Times

United Parcel Service/Federal Express

One of the most competitive U.S. industries is the overnight parcel delivery business, and two of the major forces in the business — United Parcel Service and Federal Express — have virtually opposite policies on husband/wife nepotism and on romantic relationships between co-workers.

UPS: Strict Anti-Nepotism Policy

With its fleet of chocolate-brown trucks and more than 180,000 employees worldwide, United Parcel Service claims to be the nation's leading small-package shipper. It can make this claim, said UPS Spokesman Ken Sternad, because "our people are our inventory."

Sternad said turnover is low at UPS because the company pays the highest wages in the industry, and UPS works hard to enssure that its employees feel their jobs are "very rewarding." To protect employees from workplace conflicts and to continue "running the tightest ship in the shipping business," the company has developed a closely guarded set of personnel policies.

One of these prohibits supervisors from hiring a direct relative of a current employee. Another states that "if two people marry while employed by UPS, they cannot work in the same district or department." If the couple is employed in the same area, one of the two is offered a job elsewhere in the company, Sternad explained.

The UPS nepotism policy developed gradually to meet the changing needs of the workplace, Sternad said, adding that the company feels it is "better to avoid the possibility that somebody's career could be influenced by being the relative or spouse of someone in that department."

The UPS employment application asks whether the applicant is related to a current employee at UPS. If a member of the applicant's family already works for the company, the UPS policy is explained to the applicant and his or her application is rejected.

The policy applies to all 80,000 drivers, 70,000 package loaders and sorters, and clerical and managerial employees of the Greenwich, Conn.-based firm. UPS has been privately held since its founding in 1907.

Company employees interviewed by BNA appear to be familiar with the anti-nepotism rule. Clerks and drivers can recite it. A telephone clerk in the Boston area indicated she opposes the policy. "Because it's a good company to work for, I wanted my mother to work for UPS," she explained, adding that the restriction "seems like kind of a strange rule, but I guess they're afraid of favoritism."

A UPS driver told BNA that when two people at UPS are dating, the company tries to keep them from associating. "They don't even like the drivers dating the clerks," he said.

Approximately 115,000 UPS employees are represented by the International Brotherhood of Teamsters, but the union has no formal position regarding nepotism regulations, explained Dan Darrow, director of the Teamsters' Package and Small Parcel Division. "The company has the right to impose reasonable work rules" under its contract with the Teamsters, he said. The nepotism issue is not a bargainable item and thus is not discussed during contract negotiations.

Because the union has no authority over hiring, Darrow stressed, it has no right to oppose the firm's policy of not employing workers' relatives. In addition, Darrow told BNA, the Teamsters never has filed a grievance against the rule that two employees who marry cannot work in the same division.

Marriages between two members of the bargaining unit do not appear to create any problems at UPS, Darrow said. He added, however, that he is aware of several situations in which managers who married bargaining unit employees were forced to decide which spouse would leave the company. Darrow said UPS is firm about not allowing a manager to marry an employee whom he or she supervises.

Although transfers have increased among UPS employees, company spokesman Sternad said the firm does not employ the trailing spouse. However, the company helps spouses settle into the new location by trying to place them with other companies in jobs similar to the ones they left.

Sternad declined to reveal how many married couples are employed by UPS, saying its corporate policies and statistics are proprietary information. He also said the anti-nepotism policy has worked well for the company and the firm does not plan to start hiring employees' relatives.

Another UPS spokesman, Al Winnik, told BNA the anti-nepotism rule preserves the company's policy of equal opportunity for its employees. UPS emphasizes promotion from within the company, he said, and hiring relatives could place officials in an awkward position.

"Our policy eliminates a possible source of pressure on managers and eliminates problems with favoritism or even the appearance of favoritism," Winnik said.   Since UPS is a privately held firm, "people would be in a position to give the perception of favoritism," he added.

"We don't want our managers to be influenced by their relationship to an employee, and since UPS rarely hires from outside and usually promotes from within, the limitations on the employment of relatives assures that all our employees will have an equal opportunity to be promoted," Winnik said.

UPS is a service-oriented firm that depends heavily on customer satisfaction, Winnik noted, and as the company has grown, officials have felt the anti-nepotism rule is the most effective way to make sure the best employees are promoted.

"Employees are promoted based on merit," not on their relationships, Winnik said. "We do not want our reputation as a service-oriented firm tainted by charges of favoritism."

When two UPS employees choose to marry, the company makes every effort to transfer one of them to another division or location. If relocation is not possible, the couple must decide which spouse will leave the company.

"UPS is not anti-marriage, but pro-performance and good service," Winnik offered.

Federal Express: Same Field, Different Policy

Federal Express Corp. prohibited hiring relatives of employees until 1981, when it decided the ban was "putting a somewhat unrealistic limit on [the company's] ability to find the right people," Ann Mullis, manager of personnel programs and policies, told BNA.

"We had a lot of good employees," Mullis said, and the company felt their relatives also might be good workers. Federal Express, like UPS, does not allow relatives to supervise each other, however.

Mullis said many employees among Federal Express' 43,000-member U.S. workforce are related. The company has a complaint procedure to deal with such relationships, but so far no problems have arisen, she said.

When Federal Express was thinking about dropping its ban on hiring relatives, Mullis said, some managers expressed concern about how they would treat married couples who brought domestic quarrels to work. The managers also wanted to know what they should do about husband-and-wife co-workers who "might be so much in love they couldn't contain themselves on the job," Mullis recalled.

Mullis said she told the managers to deal with such problems when and if they developed. Married couples get no preference in work schedules or annual leave. "It has worked out well for Federal Express," she said.

* * *

Quad/Graphics

Quad/Graphics, a large printing concern based in Pewaukee, Wis., has more of a family atmosphere than the average corporation. The 16-year-old company is 80 percent employee-owned and about 50 percent of its employees have relatives who work for the company. In addition, the firm currently employs 77 husband/wife couples.

President and founder Harry V. Quadracci told BNA that when he started Quad/Graphics in 1971 with just 11 employees he had no intention of starting a "family" printing business. But the company expanded so rapidly in its first years that Quadracci came to rely on his employees to recruit much-needed new help, and because of this the new employees often were their relatives.

Although the current president's father, Harry R. Quadracci, was a pioneer in the printing business, and his wife, Betty Ewen Quadracci, took an active interest in the company, Quadracci said throughout Quad/Graphics' growth and expansion, his background of working with close relatives did not influence his hiring policies directly. He said his only motivation was to attract good workers who would meet quality standards, regardless of to whom they were related.

As of November 1987, Quad/Graphics had about 3,000 non-management employees, 1,452 of whom have relatives working for the company. The firm also has about 400 management employees.

Quad/Graphics has been a highly profitable firm, growing at a compound rate of 40 percent per year. With four plants currently in operation, it is the largest privately-owned printing company in the United States and one of the 10 largest U.S. printers overall. The plants are located in Pewaukee, Sussex, and Lomira, Wis., and Saratoga Springs, N.Y., and a fifth plant in Hartford, Wis., is planned. Among the publications the company prints are *Newsweek, Time, People, Playboy, Ms.,* and *U.S. News & World Report.*

Need for New Hires

Emmy LaBode, supervisor of employee relations for Quad/Graphics, noted that the company's rapid expansion has required it to hire more people. Using its employees as references, she explained, solved its hiring needs by filling its ranks with people the employees knew best: friends and relatives.

LaBode said the practice of hiring relatives was encouraged strongly when she joined the company eight years ago. At that time, she recalled, Quad/Graphics desperately needed new workers and management asked employees if they had brothers, sisters, cousins, nieces, or nephews who could handle the jobs.

Today's manpower needs are less dramatic, she said, and the firm does not emphasize referring friends and relatives to openings as much as it did in the past, although the practice is not discouraged. The company always is looking for quality help, she said, and while being related to an employee does not guarantee a job, it also is not a bar to employment.

"As long as they're within the perameters of our hiring procedure and meet our guidelines, every individual is to be treated the same way. As long as they meet the perameters, they get the job," she said.

The process is slightly more difficult for employees' relatives because, unlike other applicants, they must be approved by Quadracci before they are hired. This requirement extends to the the staffs of department heads and supervisors who otherwise select their own staffs.

Less Flexibility with Relatives

Quadracci said he requires that he approve new hires related to employees because hiring relatives creates unique problems.

"You have to judge them on their merits, so the application of a relative is more highly scrutinized. If you take someone off the street who's unemployed and put them to work, they're taking more of a risk than the company is. If he doesn't work out, he's terminated.

"But when you hire a relative, the risk is more shared. With a termination, you could risk offending an employee, or at least, not making a relative happy," he said.

The hiring of husbands and wives was banned when Quad/Graphics began, and if two employees married one was required to leave the firm, Quadracci recalled.

The company retained its no-spouse policy until about 1982, he said, when two bindery employees announced their engagement. Quadracci said he congratulated the couple, then asked which one would be quitting.

"They didn't want to quit," he said. "They didn't realize that was in the cards. So they decided they were going to call off the wedding.

They said they'd been living together for two years, so why did they need a piece of paper?"

Quadracci said he explained the company's policy to the couple and listened to their arguments against it. After mulling the couple's predicament during a weekend, he told them theirs was a unique case and that they could stay on, but they told him he was right and one of them should quit. It was then, he said, that he decided being an equal opportunity employer meant hiring husbands and wives. Today, he observed, the company employs 77 married couples.

Although Quad/Graphics has no formal policy governing the married couples who work for it, such employment has restrictions. For example, married couples who work in the same department cannot work for the same supervisor. Couples need time away from each other, he said. Those who share too many of the same experiences can go home and commiserate over their problems. The result is that two employees' are affected adversely, instead of one. "A bad apple spoils the bunch," he said.

"We're not saints here," Quadracci said. "A supervisor can make the wrong decision as far as an employee is concerned. If you have a relative in the same department, it'd be too easy for both to be disgruntled. If you have a problem but your spouse is in another department, it's easier to be objective."

No Worker/Boss Couples

In addition, spouses cannot supervise one another. Quadracci said he was his wife's supervisor when she worked for the company and he concluded the arrangement was unsatisfactory. He thinks it would not work well for other spouses, either.

"Husband and wife are equal partners. On the job, one can't be boss and the other subordinate. It doesn't work," he said.

As a result, Quad/Graphics prefers that married couples work for different supervisors, in different departments, on different shifts, or in different plants. Those who work the same hours at the same plant cannot come to work and go home in the same car. Each must have his or her own transportation.

"Say my staff manager's husband is done at 5 p.m., and I need her till 6 p.m. So he's out there tapping his toes. It doesn't bother him, he'll say, but it bothers me. They're free to come and go as their job sees fit, not as their spouse's job sees fit," he said.

Contributes to Growth?

Quad/Graphics probably allows husbands and wives to work for it at least in part because the firm has continued to prosper and grow since it began to permit the practice. The policy has endured several unusual situations, such as a husband being supervised by his wife's ex-husband.

Linda Larson, controller of accounting whose husband works in shipping, feels that the company's success is due in part to the fact that it hires spouses. Larson, who hires employees for her department, claims that the best employees are those whose spouses work for Quad/Graphics.

Larson feels this is because spouses who come to work for Quad/Graphics already have a commitment or interest in the firm.

"When a spouse arrives here, they come with a commitment to the job much greater than an ordinary new hire. And in addition to wanting to make Quad work, they arrive knowing other people so they fit in right away," she offered.

Tensions When Spouse Not Hired

Having a policy of hiring spouses can have a negative effect when one spouse is hired and the other is rejected, Larson noted. Not hiring an employee's spouse can create tension, she said, especially because Quad/Graphics conducts many events for its workers and spouses who were not hired may feel left out and ill at ease at such functions.

Nevertheless, Larson said her tenure at the firm has taught her to look for quality and performance in applicants, regardless of whether they are married to a Quad/Graphics employee. As a result, she added, although being an employee's spouse may guarantee an interview in her department, it does not guarantee a job.

Quadracci agreed that not always hiring an employee's spouse has disadvantages. By not limiting hiring to relatives of the employees, the company has opened itself to criticism from people outside it, as well as those who work for it but do not have any relatives there. Such employees, he said, sometimes feel left out and suspect that the firm engages in favoritism and nepotism. This is another reason employees' relatives who apply for jobs are screened twice.

Another disadvantage to both spouses working for the same company, according to several Quad/Graphics employees, is that they become engulfed in discussions about work when they get home, despite the firm's efforts to keep their at-work contact brief or incidental.

Too Much Shop Talk

Small doses of shop talk are not harmful and sometimes spawn solutions to work-related problems, according to Chris Gitzlaff, traffic manager for the company's shipping department. Gitzlaff said the fact that he and his wife both work at Quad/Graphics has improved their ability to communicate with each other. But he noted that the arrangement has a drawback.

"The only trap we fall into is we talk, talk, talk, and realize all we talk about is work. I think we may tend to overdo it," he said.

Larson said she and her husband Rich have found themselves in the same situation.

"When it's hardest on us is when one of us has a problem in their job. You tend to bring it home with you and then you might have an overflow of Quad," she said. "Neither one of us has a job that you can leave behind you when you walk in the door."

Conversely, because she and her husband work for the same employer, discussions of his on-the-job problems mean more to her, she explained. Similarly, his problems also may apply to her and may affect her job as well.

Employees with spouses at Quad/Graphics interviewed by BNA said one of the biggest advantages of working for the same employer is that they can communicate with each other more. They understand more of their spouse's problems with the job, and they are better able to deal with those problems objectively, they said.

Another advantage, according to Irene Gitzlaff, case management administrator for employee services, is that spouses' work schedules can be arranged to reduce many of the child-raising problems often associated with families where both parents work. While some employees are on a five-day, 40-hour work week, others work three 12-hour days and then are off for four days. For example, she worked three eight-hour days when she began with Quad/Graphics and her husband worked the three 12-hour shifts. Nevertheless, they were able to take care of their children and not hire a sitter because they worked on alternate days.

Gitzlaff added that when the children were younger the family also took advantage of Quad/Care, a day-care facility near the Sussex and Pewaukee plants that serves nearly 200 children of Quad/Graphics employees each week.

Quadracci said the company would have established the facility even if it did not hire employees' relatives, adding that few other company policies have been changed because the firm's practice of hiring relatives. The company has not revised its policies much, he said, because it has always tried to be sensitive to its employees' needs.

Vacation Scheduling

"We're not going to tell one spouse to take a vacation this week and the other the next," Quadracci said. "On the other hand, we don't expect them to take a vacation based only on the husband's vacation. We ask them to check to find out when it's best for them to both go. We don't want to see being related become a problem.

"When a husband gets transferred from nights onto days and the wife stays on nights, she can't demand that she be brought onto days. But management should be sensitive to the fact that it's very difficult for one to work days while the other is working nights."

Quadracci's sensitivity to employees' wishes is not wasted on the workers. Each employee interviewed showed a strong loyalty to the company, perhaps best expressed by the fact that although each had a relative working there, they all said it was often difficult to select the best-qualified relatives to recommend for employment at Quad/Graphics.

According to LaBode, employees are very careful in deciding which relatives to recommend because they take pride in their work. Each recommendation, she said, is seen as a reflection on that employee.

"I firmly believe they wouldn't recommend, relative or not, someone who is unsuitable to work here. I've even had people tell me they wouldn't recommend relatives for jobs.

"I have six other sisters and I wouldn't recommend them. It's not that they're not good gals, but I don't think they'd fit this environment. You just don't want to put yourself in the position where I recommend a sister and know she wouldn't work out, but do it because she needs a job. We have too much pride in this job to do that," she said.

The employees know what is expected of them at Quad/Graphics, Quadracci said, and they know what would be expected of prospective employees.

* * *

Steelcase, Inc.

Steelcase, Inc., headquartered in Grand Rapids, Mich., is one of the largest manufacturers of office furniture in the world. It employs 8,000 people at its plants and offices in Grand Rapids and about 13,500 total throughout North America.

James Soule, vice president for human resources, told BNA that although Steelcase does not have a formal policy of hiring relatives of employees, in "historical practice" it often has done so.

Soule said between 350 and 400 married couples now work for the company in Grand Rapids, many of whom met while working at Steelcase.

Christine Kroft, manager of employee communications for Steelcase, noted that the company's employee newsletter lists couples who have met at the company and are planning to marry, as well as births to Steelcase couples.

"We really do try to play it up," said Kroft, whose husband also works for Steelcase.

Soule said that although the company does not have a formal policy on nepotism, in 1981 it institutionalized what for all practical purposes was an informal system for hiring workers' relatives.

Called the sponsorship program, the plan applies only to hourly workers — mostly blue-collar employees who work on the assembly lines — who have been with the company at least 15 years.

Turnover Rate Low

Soule noted that the annual turnover rate at Steelcase is only about 3.8 percent. He said employees always have tried to have their relatives work at the company and in 1981 the company began asking its hourly workers to sponsor individuals, usually relatives, as potential employees. In addition to spouses, sons, daughters, sisters, brothers, and other relatives have been hired under the program.

Soule recalled that asking all hourly employees to sponsor a relative created problems. Because of the company's low turnover rate, a list of 1,800 people waiting for jobs emerged soon after the program began, creating a three- to four-year backlog of applicants.

As a result, in 1984 the company limited the program to hourly employees with at least 15 years' service. The pool of job applicants currently has only about 200 persons in it.

Steelcase now hires about 80 percent of its hourly workers through the sponsorship program, while the remaining 20 percent are obtained through outreach programs to community groups such as Vietnam veterans organizations, the Urban League, and the Inter-Tribal Council.

Soule said the company has only a few restrictions on relatives working together. The firm's hiring policy for full-time production employees states that if the spouse of a Steelcase employee is submitted for sponsorship to the pool, "an agreement must be reached that if employed both spouses cannot work in the same plant nor attempt to transfer to that plant once employed." Soule noted, however, that a "grandfather" clause exempts married couples already working in the same plant.

Transfers Arranged

If an employee is supervising his or her spouse, "we'll work with either spouse" to arrange a transfer, and as a result no one has ever had to leave the company because of this restriction, Soule said.

In general, he added, it is acceptable for spouses to be co-workers, but if a supervisor determines that one or the other's work performance is suffering because of the marital relationship, a transfer for one of the spouses can be arranged.

Dan and Bonnie Phillips both work in one of Steelcase's Grand Rapids plants, and have been married for six years. Dan has been employed by Steelcase for 20 years, and Bonnie for nine years. They originally worked together in a Steelcase plant in Orange County, Calif., but they transferred to Grand Rapids seven years ago.

According to Dan, during the time they have been married, he has been Bonnie's assistant foreman, and in the past she has been his quality control inspector for an assembly line that manufactures desks.

"We prefer working together as to not working together," Bonnie commented.

Nevertheless, Dan and Bonnie said they have experienced some problems with co-workers because of the structure of their work relationship.

For example, Steelcase assembly line workers can earn extra money by producing beyond their weekly quotas, something that most of them are able to do, according to the company. Most assembly line workers earn about $100 extra per week this way, Dan said.

Wife's Bonuses Earned

He said Bonnie is a fast worker and has earned large bonuses on a regular basis. One of their co-workers accused Dan of giving Bonnie easier work than the other employees so she could earn more money. While Dan said the accusation was false, he added that now he is careful to rotate workers' tasks because "you don't want to leave anything to doubt."

Bonnie said, "A lot of people make accusations, but they don't have anything" to base them on. The couple indicated that it probably is human nature for co-workers to suspect favoritism in their case. Bonnie noted, however, that no one has ever gone any higher than Dan to complain about alleged favoritism.

The Phillips and Christine Kroft, whose husband is a computer specialist in a different department, said having one's spouse work for the same company can be helpful in the work itself.

"I can be very supportive for him, he can be very supportive for me," Kroft offered, because they both "understand the company philosophy."

Dan Phillips said because Bonnie and he work together, they can spot ways to improve quality on the line more quickly by comparing notes with each other.

Company Loyalty Enhanced

Bonnie added that she and her husband "know quite a few [married] couples" at Steelcase and that most of them like the fact that they work for the same company.

Working together, said Dan, "does make you more loyal to the company."

Jeff and Cheri Shipman are another couple who work for Steelcase, she as an executive secretary and he as a financial analyst in a different department. The Shipmans met at Steelcase, where she has worked for seven years and he for 2 years. They have been married for a little over a year, but never worked in the same department. "We just ran past each other in the hall" and then got acquainted, Jeff explained.

Cheri Shipman said she also has noticed that "a lot of married couples" work at Steelcase.

Although the Shipmans work the same hours, they drive to work separately and take separate lunch hours, primarily because Jeff works later more often than Cheri.

Cheri said problems would arise if Jeff were her boss; because of this they have decided never to apply for jobs in each others' department.

Soule said hiring relatives is a policy that "has worked for us," and he sees no reason it would not work for other companies.

However, he noted that having large numbers of relatives working together creates some problems. For example, he said, if the son or daughter of a long-time worker is disciplined, the parent might ask, "How come my kid is getting this kind of discipline?"

Soule said company management previously in such situations asked the parents to tell their children to improve their performance. Due to legal considerations concerning workplace privacy, however, "we can't do that" anymore, he said.

He said problems sometimes arise on assembly lines if both the husband and wife want to take their vacation at the same time. For example, he said late fall is deer hunting season, and many employees ask for time off. Under company policy, the member of a husband-and-wife couple with more seniority gets to go deer hunting. As a result, he said, "mother gets to go and father doesn't."

According to Soule, simultaneous vacations are less of a problem with white-collar couples. Their work may accumulate while they are away, he said, but this does not create the same type of problem that occurs when two married people who work on the assembly line take vacations at the same time.

* * *

El Paso Times

The *El Paso Times* is among the smaller, less-prominent newspapers that accommodate changing news staff demographics by allowing married couples to work together.

To management at the *Times*, married couples in the newsroom create no more personnel problems than any other group of employees.

The *Times* was established in 1880 and has a staff of more than 400 in seven departments. A member of the Gannett Group, it is the city's morning daily, with a circulation of 86,000. It has a joint operating agreement with The *El Paso Herald Post*, the city's evening daily, for office and production facilities. The *Herald Post* is a member of the Scripps-Howard news organization; the *Times* and the *Herald Post* are El Paso's only daily newspapers.

Working in close quarters, the *Times*' news staff of 66 is located on the top floor of a three-story building in the city center. Reporters crowd four, 15-foot-long work stations surrounded by three partitioned offices that house editorial staff and a small darkroom.

No Formal Policy

According to Paula Moore, the paper's managing editor, the Gannett Corp. has no written nepotism policy, leaving such matters up to the discretion of individual newspaper management. While some of the organization's papers have formal policies, the *Times* does not.

"We do not let the fact [that] someone is married to someone else stand in the way of hiring the best people," Moore offered. "Our policy is to hire the best possible person for a position."

Moore and her husband John have worked at the paper for 10 years, during which as many as five married couples have been on the news staff at one time; currently there are two couples. The Moores met while working at the Clovis, N.M., *News Journal* in 1971 and have been married for 15 years.

John Moore said having married couples on the *Times*' news staff was not planned. Of the five couples who have worked there since 1977, three were married before they joined the organization. One couple got married while the wife was on the staff, but her husband was not hired until several months after they wed. In each case, Moore pointed out, the spouses worked in different departments.

When the Moores joined the paper, John was hired as regional editor and Paula as a feature writer. He later was promoted to city editor, and she eventually was named features editor and, later, news editor. Subsequently, the managing editor position opened up and both of them applied for the job.

"Gannett said we were both qualified for it," John said, "and created co-managing editors. It wasn't two people in one job. We split the direct management of the news departments into two jobs with full and equal responsibility."

The Moores served as co-editors for seven years until April 1987, when John decided to learn newspaper production management. They do not think that the fact they were married while they were co-managing editors had any effect on their co-workers' attitudes toward them.

"I can't recall a situation," John said, "when someone perceived we took a similar position on an issue because we were married. I think others took it for granted we made decisions because professionally it was the right thing to do.

"Other people thought we were individuals who just happened to be married. We had both been here several years, the staff was well-acquainted with us, and it was a normal working situation. If married couples go about their jobs responsibly and professionally, no one can criticize their marital situation," he said.

He emphasized that his decision to learn a new aspect of the business did not stem from any dissatisfaction with working jointly with Paula. "We didn't have any problems," he stated, "and I don't think we were creating any problems for the newspaper. We've worked together for 16 years and are still working together at least indirectly. We have the same interests, although different approaches.

"I'm now dealing with producing on paper what she produces in the newsroom. I'm seeing a different perspective on it, but I wouldn't hesitate at all to go back to the newsroom with both of us in it," he said.

For 18 months before John moved into production, Paula was operating head of the newsroom, a job she continues to hold. "He was actually reporting to me," she said, "but for two papers before this, I worked for him."

Call It A Draw

Asked if one of the two arrangements was preferable to the other, Paula said, "Before coming here, we were in different places, literally, and in a much bigger newsroom. I think I would call it a draw. We've never discussed which we would prefer to do again."

She added that they enjoy not being in the same department now. "It's not that we wouldn't ever work that closely again, but it is different, nice for a change. He is still interested in what is going on in the newsroom and probably more interested in hearing me talk about it."

Added John, "Now that I have been out of it for awhile, I think some of our interests have diverged, and there has been some relief from the day-to-day pressures."

Paula said despite pressure-packed and long, unpredictable workdays of news reporting, both spouses can be happier and more productive employees than if one spouse had a job with more regular hours.

Hours vary at the *Times*. Salaried editorial staff may not have any set schedule, and this often leads to 16-hour days. *Times* reporters are paid hourly and overtime is limited, a situation that results in overlapping shifts. Some reporters start to work at 8 a.m., others start at noon, and a late shift arrives at 4 p.m.

"Newspapering is a profession that requires a lot of commitment," Paula stressed. "People who are in it together understand the pressures. And often here at the *Times* some of the best people have been those who are married. I think it is normal the top performers would gravitate toward one another.

"You know what the other person is doing and why," Paula added. "You can be supportive, and you certainly have a lot in common. It is better than the situation in which only one of you can work at the paper, and the other has to go make pizzas because the nepotism rules keep you from working together. Those are certainly advantages, and they are major ones."

John added, "I think in any similar profession where there is a lot of pressure and odd working hours, people naturally are going to be attracted to others in their line of work. They don't have the time to communicate with other people as much, because it's an all-consuming kind of thing. That's why doctors marry doctors, and lawyers marry lawyers."

Paula said the disadvantages for married couples derive in part from the advantages. Married co-workers may "talk shop" too much, and the relationship may seem to lack fresh ideas and attitudes. "So maybe there is a tendency to burn out in the relationship more quickly. But I think in most cases when you have two career people in the same profession, the advantages outweigh the disadvantages. Certainly it's not all a bowl of cherries," she said.

Changing Light Bulbs

She pointed out, however, the same situations can arise in any relationship with two-career couples, whether they are co-workers or not. "There is nobody at home to make sure the light bulbs are working, and that can be very trying regardless of what your jobs are," she noted.

Also, due to the stress of the work, couples who work together on newspapers may lose their tempers more easily at each other because they feel more comfortable with each other. "You are not used to holding back with that person," said Paula, "but I can't say I've seen it happen in the newsroom any more with married couples than with others — maybe less often. Married relationships tend to be more stable."

"I think there comes a point," John added, "when couples working together is not the best way. Sharing the same pressures can be an advantage, but it can also be a disadvantage because the same pressures become one instead of two."

During one period, Paula was the *Times'* city editor and John was the news editor, the two newspaper jobs traditionally most at odds. "There were times we had arguments," John pointed out. "She was editing copy my staff had written. Naturally, with any city editor and news editor there are conflicts about what is the right or wrong way to handle a piece of copy. But that is pure professional disagreement."

The most difficult situation involving co-worker couples probably is when one spouse must be reprimanded. An uneasiness emerges about how the partner may respond. It happened with the Moores. "We had to reprimand one spouse severely," Paula stated, "and we wondered at that point what kind of reaction we might receive from the other. But we got none whatsoever, and that was to their credit."

She emphasized that the same concern exists with unrelated employees who are good friends. Close relationships develop in the newsroom, and Paula indicated that at times dating relationships may be more volatile than marriages.

Asked if the next marriage of two staff members would raise red flags, she said, "I think it would raise a pink one. We would want to take a look at it and make sure they would continue to do the job they had been. But we would not assume it would create problems."

Ben and Nan Keck joined the *Times* staff four years ago after meeting at *The Amarillo News Globe*, where they began working together 10 years ago. They were married for three years while there, but stopped working together because the company's nepotism policy prohibited two married persons from working full-time on the news staff.

"I was news editor, and Ben was city editor, which were basically lateral positions," Nan said, "but they said one of us had to go part-time."

They asked the publisher to modify the policy but their request was denied. They were given the right to decide which of them went on part-time duty, but a promotion offered to Ben made it economically preferable for Nan to reduce her work week to 39 hours a week, a "hair-splitting difference," from full-time, as she described it.

"I was demoted," Nan recalled, "because they didn't want a part-time news editor. So I went back to reporting."

Nan later was named assistant city editor, but without the customary pay increase because she still was considered part time. "I got no sick leave, and my vacation time was calculated differently," she noted.

Ben said, "They would not promote her when the city editor left, although she was the most qualified and recommended by me because I was then over the city editor. But they wouldn't do it because she was married to me. My recommendation had nothing to do with our being married; it had to do with her abilities."

Ben thinks the denial of Nan's promotion was due as much to management's general opposition to promoting women as it was to the nepotism policy.

"Women had been in the job before, and they just didn't get along with the top bosses too well," he said.

The Kecks put up with the situation "as long as we could" before being lured to the *Times* by friends and colleagues in El Paso who had learned of two openings there.

Not Hired As Couple

"They told us when we came here," Ben said, "they were not hiring us as a couple; they were hiring us as individuals. If only one of us worked out after the three-month probation period, fine. We accepted that."

Nan added, "It's working out great for us. I know there is a consideration that if you lose one person, you are losing two when you hire married couples. I guess they were willing to take a gamble on that."

Nan began at the *Times* as copy editor and Ben as an assistant city editor. Later, she was promoted and Ben, tired of the "headaches of management," returned to being a reporter. Ben observed that

"Here it hasn't mattered where one of us goes in terms of moving up or down. If we ever decided to do something like a small newspaper together outside a corporation, I know how she works, and she knows how I work. We could be a pretty good team."

The Kecks share Paula Moore's view that working together in the newsroom can be taxing to the relationship at times. When couples are involved intensely in the same effort, they tend to take work issues home.

"Sometimes the only thing we are talking about is work, and it is the same work," Ben admitted. "If I were a lawyer working across the street, I could pick her up for lunch; and we could talk about something different. As it is, it's all newspaper talk. Sometimes it builds, but you go away on vacation for a week and blow it off."

Because Ben reports to the city desk and Nan works on the copy desk, she often edits his copy, but they insist they do not allow their personal relationship to interfere with their duty as professionals to produce the best possible product.

"I guess there will be times when I'll be editing his copy, and I'll want to take some things out because I don't understand it or think it's backed up," Nan said, "but he happens to be a real good reporter, so it doesn't happen that often. He understands my job, and I know what he is trying to do. It doesn't mean we don't occasionally shout at each other in the newsroom under deadline pressure, but it has never caused a problem."

Regarding co-workers' views on working for a married couple, Nan said she could not recall any problems aside from "trivial things."

"When he was city editor," she said, "he didn't like having his byline on his stories, because he just figured writing stories was part of his job. So there were times the copy editors tried to get me to persuade him to put bylines on his stories. But those were trivial."

Paula Moore thinks discussions concerning nepotism in the workplace have increased. "My husband and I worked together for 15 years at three different papers. So for us it certainly is not new. But it seems to be a trendy topic, which leaves me to believe people are discovering it for the first time," she said.

John Moore said employers should recognize the merits of hiring working couples. "From a business standpoint and a management standpoint," he said, "there is great potential in two employees marrying, and they shouldn't be penalized for that. I think if any kind of an authoritative study were done, it would show a majority of married couples in the same workplace were more valuable than some of the single people. If you say married couples may not work in the same place, I think you are going to lose a lot of good people."

* * *

Appendix A

Text of Court Cases

Bundy v. Jackson

EEOC v. Rath Packing

Rulon-Miller v. IBM

Meritor Savings Bank v. Vinson

BUNDY v. JACKSON

U.S. Court of Appeals, District of Columbia Circuit

BUNDY v. JACKSON, Director, D.C. Director of Corrections, No. 79-1693, January 12, 1981

CIVIL RIGHTS ACT OF 1964

1. Sex discrimination — Sexual advances — Conditions of employment ▶ 108.4159

District of Columbia Department of Corrections discriminated against female employee on basis of sex with respect to "terms, conditions, or privileges of employment" when its supervisors sexually harassed her without objection from department director, and employee does not have to prove that she resisted harassment and that resistance caused loss or denial of tangible job benefits.

2. Remedy — Compensatory damages ▶ 210.655

Award of damages for emotional harm resulting from violation of Title VII is precluded by statute's authorization of "equitable relief."

3. Attorneys' fees — Prevailing party ▶ 108.8940

Female employee who established claim of sexual harassment without having to prove loss or denial of tangible job benefits is prevailing party for purpose of award of attorneys' fees.

4. Remedy — Injunction — Mootness ▶ 108.695 ▶ 205.101

Female employee's request for injunctive relief against sexual harassment is not moot despite her failure to complain of further harassment since filing of administrative complaint, where there is no certainty that harassment will not recur in view of both her employer's failure to take affirmative steps to prevent recurrence and continued employment of all of workers who engaged in harassment.

5. Remedy — Sexual harassment — EEOC guidelines ▶ 108.508 ▶ 225.301

To remedy sexual harassment against female employee of District of Columbia Department of Corrections, federal district court should apply EEOC's Final Guidelines on Sexual Harassment in the Workplace and therefore should order director of department (1) to raise affirmatively subject of sexual harassment with all his employees and inform them that sexual harassment is illegal, (2) to establish and publicize complaint mechanism, (3) to take all necessary steps promptly to investigate and correct any harassment, including warnings and appropriate discipline directed at offending party, and generally to develop other means of preventing harassment, and (4) to ensure that complaints of sexual harassment receive thorough and effective treatment within formal process already established by department to comply with U.S. Civil Service Commission regulations.

6. Remedy — Retention of jurisdiction ▶ 250.781

Federal district court, which has been instructed to issue injunction requiring District of Columbia Department of Corrections to take preventive and corrective action with respect to complaints of sexual harassment, should retain jurisdiction so that it may review plans of director of department for complying with injunction.

7. Sex discrimination — Sexual advances — Promotion — Prima facie case ▶ 108.4159 ▶ 108.4164 ▶ 108.7333

Female employee will establish prima facie case that she was denied promotion in retaliation for her refusal of sexual advances by her supervisors if she shows that she was victim of pattern or practice of sexual harassment attributable to employer and that she applied for and was denied promotion for which she was technically eligible and of which she had reasonable expectation, but she need not prove that other employees who were no better qualified, but who were not similarly disadvantaged, were promoted at time that she was denied promotion.

8. Sex discrimination — Sexual advances — Promotion — Rebuttal ▶ 108.4159 ▶ 108.4164 ▶ 108.7335

Employer can rebut female employee's prima facie showing that she was denied promotion in retaliation for her refusal of sexual advances by her supervisors by establishing through clear and convincing evidence that, despite employee's technical eligibility for promotion, in practice it set qualification criteria for promotion more stringent than employee could meet, and it can support its rebuttal case by showing that any other employees who were promoted at approximately time that female employee was denied promotion and who were not themselves victims of pattern of sexual harassment in fact met these more stringent criteria.

Appeal from the U.S. District Court for the District of Columbia (19 FEP Cases 828). Remanded.

Barry H. Gottfried (Arthur D. Chotin and Arthur Kahn, with him on brief), Washington, D.C., for appelant.

Leo N. Gorman, Assistant Corporation Counsel (Judith W. Rogers, Corporation Counsel of the District of Columbia, and Richard W. Barton, Deputy Corporation Counsel, with him on brief), for appellee.

Vella M. Fink (Leroy D. Clark, General Counsel, Joseph T. Eddins, Associate General Counsel, Beatrice Rosenberg, Assistant General Counsel, and Marilyn S.G. Urwitz, on brief), for EEOC, amicus curiae, urging reversal.

Linda F. Thome, Washington, D.C., on brief for Women's Legal Defense Fund, amicus curiae, urging reversal.

Before WRIGHT, Chief Judge, and SWYGERT* and ROBINSON, Circuit Judges.

Full Text of Opinion

WRIGHT, Chief Judge: — In Barnes v. Costle, 561 F.2d 983, 15 FEP Cases 345 (D.C. Cir. 1977), we held that an employer who abolished a female employee's job to retaliate against the employee's resistance of his sexual advances violated Title VII of the Civil Rights Act of 1964, as amended, 42 U.S.C. §2000e et seq. (1976 & Supp. III 1979). The appellant in this case asserts some claims encompassed by the Barnes decision, arguing that her rejection of unsolicited and offensive sexual advances from several supervisors in her agency caused those supervisors unjustifiably to delay and block promotions to which she was entitled. Equally important, however, appellant asks us to extend Barnes by holding that an employer violates Title VII merely by subjecting female employees to sexual harassment, even if the employee's resistance to that harassment does not cause the employer to deprive her of any tangible job benefits.

The District Court in this case made an express finding of fact that in appellant's agency "the making of improper sexual advances to female employees [was] standard operating procedure, a fact of life, a normal condition of employment," Finding of Fact No. 38, Appellant's Appendix (App.) 15, and that the director of the agency, to whom she complained of the harassment, failed to investigate her complaints or take them seriously, id. No. 44, App. 16. Nevertheless, the District Court refused to grant appellant any declaratory or injunctive relief, concluding that sexual harassment does not in itself represent discrimination "with respect to * * * terms, conditions, or privileges of em-

ployment" within the meaning of Title VII, 42 U.S.C. §2000e-2(a)(1) (1976). Further, the court denied appellant's request for back pay to compensate for the allegedly improper delay in her promotion to GS-9, and for elevation to GS-11 and back pay for the delay in that promotion, holding that the employer had independent, legitimate reasons for delaying and denying the promotions.

Because we believe the District Court wrongly construed Title VII on the claim for declaratory and injunctive relief and failed to apply the proper burden of proof analysis to the promotion claims, we reverse.[1]

I. BACKGROUND

Appellant Sandra Bundy is now, and was at the time she filed her lawsuit, a Vocational Rehabilitation Specialist, level GS-9, with the District of Columbia Department of Corrections (the agency). Bundy began with the agency as a GS-4 Personnel Clerk in 1970, was promoted to GS-5 that same year, and became a GS-6 Staffing Technician in 1973. After training as a technician in employment staffing, she became a GS-7 Employment Development Specialist (the predecessor classification to Vocational Rehabilitation Specialist) in 1974, and achieved her current GS-9 level in 1976, one year after she filed her formal complaint of sexual harassment with the agency. In recent years Bundy's chief task has been to find jobs for former criminal offenders.

The District Court's finding that sexual intimidation was a "normal condition of employment" in Bundy's agency finds ample support in the District Court's own chronology of Bundy's ex-

---

[1] Bundy's complaint and, originally, her appeal also included a claim that the agency had illegally delayed her promotion to GS-9, for which she was found fully qualified in January 1976, until July of that year, in alleged retaliation against her filing a discrimination complaint. Aquila Gilmore, who was Chief Equal Employment Opportunity Officer for the agency, admitted at trial that he delayed the promotion in response to Bundy's filing of her complaint, Finding of Fact No. 46, Appellant's Appendix (App.) 17, but contended that he had done so in the good faith belief that the delay was authorized under District of Columbia regulations, Defendant's Exh. No. 18, Appellant's Supplemental Appendix (SA) 296. Before oral argument, however, appellee District of Columbia conceded that Gilmore had been wrong in delaying the promotion and offered Bundy back pay for the delay. The District believes, however, that Bundy is entitled only to four, rather than five, months' back pay since, even if Gilmore had not delayed the promotion, normal procedures would have delayed Bundy's formal elevation for one month after she was declared officially qualified. On remand the District Court can determine the proper amount of back pay as a remedy for appellee's error here.

periences there. Those experiences began in 1972 when Bundy, still a GS-5, received and rejected sexual propositions from Delbert Jackson, then a fellow employee at the agency but now its Director and the named defendant in this lawsuit in his official capacity. Findings of Fact Nos. 28–29, App. 11–12. It was two years later, however, that the sexual intimidation Bundy suffered began to intertwine directly with her employment, when she received propositions from two of her supervisors, Arthur Burton and James Gainey.

Burton became Bundy's supervisor when Bundy became an Employment Development Specialist in 1974. Shortly thereafter Gainey became her first-line supervisor and Burton her second-line supervisor, although Burton retained control of Bundy's employment status. Id. Nos. 32–33, App. 12. Burton began sexually harassing Bundy in June 1974, continually calling her into his office to request that she spend the workday afternoon with him at his apartment and to question her about her sexual proclivities. Id. No. 34, App. 12–13.[2] Shortly after becoming her first-line supervisor Gainey also began making sexual advances to Bundy, asking her to join him at a motel and on a trip to the Bahamas. Id. No. 35, App. 13–14. Bundy complained about these advances to Lawrence Swain, who supervised both Burton and Gainey. Swain casually dismissed Bundy's complaints, telling her that "any man in his right mind would want to rape you," id. No. 37, App. 14, and then proceeding himself to request that she begin a sexual relationship with him in his apartment. Id. No. 36, App. 14. Bundy rejected his request.

[OTHER WOMEN]

We add that, although the District Court made no explicit findings as to harassment of other female employees, its finding that harassment was "standard operating procedure" finds ample support in record evidence that Bundy was not the only woman subjected to sexual intimidation by male supervisors.[3]

In denying Bundy any relief, the District Court found that Bundy's supervisors did not take the "game" of sexually propositioning female employees "seriously," and that Bundy's rejection of their advances did not evoke in them any motive to take any action against her. Id. No. 38, App. 15. The record, however, contains nothing to support this view, and indeed some evidence directly belies it. For example, after Bundy complained to Swain, Burton began to derogate her for alleged malingering and poor work performance, though she had not previously received any such criticism. App. 30. Burton also arranged a meeting with Bundy and Gainey to discuss Bundy's alleged abuse of leave, though he did not pursue his charges at this meeting. App. 94–95.

Beyond these actions, Bundy's supervisors at least created the impression that they were impeding her promotion because she had offended them, and they certainly did nothing to help her pursue her harassment claims through established channels. Bundy became eligible for promotion to GS-9 in January 1975. App. 178. When she contacted Gainey to inquire about a promotion he referred her to Burton, who then referred her back to Gainey, who then told her that because of a promotion freeze he could not recommend her for a promotion. App. 41–43. One month later, however, Bundy learned that the personnel office had indeed recommended other employees for promotion despite the freeze. App. 44. Bundy then informally consulted an Equal Employment Opportunity (EEO) Officer who was working in her office, and then requested a meeting with Claude Burgin, Swain's supervisor. On February 18, 1975 Bundy met with Burton and Burgin and told the latter that Burton and Gainey had sexually harassed her and denied her a promotion because she

---

[2] Burton called Bundy into his office to ask about her weekend activities and, in particular, whether she liked horses. When she responded that she indeed rode horses, he said that he had heard that women rode horses to obtain sexual relief. He told her he had books and pictures at home to support this theory and suggested that she come to his apartment to see them. Burton specifically asked her to come to his apartment to look at the books and pictures during the workday afternoon instead of performing her job-related field activities. Moreover, he repeated his importunings by telephone after obtaining Bundy's unlisted home number.

[3] Carolyn Epps, who worked for the agency between 1967 and 1974, testified that after she asked her supervisor, Lawrence Swain, about the possibility of a promotion he began making unsolicited physical and verbal advances toward her, App. 93–96, and that she received verbal sexual advances from supervisor Claude Burgin after she discussed her promotion with him. App. 94. Epps also testified that she heard Swain ask other female employees to come to his apartment for drinks and saw him pressing his body against their bodies in his office. App. 96–97. In 1974 Epps applied to become an administrative aide-stenographer, which would have meant a promotion from GS-6 to GS-7. She testified that, although she was qualified for the job, it went instead to another female employee who had received sexual advances from Swain and who, unlike Epps, did not know stenography. App. 100–101.

Ann Blanchard worked for the agency from 1971 to 1973, supervised by James Gainey and Arthur Burton. Burton made sexual advances toward her and also apparently intimidated her by stating that another employee whom he would not identify had told Burton that Blanchard had been conducting a sexual relationship with one of her agency clients. App. 105–106.

had resisted their advances. Burgin simply responded that she was denied the promotion because her work was unsatisfactory, and that she was free to pursue the matter further if she cared to. App. 46-48. Bundy then informally complained about the sexual harassment to Aquila Gilmore, the Chief EEO Officer in the agency. Gilmore, however, simply advised that her charges might be difficult to prove, and cautioned her against bringing unwarranted complaints. He never brought the issue to the attention of Delbert Jackson, by then Director of the agency. App. 187-190.

[MEETING]

On April 11, 1975 Bundy met with Jackson and showed him the draft of a letter summarizing her complaint. Jackson then arranged an April 14 meeting with Burgin, Burton, and Bundy, Finding of Fact No. 39, App. 14, but Gilmore, who had become Chief of Manpower Management at the agency, and Charles Rogers, Assistant Director of Operations, also attended the meeting. Bundy, purportedly embarrassed at the unexpected presence of the latter two men, did not take the opportunity of discussing her sexual harassment claims at this meeting, nor did Jackson or Gilmore raise the issue. Instead, the meeting focused on Bundy's possible promotion and her alleged work deficiencies. Id. No. 40, App. 15-16. On April 23 Gainey and Burton completed a memorandum offering Bundy's inadequate work performance as the reason for denying her a promotion to GS-9. Plaintiff's Exh. 2, Appellant's Supplemental Appendix (SA) 217. Bundy responded to this memorandum, arguing that her supervisors had never presented her with any written criticism of her performance until she raised the harassment issue. See App. 145-148.[4]

Bundy proceeded to pursue her complaint beyond her immediate supervisors. She registered an informal complaint with EEO Officer Philip Matthews, App. 64-65,[5] and then filed a formal complaint and supplemental complaints with the agency. Jackson, having learned of the formal complaints, took no steps to investigate them beyond simply asking Burton, Gainey, and Swain whether they had made improper advances to Bundy. Finding of Fact No. 44, App. 16-17; App. 125-127. Bundy was finally promoted to GS-9 in July 1976. Having received "satisfactory" ratings for her work performance, she became eligible for promotion to GS-11 in July 1977, but has not yet received that promotion.

Bundy filed her complaint in the District Court on August 3, 1977.[6]

II. CLAIM FOR DECLARATORY AND INJUNCTIVE RELIEF

The District Court appeared to find that even Bundy took a casual attitude toward the pattern of unsolicited sexual advances in the agency, Finding of Fact No. 47, App. 17, thereby implying that these advances by themselves did no harm to female employees. We find little or no basis in the record for the District Court's finding or implication, especially since Bundy's testimony that the sexual harassment she endured did her serious emotional harm, App. 40, was essentially unrefuted. In any event, the essential basis for the District Court's refusal to hold that the sexual harassment was in itself a violation of Title VII, Conclusion of Law No. 5, App. 18, was not this factual finding, but the District Court's construction of Title VII.

The key provision of Title VII states:

It shall be an unlawful employment practice for an employer —'

(1) to fail or refuse to hire or to discharge any individual, or otherwise to discriminate against any individual with respect to [her] compensation, terms, conditions, or privileges of employment, because of such individual's * * * sex * * *[.]

42 U.S.C. §2000e-2(a)(1) (1976). The specific provision of Title VII applying to employment with the District of Columbia, as well as to a federal agency as in Barnes v. Castle, supra, states:

All personnel actions affecting employees * * * in those units of the Government of the District of Columbia having positions in the competitive service * * * shall be made free from any discrimination based on race, color, religion, sex, or national origin.

---

[4] The memorandum criticized Bundy for failing to file proper weekly and monthly reports, to serve clients properly, and to make sufficient field visits. Plaintiff's Exh. No. 2, SA 217. Bundy responded that all her co-workers normally had difficulties filing reports because of inefficiencies in the filing system, that it was not possible to give any better service to her excessive number of clients in the 15-30 minutes allotted for consultation with each one, and that her supervisors never provided her with any express requirements or goals for the number of her field visits. App. 61-64.

[5] Even after Bundy consulted Matthews, Burton apparently continued to intimidate her, accusing her of failing to honor a duty assignment. App. 149-150, which Bundy testified she had never been given. Plaintiff's Exh. No. 9, SA 250.

[6] Since the agency took no final action on her complaint, and since she waited more than 180 days after she filed the complaint with the agency, Bundy fully exhausted her administrative remedies before proceeding in District Court. 42 U.S.C. §2000e-16(c) (1976); Civil Service Commission Regulations §713.281, Federal Personnel Manual Supp. 990-1 (1978).

Id. §2000e-16(a). Despite the difference in language between these two sections, we have held that Title VII places the same restrictions on federal and District of Columbia agencies as it does on private employers, Barnes v. Costle, supra, 561 F.2d at 988, 15 FEP Cases at 349, and so we may construe the latter provision in terms of the former. We infer that the District Court in this case did the same, and that it refused Bundy declaratory and injunctive relief because it believed that sexual harassment not leading to loss or denial of tangible employment benefits for the harassed employee fell outside the scope of discrimination with respect to "terms, conditions, or privileges of employment."

Because Paulette Barnes had had her job terminated after she refused her supervisor's sexual importunings, we were not required in Barnes to construe the phrase "terms, conditions, or privileges of employment." Instead, our task of statutory construction in Barnes was to determine whether the disparate treatment Barnes suffered was "based on * * * sex." Id. at 989, 15 FEP Cases at 349. We heard arguments there that whatever harm Barnes suffered was not sex discrimination, since Barnes' supervisor terminated her job because she had refused sexual advances, not because she was a woman. We rejected those arguments as disingenuous in the extreme. The supervisor in that case made demands of Barnes that he would not have made of male employees. Id. "But for her womanhood * * * [Barnes'] participation in sexual activity would never have been solicited. To say, then, that she was victimized in her employment simply because she declined the invitation is to ignore the asserted fact that she was invited only because she was a woman subordinate to the inviter in the hierarchy of agency personnel." Id. at 990, 15 FEP Cases at 350–351 (emphasis added; footnotes omitted).[7]

[DISCRIMINATION]

We thus made clear in Barnes that sex discrimination within the meaning of Title VII is not limited to disparate treatment founded solely or categorically on gender. Rather, discrimination is sex discrimination whenever sex is for no legitimate reason a substantial factor in the discrimination. Id. at 990 & n.50, 15 FEP Cases at 350, citing Phillips v. Martin Marietta Corp., 400 U.S. 542, 3 FEP Cases 40 (1971); see 29 C.F.R. §1604.4(a) (1979) ("so long as sex is a factor in the application of [an employer's decision], such application involves a discrimination based on sex"). Other circuits have agreed. Tomkins v. Public Service Electric & Gas Co., 568 F.2d 1044, 16 FEP Cases 22 (3d Cir. 1977); Garber v. Saxon Business Products, Inc., 552 F.2d 1032, 15 FEP Cases 344 (4th Cir. 1977); see Miller v. Bank of America, 600 F.2d 211, 20 FEP Cases 462 (9th Cir. 1979).

[1] We thus have no difficulty inferring that Bundy suffered discrimination on the basis of sex. Moreover, applying Barnes, we have no difficulty ascribing the harassment — the "standard operating procedure" — to Bundy's employer, the agency. Although Delbert Jackson himself appears not to have used his position as Director to harass Bundy, an employer is liable for discriminatory acts committed by supervisory personnel, Barnes v. Costle, supra, 561 F.2d at 993, 15 FEP Cases at 353, and there is obviously no dispute that the men who harassed Bundy were her supervisors. Barnes did suggest that the employer might be relieved of liability if the supervisor committing the harassment did so in contravention of the employer's policy and without the employer's knowledge, and if the employer moved promptly and effectively to rectify the offense. Id.; see Croker v. Boeing Co. (Vertol Div.), 437 F.Supp. 1138, 1194, 15 FEP Cases 165, 211 (E.D. Pa. 1977). Here, however, Delbert Jackson and other officials in the agency who had some control over employment and promotion decisions had full notice of harassment committed by agency supervisors and did virtually nothing to stop or even investigate the practice.[8] See id. at 1191,

---

[7] We also rejected the argument that sexual harassment could not be gender discrimination simply because a woman could also harass a man, or because any homosexual supervisor could harass an employee of the same gender. We noted that in each instance the question is one of but-for causation: would the complaining employee have suffered the harassment had he or she been of a different gender? Barnes v. Costle, 561 F.2d 983, 990 n.55, 15 FEP Cases 345, 351 (D.C. Cir. 1977). Only by a reductio ad absurdum could we imagine a case of harassment that is not sex discrimination — where a bisexual supervisor harasses men and women alike. Id.

---

[8] This case thus also satisfies the more stringent test of employer respondeat superior liability Judge MacKinnon advocated in his concurrence in Barnes v. Costle, supra note 7, 561 F.2d at 995–1001, 15 FEP Cases at 354–360. The employer, in full knowledge of the alleged offense and having received a formal complaint, was in the best position to correct the offenses, yet impeded the complaint — and even abetted the offenses.

We note in this context that the District Court's finding that Jackson, among others, did not take the harassment ritual "seriously" is a remarkable non sequitur.

Jackson never took any further steps whatsoever to ascertain whether Bundy's complaints were valid, nor did he take plaintiff's complaint seriously enough to ask for a copy of the written re-

15 FEP Cases at 209. And though there was ample evidence in this case that at least two other women in the agency suffered from this harassment, see note 3 supra, Barnes makes clear that the employer could be held liable even if Bundy were the only victim, since Congress intended Title VII to protect *individuals* against class-based prejudice. Barnes v. Costle, supra, 561 F.2d at 993, 15 FEP Cases at 353.[9]

[NOVEL QUESTION]

We thus readily conclude that Bundy's employer discriminated against her on the basis of sex. What remains is the novel question whether the sexual harassment of the sort Bundy suffered amounted by itself to sex discrimination with respect to the *"terms, conditions, or privileges of employment."* Though no court has as yet so held, we believe that an affirmative answer follows ineluctably from numerous cases finding Title VII violations where an employer created or condoned a substantially discriminatory work *environment*, regardless of whether the complaining employees lost any tangible job benefits as a result of the discrimination.

Bundy's claim on this score is essentially that "conditions of employment" include the psychological and emotional work environment — that the sexually stereotyped insults and demeaning propositions to which she was indisputably subjected and which caused her anxiety and debilitation, App. 40, illegally poisoned that environment. This claim invokes the Title VII principle enunciated by Judge Goldberg in Rogers v. Equal Employment Opportunity Com'n, 454 F.2d 234, 4 FEP Cases 92 (5th Cir. 1971), cert. denied, 406 U.S. 957, 4 FEP Cases 771 (1972). The plaintiff in Rogers, a Hispanic, did not claim that her employer,

a firm of opticians, had deprived her of any tangible job benefit. Rather, she claimed that by giving discriminatory service to its Hispanic *clients* the firm created a discriminatory and offensive work environment for its Hispanic *employees*. Granting that the express language of Title VII did not mention this situation, Judge Goldberg stated:

Congress chose neither to enumerate specific discriminatory practices, nor to elucidate in extenso the parameter of such nefarious activities. Rather, it pursued the path of wisdom by being unconstrictive, knowing that constant change is the order of our day and that the seemingly reasonable practices of the present can easily become the injustices of the morrow. Time was when employment discrimination tended to be viewed as a series of isolated and distinguishable events, manifesting itself, for example, in an employer's practices of hiring, firing, and promoting. But today employment discrimination is a far more complex and pervasive phenomenon, as the nuances and subtleties of discriminatory employment practices are no longer confined to bread and butter issues. As wages and hours of employment take subordinate roles in management-labor relationships, the modern employee makes ever-increasing demands in the nature of intangible fringe benefits. Recognizing the importance of these benefits, we should neither ignore their need for protection, nor blind ourselves to their potential misuse.

454 F.2d at 238, 4 FEP Cases at 94. The Fifth Circuit then concluded that the employer had indeed violated Title VII, Judge Goldberg explaining that "terms, conditions, or privileges of employment"

is an expansive concept which sweeps within its protective ambit the practice of creating a work environment heavily charged with ethnic or racial discrimination. * * * One can readily envision working environments so heavily polluted with discrimination as to destroy completely the emotional and psychological stability of minority group workers * * *.

Id.; accord, Carroll v. Talman Federal Savings & Loan Ass'n, 604 F.2d 1028, 1032-1033 & n.13, 20 FEP Cases 764, 767-768 (7th Cir. 1979), petition for cert. pending (forcing female bank employees to wear uniforms while allowing males to wear own suits violates Title VII by perpetuating demeaning sexual stereotypes; "terms and conditions of employment" mean more than tangible compensation and benefits); Cariddi v. Kansas City Chiefs Football Club, Inc., 568 F.2d 87, 16 FEP Cases 462 (8th Cir. 1977) (though employee could only prove isolated incidents, a pattern of offensive ethnic slurs would violate his Title VII rights); Firefighters Institute for Racial Equality v. City of St. Louis, 549 F.2d 506, 514-515, 14 FEP Cases 1486, 1492-1493 (8th Cir.), cert. denied, 434 U.S. 819, 15 FEP Cases 1184 (1977) (segregated employee eating clubs condoned — though not or-

---

port of the investigation which was conducted. This is a further indication that Jackson, as had others before him, considered sexual advances by males in the office to female employees as a game that was played and not to be taken seriously.

Finding of Fact No. 44, App. 16. To state the all too obvious, Jackson may have avoided all investigation precisely because he realized that proof of a practice of sexual harassment would be a serious matter for his agency indeed. Alternatively, if he in fact did consider the whole matter trivial, he was only compounding Bundy's difficulty in obtaining relief from harassment and thus, in a sense, compounding the Title VII violation.

[9] We note that although a pattern or practice of harassment directed at a single employee can violate Title VII, casual or isolated manifestations of a discriminatory environment, such as a few ethnic or racial slurs, may not give rise to a cause of action. Cariddi v. Kansas City Chiefs Football Club, Inc., 568 F.2d 87, 88, 16 FEP Cases 462, 462-463 (8th Cir. 1977); Fekete v. U.S. Steel Corp., 353 F.Supp. 1177, 1186, 5 FEP Cases 639, 647-648 (W.D. Pa. 1973); see Int'l Brhd of Teamsters v. United States, 431 U.S. 324, 336 n.16, 14 FEP Cases 1514, 1519 (1977).

ganized or regulated — by employer violate Title VII by creating discriminatory work environment); Gray v. Greyhound Lines, East, 545 F.2d 169, 176, 13 FEP Cases 1401, 1406 (D.C. Cir. 1976) (pattern of racial slurs violates Title VII rights to nondiscriminatory environment); United States v. City of Buffalo, 457 F.Supp. 612, 631-635, 19 FEP Cases 776, 789-792 (W.D. N.Y. 1978) (black employees entitled to work environment free of racial abuse and insult); Compston v. Borden, Inc., 424 F.Supp. 157, 17 FEP Cases 310 (S.D. Ohio 1976) (demeaning religious slurs by supervisor violate Title VII); Steadman v. Hundley, 421 F.Supp. 53, 57, 18 FEP Cases 1370, 1371 (N.D. Ill. 1976) (racial slurs may lead to Title VII violation); cf. Harrington v. Vandalia-Butler Board of Educ., 585 F.2d 192, 194 n.3, 18 FEP Cases 348, 349 (6th Cir. 1978), cert. denied, 441 U.S. 932, 19 FEP Cases 888 (1979) (giving female physical education teachers inferior locker and shower facilities is illegal discrimination; Title VII reaches "actual working conditions," not just equal opportunity for employment); Waters v. Heublein, Inc., 547 F.2d 466, 13 FEP Cases 1409 (9th Cir.), cert. denied, 433 U.S. 915, 15 FEP Cases 31 (1977) (white plaintiff has standing to sue employer who discriminates against blacks, since she has statutory right to work environment free of racial prejudice); Swint v. Pullman-Standard, 539 F.2d 77, 13 FEP Cases 604 (5th Cir. 1976) (discriminatory job assignments violate Title VII even where no discrimination in salary; Title VII claimant need not prove tangible economic harm).[10]

[RELEVANCE OF CASES]

The relevance of these "discriminatory environment" cases to sexual harassment is beyond serious dispute. Racial or ethnic discrimination against a company's minority clients may reflect no intent to discriminate directly against the company's minority employees, but in poisoning the atmosphere of employment it violates Title VII. Sexual stereotyping through discriminatory dress requirements may be benign in intent, and may offend women only in a general, atmospheric manner, yet it violates Title VII. Racial slurs, though intentional and directed at individuals,

may still be just verbal insults, yet they too may create Title VII liability. How then can sexual harassment, which injects the most demeaning sexual stereotypes into the general work environment and which always represents an intentional assault on an individual's innermost privacy, not be illegal?

Moreover, an important principle articulated in Rogers v. Equal Employment Opportunity Com'n, supra, suggests the special importance of allowing women to sue to prevent sexual harassment without having to prove that they resisted the harassment and that their resistance caused them to lose tangible job benefits. Judge Goldberg noted that even indirect discrimination is illegal because it

> may constitute a subtle scheme designed to create a working environment imbued with discrimination and directed ultimately at minority group employees. As patently discriminatory practices become outlawed, those employers bent on pursuing a general policy declared illegal by Congressional mandate will undoubtedly devise more sophisticated methods to perpetuate discrimination among employees. * * *

454 F.2d at 239, 4 FEP Cases at 95. Thus, unless we extend the Barnes holding, an employer could sexually harass a female employee with impunity by carefully stopping short of firing the employee or taking any other tangible actions against her in response to her resistance, thereby creating the impression — the one received by the District Court in this case — that the employer did not take the ritual of harassment and resistance "seriously."

Indeed, so long as women remain inferiors in the employment hierarchy, they may have little recourse against harassment beyond the legal recourse Bundy seeks in this case. The law may allow a woman to prove that her resistance to the harassment cost her her job or some economic benefit, but this will do her no good if the employer never takes such tangible actions against her. And this, in turn, means that so long as the sexual situation is constructed with enough coerciveness, subtlety, suddenness, or onesidedness to negate the effectiveness of the woman's refusal, or so long as her refusals are simply ignored while her job is formally undisturbed, she is not considered to have been sexually harassed.

C. MacKinnon, Sexual Harassment of Working Women 46-47 (1979). It may even be pointless to require the employee to prove that she "resisted" the harassment at all. So long as the employer never literally forces sexual relations on the employee, "resistance" may be a meaningless alternative for her. If the employer demands no response to his verbal or physical gestures other than good-natured tolerance, the

---

[10] The Equal Employment Opportunity Commission (EEOC) itself, to whose interpretation of Title VII we owe considerable deference, Griggs v. Duke Power Co., 401 U.S. 424, 433-434, 3 FEP Cases 175, 179 (1971), has consistently held that the statute grants an employee a working environment free of discrimination. E.g., EEOC Decision No. 74-84, CCH EEOC Decisions ¶6450 (1975); EEOC Decision No. 72-0779, CCH EEOC Decisions ¶6321, 4 FEP Cases 317 (1971).

woman has no means of communicating her rejection. She neither accepts nor rejects the advances; she simply endures them. She might be able to contrive proof of rejection by objecting to the employer's advances in some very visible and dramatic way, but she would do so only at the risk of making her life on the job even more miserable. Id. at 43–47. It hardly helps that the remote prospect of legal relief under Barnes remains available if she objects so powerfully that she provokes the employer into firing her.

The employer can thus implicitly and effectively make the employee's endurance of sexual intimidation a "condition" of her employment. The woman then faces a "cruel trilemma." She can endure the harassment. She can attempt to oppose it, with little hope of success, either legal or practical, but with every prospect of making the job even less tolerable for her. Or she can leave her job, with little hope of legal relief[11] and the likely prospect of another job where she will face harassment anew.

[GUIDANCE ON DECREE]

[2–4] Bundy proved that she was the victim of a practice of sexual harassment and a discriminatory work environment permitted by her employer. Her rights under Title VII were therefore violated. We thus reverse the District Court's holding on this issue and remand it to that court so it can fashion appropriate injunctive relief.[12] And on this novel issue, we think it advisable to

offer the District Court guidance in framing its decree.[13]

The Final Guidelines on Sexual Harassment in the Workplace (Guidelines) issued by the Equal Employment Opportunity Commission on November 10, 1980, 45 Fed. Reg. 74676–74677 (1980) (to be codified at 29 C.F.R. §1604.11(a)–(f)), offer a useful basis for injunctive relief in this case. Those Guidelines define sexual harassment broadly:

Unwelcome sexual advances, requests for sexual favors, and other verbal or physical conduct of a sexual nature constitute sexual harassment when (1) submission to such conduct is made either explicitly or implicitly a term or condition of an individual's employment, (2) submission to or rejection of such conduct by an individual is used as the basis for employment decisions affecting such individual, or (3) such conduct has the purpose or effect of unreasonably interfering with an individual's work performance or creating an intimidating, hostile, or offensive work environment.

Guidelines, supra, 45 Fed. Reg. at 74677 (to be codified at 29 C.F.R. §1604.11(a)). The Guidelines go on to reaffirm that an employer is responsible for discriminatory acts of its agents and supervisory employees with respect to sexual harassment just as with other forms of discrimination, regardless of whether the employer authorized or knew or even should have known of the acts, id. (to be codified at 29 C.F.R. §1604.11(d)), and also remains responsible for sexual harassment committed by nonsupervisory employees if the employer authorized, knew of, or should have known of such harassment, id. (to be codified at 29 C.F.R. §1604.11(d)). The general goal of these Guidelines is preventive. An employer may negate liability by taking "immediate and appropri-

---

[11] Compare In re Carmita Wood, Case No. 75-92437, New York State Dep't of Labor Unemployment Insurance Appeals Board, Decision and Notice of Decision (March 7, 1975) (employee who claimed sexual harassment forced her to leave job was held to have resigned voluntarily and thus was ineligible for compensation), with Appeals Board Decision No. P-B-139 (California), reversing Decision of the Referee. In re Nancy J. Fillhouer, Case No. SJ-5963, William J. Costello, Referee (San Jose Referee Office, April 28, 1975) (granting such claim).

[12] Title VII allows the courts to award a victorious plaintiff reinstatement, back pay, or "any other equitable relief as the court deems appropriate." 42 U.S.C. §2000e–5 (g) (1976). Back pay and reinstatement are, of course, irrelevant to the discriminatory environment issue, and we follow the great majority of the federal courts in construing "equitable relief" to preclude any award of damages for emotional harm resulting from a Title VII violation. E.g., Harrington v. Vandalia-Butler Board of Educ., 585 F.2d 192, 18 FEP Cases 348 (6th Cir. 1978), cert. denied, 441 U.S. 932, 19 FEP Cases 888 (1979); Curran v. Portland Superintending School Committee, 435 F.Supp. 1063, 1077–1078, 15 FEP Cases 644, 654 (D. Me. 1977), Wright v. St. John's Hospital, 414 F.Supp. 1202, 1208, 14 FEP Cases 5, 10 (D. Okla. 1976); see Equal Employment Opportunity Com'n v. Detroit Edison Co., 515 F.2d 301, 308–309, 10 FEP Cases 239; 243–244 (6th Cir. 1975), vacated and remanded, 431 U.S. 951, 14 FEP Cases 1686 (1976). We add that, since our holding makes Bundy a prevailing party in this suit, the District Court on remand may entertain a request for attorney's fees. 42 U.S.C. §2000e–5(k) (1976).

[13] Appellee has argued that an injunction is improper and unnecessary in this case since Bundy has complained of no instances of sexual harassment since 1975 and there is therefore no reason to think further harassment will occur. Common sense tells us that the men who harassed Bundy may well have ceased their actions solely because of the pendency of her complaint and lawsuit. Moreover, the law tells us that a suit for injunctive relief does not become moot simply because the offending party has ceased the offending conduct, since the offending party might be free otherwise to renew that conduct once the court denied the relief. Allee v. Medrano. 419 U.S. 802, 810–811, 86 LRRM 2215 (1974). The request for injunctive relief will be moot only where there is no reasonable expectation that the conduct will recur. United States v. W. T. Grant Co., 345 U.S. 629 (1953), or where interim events have "completely and irrevocably eradicated the effects of the alleged violation," County of Los Angeles v. Davis. 440 U.S. 625, 631, 19 FEP Cases 282, 285 (1979). We perceive no such certainty here, most obviously because Bundy's agency has taken no affirmative steps to prevent recurrence of the harassment, and because all the harassing employees still work for the agency. The issuance of Mayor's Order No. 79-89 (May 24, 1979), see text and note at note 14 infra, does not provide any certainty that the offending conduct will not recur.

ate corrective action" when it learns of any illegal harassment, id., but the employer should fashion rules within its firm or agency to ensure that such corrective action never becomes necessary, id. (to be codified at 29 C.F.R. §1604.11(f)).

[5] Applying these Guidelines to the present case, we believe that the Director of the agency should be ordered to raise affirmatively the subject of sexual harassment with all his employees and inform all employees that sexual harassment violates Title VII of the Civil Rights Act of 1964, the Guidelines of the EEOC, the express orders of the Mayor of the District of Columbia,[14] and the policy of the agency itself. The Director should also establish and publicize a scheme whereby harassed employees may complain to the Director immediately and confidentially. The Director should promptly take all necessary steps to investigate and correct any harassment, including warnings and appropriate discipline directed at the offending party, and should generally develop other means of preventing harassment within the agency.

[COMPLAINT ADJUDICATION]

Perhaps the most important part of the preventive remedy will be a prompt and effective procedure for hearing, adjudicating, and remedying complaints of sexual harassment within the agency. Fortunately, the District Court need not establish an entire new procedural mechanism for harassment complaints. Under Civil Service Commission Regulations §§713.211–713.823, Federal Personnel Manual Supplement 990-1 (1978), the Department of Corrections, like all other federal and District of Columbia agencies, is required to establish procedures for adjudication of complaints of denial of equal employment opportunity, whether the ground of discrimination is race, color, religion, sex, or national origin. The required procedures guarantee the complainant a prompt and effective investigation, an opportunity for informal adjustment of the discrimination, and, if necessary, a

formal evidentiary hearing. Moreover, if the complaint proves meritorious the agency may be required to take disciplinary action against any employee found to have committed discriminatory acts. Id. §713.222(c). Finally, the agency must inform any employee denied relief within the agency of his or her right to file a civil action in the District Court. Id. §713.282.

[6] Since we have held that sexual harassment, even if it does not result in loss of tangible job benefits, is illegal sex discrimination, the District Court may simply order the Director of the agency to ensure that complaints of sexual harassment receive thorough and effective treatment within the formal process the agency has already established to comply with the Civil Service Commission regulations. Finally, we believe the District Court should retain jurisdiction of the case so that it may review the Director's plans for complying with the injunction.[15]

---

[14] On October 31, 1975 the Mayor of the District of Columbia issued Mayor's Order No. 75-230, prohibiting employment discrimination on the basis of sex and other improper factors in all District agencies. On May 24, 1979 Mayor Barry amended Order No. 75-230 with Mayor's Order No. 79-89, which construes illegal sexual discrimination to include sexual harassment, requires the District's Office of Human Rights to receive and adjudicate any complaints of sexual harassment of District employees according to the procedures set forth in Mayor's Order No. 75-230, and requires all agency heads to establish and implement intra-agency means of investigating and adjudicating complaints of harassment. These orders are a useful supplement to the EEOC Guidelines and a District Court injunction.

[15] We offer the following as appropriate language for the injunction:

The court decrees that the defendant Delbert Jackson, Director of the District of Columbia Department of Corrections, along with his supervising employees, agents, and all those subject to his control or acting in concert with him, are enjoined from causing, encouraging, condoning, or permitting the practice of sexual harassment of female employees by male supervisors and employees within the Department: to wit, any unwelcome sexual advances, requests for sexual favors, or other verbal or physical conduct of a sexual nature when submission to such conduct is explicitly or implicitly a requirement of the individual's employment, or used as a basis for any employment decision concerning that individual, or when such conduct has the purpose or effect of unreasonably interfering with the individual's work performance or creating an intimidating or hostile or offensive work environment.

Defendant is further required:

1. To notify all employees and supervisors in the Department, through individual letters and permanent posting in prominent locations throughout Department offices, that sexual harassment, as explicitly defined in the previous paragraph, violates Title VII of the Civil Rights Act of 1964, regulatory guidelines of the Equal Employment Opportunity Commission, the express orders of the Mayor of the District of Columbia, and the policy of the Department of Corrections.

2. To ensure that employees complaining of sexual harassment can avail themselves of the full and effective use of the complaint, hearing, adjudication, and appeals procedures for complaints of discrimination established by the Department of Corrections pursuant to Civil Service Regulations §§713.211–713.823.

3. To develop appropriate sanctions or disciplinary measures for supervisors or other employees who are found to have sexually harassed female employees, including warnings to the offending person and notations in that person's employment record for reference in the event future complaints are directed against that person.

4. To develop other appropriate means of instructing employees of the Department on the harmful nature of sexual harassment.

Defendant shall return to this court within 60 days to report on the steps he has taken in compliance with this order and to present his plans for the additional measures required by Paragraph 4 above. The court shall retain jurisdiction of this case.

III. CLAIMS FOR BACK PAY AND PROMOTION

Beyond claiming that the sexual harassment she suffered was illegal in itself, Bundy claims that her supervisors illegally retaliated against her refusal of their sexual propositions by delaying her promotion to GS-9 level, and that they continue to retaliate by denying her a promotion to GS-11. Bundy thus requests back pay for the delay in promotion to both levels, and an order requiring her immediate promotion to GS-11. The District Court held against Bundy on these claims, essentially finding that the supervisors were not offended by Bundy's refusal of their advances, and hence had no motive to retaliate against her, and that Bundy's flawed qualifications and work performance gave them legitimate reasons for delaying and denying the promotions. Bundy now argues that the District Court's factual findings were clearly erroneous, FED. R. CIV. P. 52(a), and notes that in a discrimination case the appellate court may make an independent review of the record to determine whether the District Court was correct in finding the "ultimate fact" of discrimination or no discrimination. Kinsey v. First Regional Securities, Inc., 557 F.2d 830, 836, 14 FEP Cases 1143, 1146 (D.C. Cir. 1977). The parties presented to the District Court, and present to us now, a fairly confusing set of facts with respect to the promotion claims. We review them only very briefly.

Bundy became eligible for promotion to GS-9 in January 1975 after 12 months as a GS-7. She was not promoted until July 1976.[16] At the time she became technically eligible for a promotion she was told that a temporary job freeze made even a recommendation of promotion impossible. Nevertheless, other employees in her unit were recommended for promotion and even promoted during the purported freeze. App. 41-44. Specifically, William Hill, another Vocational Rehabilitation Specialist, was promoted to GS-9 in May 1975 after 15 months as a GS-7 and three months of technical eligibility, App. 184, and William Goff, who was hired as a GS-9 Vocational Rehabilita-

tion Specialist, was promoted to GS-11 in July 1975 after 15 months as a GS-9, App. 183. Bundy cites evidence that she performed the same work as these men, and that she performed it every bit as well as they did. App. 107-108.

[QUALITY OF WORK]

The trial court found that Bundy's work was in fact deficient, and that her qualifications were inferior to those of Hill and Goff. It found that Bundy had taken excessive sick leave, failed to file required reports, made insufficient field contacts, and neglected to report her duty assignments, Findings of Fact Nos. 16-19, App. 10, and that her supervisors had properly informed her of these deficiencies, id. No. 20, App. 10. It also found that Hill and Goff, unlike Bundy, had had considerable experience working with ex-offenders or disadvantaged youths before they joined the agency, and that Goff, unlike Bundy, possessed a college degree. The District of Columbia now supports the District Court decision by noting that Bundy's consistent "satisfactory" work ratings are not in themselves a sufficient basis for promotion, Defendant's Exh. No. 17, SA 294, and that had Bundy been promoted in January 1975 she would have achieved the promotion faster than any employee in her unit, male or female, and *much* earlier than several male employees, Defendant's Exh. No. 14, SA 288. Bundy responds that there is no basis for the District's challenges to her work performance, that — in the testimony of her colleague Ann Blanchard — all employees in the unit had difficulty with filing and other procedures, App. 107-114, and that her allegedly excessive sick leave was in fact due to emotional stress she suffered as a result of sexual harassment, App. 39-40.

As for her desired promotion to GS-11, Bundy notes that such a promotion was granted in 1977 to another employee, Curtis Davis, whose responsibilities and performance, she argues, were similar to hers. In finding against her on this issue, the District Court found that because Bundy, unlike Davis, worked mostly with so-called "regular procedure" cases rather than "special procedure" cases, as defined by the Civil Service Commission, she was not eligible for GS-11. Findings of Fact Nos. 10-11, App. 9; Conclusion of Law No. 4, App. 17.

The relevant distinction between Bundy's and Davis' work is apparently that Bundy worked primarily with clients over 26 years old and Davis solely with clients under 26. App. 73-75. Bundy insists that the District Court misconstrued the Civil Service classifi-

---

[16] Bundy thus believes she is entitled to back pay for the period between January 1975 and July 1976. However, as we noted earlier, see note 1 supra, the District has conceded that Bundy should have been promoted at least as of February 1976, since the agency improperly denied her January 1976 promotion request in wrongful response to her filing of a discrimination claim. Thus the request for back pay to compensate for the delay in promotion to GS-9 allegedly due to her refusal of her supervisors' sexual advances really involves the 12-month period from January 1975 to January 1976.

cations in concluding that the age of the clients automatically and by itself determines a Vocational Rehabilitation Specialist's eligibility for GS–11. She argues that the Civil Service Commission's notion of "special procedure" cases is in fact flexible, including clients of any age who present such special placement problems as illiteracy or emotional disability. Since many of her adult clients have such problems, App. 192–193, 207–208, she believes the District Court erred in categorically presuming that she was ineligible for GS–11.[17] Although this issue may appear to be one of construing the Civil Service classification rules, it is also a factual question of the similarity or difference between Bundy's and Davis' responsibilities.

In a case of such factual dispute, we of course owe great deference to the trial court's findings. Indeed, we must affirm the trial court's conclusion on the question of discrimination if the so-called "subsidiary facts" are not clearly erroneous, if the inferences drawn from them are reasonable, and if the findings and inferences reasonably support the "ultimate" factual finding on discrimination. Kinsey v. First Regional Securities, Inc., supra, 557 F.2d at 835–836, 14 FEP Cases at 1146. Nevertheless, were we to make a final disposition of Bundy's back pay and promotion claims, even under this highly deferential standard we might be inclined to overrule the District Court. Most important, we would readily reject as clearly erroneous the District Court's findings that the supervisors in Bundy's agency never took the ritual of harassment seriously and that they therefore had no motive for retaliating against Bundy. Findings of Fact Nos. 38, 44, App. 15, 16. Moreover, we would at least be inclined to question the District Court's findings on Bundy's allegedly poor work performance, id. Nos. 16–20, App. 10, since the only important evidence of flaws in her work was the self-serving testimony of supervisors who had themselves been her harassers.

[BURDEN OF PROOF]

However, we cannot make a final disposition of these claims, because the District Court, whether right or wrong

in its factual findings, failed to allocate properly the burden of proof according to Title VII principles. The District Court's findings of fact and conclusions of law in no way indicate that the court properly defined the requirements of the plaintiff's prima facie case, or the burden the employer bears in rebutting a prima facie case. McDonnell Douglas Corp. v. Green, 411 U.S. 792, 802, 805, 5 FEP Cases 965, 969, 970 (1973); Hackley v. Roudebush, 520 F.2d 108, 157–158, 11 FEP Cases 487, 525–526 (D.C. Cir. 1975). We therefore must remand the case to the District Court to enable it to conduct further evidentiary proceedings in accordance with the proper allocation of burden of proof. However, adjusting the general burden of proof principles of McDonnell Douglas Corp. v. Green, supra, to unusual factual situations is a matter of some difficulty, and this sexual harassment claim is indeed exceptionally unusual among Title VII cases. We therefore shall attempt to guide the District Court in this matter.

Recognizing the difficulty a plaintiff faces in proving the motives behind an employer's actions, McDonnell established the general principle that in an employment discrimination case under Title VII the employee must first make out a prima facie case.

This may be done by showing (i) that he belongs to a racial minority; (ii) that he applied and was qualified for a job for which the employer was seeking applicants; (iii) that, despite his qualifications, he was rejected; and (iv) that, after his rejection, the position remained open and the employer continued to seek applicants from persons of complainant's qualifications. * * *

411 U.S. at 802, 5 FEP Cases at 969 (footnote omitted). As the Supreme Court noted in a later case, this prima facie showing does not in itself prove illegal discrimination. Rather, it constitutes proof of actions taken by the employer from which we can reasonably infer a discriminatory animus, because common experience tells us that such actions normally have a discriminatory motive. Furnco Construction Corp. v. Waters, 438 U.S. 567, 579–580, 17 FEP Cases 1062, 1067 (1978). Once the prima facie case is made out, the burden shifts to the employer to articulate legitimate, nondiscriminatory reasons for denying the applicant the position. McDonnell Douglas Corp. v. Green, supra, 411 U.S. at 802, 5 FEP Cases at 969. If the employer meets that burden, he has rebutted the prima facie case. But the employee must still have a "full and fair opportunity" to prove in response that the purported legitimate reason was in fact a mere pretext for discrimination. Id. at 805, 5 FEP Cases at 970. Normally, the plaintiff must make out his prima facie case by a preponderance of the ev-

---

[17] As we noted earlier, see note 6 supra, Bundy properly exhausted her administrative remedies on her harassment claims. We reject the District's argument that Bundy cannot request an order of promotion to GS–11 in this discrimination suit because she did not previously request reclassification with the Civil Service Commission, since her classification argument is an incident of her harassment claims.

idence. The employer's burden to articulate a legitimate, nondiscriminatory reason for his action is simply the burden of going forward with the evidence. Board of Trustees v. Sweeney, 439 U.S. 24, 18 FEP Cases 520 (1978) (per curiam); id. at 29, 18 FEP Cases at 522 (Stevens, J., dissenting). Once the employer has submitted evidence tending to show that he had a legitimate reason for his action, the burden of going forward with the evidence shifts back to the plaintiff. Under McDonnell, the ultimate burden of persuasion always remains with the plaintiff.

The literal McDonnell formula, of course, is designed for a claim of discriminatory refusal to hire due to alleged racial prejudice. It does not precisely apply to a claim, like Bundy's, of discriminatory refusal to promote. Even more important, the McDonnell formula presumes the standard situation where the alleged discrimination is due to the bare fact of the claimant's membership in a disadvantaged group. It therefore also fails to fit with precision the very unusual, perhaps unique, situation of sexual harassment, where the alleged basis of discrimination is not the employee's gender per se, but her refusal to submit to sexual advances which she suffered in large part because of her gender. McDonnell itself, however, recognizes very realistically that the courts must adjust the definition of a prima facie case and the allocation of burden of proof to the differing situations that may arise in Title VII cases, 411 U.S. at 802 n.14, 5 FEP Cases at 969, and with that recognition in mind we proceed to consider the proper proof standards for this case.

[REFUSAL TO PROMOTE]

Adjusting the McDonnell formula to cases of discriminatory refusal to promote is relatively simple. Thus to make out a prima facie case the plaintiff must show that she belongs to a protected group, that she was qualified for and applied for a promotion, that she was considered for and denied the promotion, and that other employees of similar qualifications who were not members of the protected group were indeed promoted at the time the plaintiff's request for promotion was denied. Kunda v. Muhlenberg College, 463 F.Supp. 294, 307, 18 FEP Cases 1297, 1307 (E.D. Pa. 1978). Qualification for promotion, of course, may not be a strictly precise concept, and will depend on the rules and customs of a particular employer. In the present case, for example, a Vocational Rehabilitation Specialist's technical eligibility for promotion to a GS-9 level never automatically means promotion, nor does mere "satisfactory" performance in the complainant's current job ever guarantee promotion. But proof of these factors certainly helps establish a prima facie case. On the other hand, there can be no absolutely precise and uniform time period before and after the denial of the complainant's promotion during which plaintiffs must show that similarly qualified nondisadvantaged employees were promoted. But a court can certainly determine a reasonable period on the facts of a particular case.

This minor adjustment in the McDonnell formula for promotion cases could, of course, end our analysis of the issue of Bundy's claims for back pay and promotion; since she is obviously a member of a protected group — women — Bundy could go on to prove the other requisite factors. See Williams v. Bell, 587 F.2d 1240, 1245-1246 n.45, 17 FEP Cases 1662, 1665-1666 (D.C. Cir. 1978) (dictum). Nevertheless, to treat Bundy's case as if it were equivalent to an ordinary case of alleged gender discrimination is manifestly unfair. Unlike a woman claiming general gender discrimination, Bundy has already proved that she is a victim of illegal discrimination as a matter wholly independent of her claim for back pay and promotion. We think she should therefore enter the ritual of order of proof at an advantage over the typical Title VII plaintiff who claims categorical gender discrimination which can only be proved as an incident of the discriminatory denial of promotion or other tangible benefit.

[DAY CASE]

We have already essentially taken this view in an analogous case. In Day v. Mathews, 530 F.2d 1083, 12 FEP Cases 1131 (D.C. Cir. 1976), a black employee of the Department of Health, Education and Welfare had sought promotion. He alleged, and HEW conceded, that HEW officials had discriminated against him on account of his race by impeding his request through administrative delays and unfairly low ratings of his performance. Id. at 1084, 12 FEP Cases at 1131. Nevertheless, HEW argued that Day would not have gotten the promotion even if he had not been the victim of discrimination; apparently HEW believed the discrimination was a gratuitous act by prejudiced officials and that Day was in any event not qualified for the promotion. In remanding the case to the District Court for further evidentiary proceedings under the proper legal standard of proof, we held that, since the employer had already been proved a discriminator, the plaintiff's prima facie case with respect to the denial of promotion had in effect already been made out, and that the burden should immediately shift to the employer to prove that Day's qualifications were such that he would not have been promoted even if he had not been the victim of discrimination. Id. at 1085, 12 FEP Cases at 1132. Moreover, in this special circumstance we held that the burden of persuasion, not just the burden of going forward with the evidence, shifted to the employer. And we held that the employer must meet his burden by clear and convincing evidence, rather than simply by a preponderance of the evidence. Id. See Baxter v. Savannah Sugar Refining Corp., 495 F.2d 437, 444–445, 8 FEP Cases 84, 89 (5th Cir.), cert. denied, 419 U.S. 1033, 8 FEP Cases 1142 (1974) (once employer is proved to have discriminated against plaintiff class, he bears burden of presenting clear and convincing evidence on issue of discrimination against individual plaintiffs). We stressed in Day that since the employer's own proved discriminatory actions were largely responsible for the plaintiff's typical dilemma of having to prove the motive underlying the employer's past action, "any resulting uncertainty [should] be resolved against the party whose action gave rise to the problem." 530 F.2d at 1086, 12 FEP Cases at 1133 (footnote omitted). We thereby recognized that where a Title VII defendant is proved a discriminator as a matter independent of the plaintiff's claim of discriminatory denial of a tangible job benefit, the court should ease the plaintiff's burden on that latter claim.[18]

---

[18] In Pettit v. United States, 488 F.2d 1026, 6 FEP Cases 1166 (Ct.Cl. 1973), the Court of Claims addressed a claim analogous to Bundy's. The plaintiff, seeking relief from an allegedly discriminatory denial of a promotion, proved as an independent matter that supervisors in his agency had subjected him to a blatantly discriminatory work environment by making offensive racial jokes and insults and giving him inferior work facilities. Id. at 1028, 6 FEP Cases at 1168. In assessing his claim for back pay and promotion the court accordingly and appropriately modified the McDonnell formula as follows:

We, therefore, hold that a prima facie case of failure to promote because of racial discrimination is made by showing: (i) that plaintiff belongs to a racial minority, (ii) that he was qualified for promotion and might have reasonably expected selection for promotion under the defendant's on-going competitive promotion system, (iii) that he was not promoted, and (iv) the supervisory level employees having responsibility to exercise judgment under the promotion system betrayed in other matters a predisposition towards discrimination against members of the involved minority. • • •

Id. at 1033, 6 FEP Cases at 1172; accord, Detroit Police Officers Ass'n v. Young, 446 F.Supp. 979, 1003, 16 FEP Cases 1005, 1020 (E.D. Mich. 1978). The last element in this formula is the innovation most relevant to Bundy's case: the plaintiff can make out the prima facie case in part by showing discrimination independent of the back pay claim but obviously relevant to the question of the employer's motive in denying the plaintiff promotion. But we also note the important omission in this formula. Unlike the McDonnell formula, this one does not require the plaintiff to draw the relevant comparison between

[7] We would adjust the McDonnell formula to Bundy's claim as follows: To establish a prima facie case of illegal denial of promotion in retaliation against the plaintiff's refusal of sexual advances by her supervisors, the plaintiff must show (1) that she was a victim of a pattern or practice of sexual harassment attributable to her employer (Bundy has, of course, already shown this); and (2) that she applied for and was denied a promotion for which she was technically eligible and of which she had a reasonable expectation. If the prima facie case is made out, the employer then must bear the burden of showing, by clear and convincing evidence, that he had legitimate nondiscriminatory reasons for denying the claimant the promotion. As in McDonnell, if the employer successfully rebuts the prima facie case, the claimant should still have the opportunity to prove that the employer's purported reasons were mere pretexts.

[DIFFERENCE]

[8] The most important difference between this formula and the McDonnell formula is that we are not requiring the plaintiff to show as part of her prima facie case that other employees who were no better qualified, but who were not similarly disadvantaged, were promoted at the time she was denied a promotion. We relieve the plaintiff of the need to prove such facts because, as we have explained, we think her burden should be eased where she can prove not only that she is a member of a disadvantaged group, but also that she has personally suffered illegal discrimination through the harassment itself. We simply require the plaintiff to show that according to the employer's formal rules she was eligible for promotion and that, within the context of the employer's actual practical pattern of promotion, she had a reasonable expectation of the promotion she sought. In rebutting the prima facie case — if the plaintiff makes it out — the employer would then have to show by clear and convincing evidence that, despite the employee's technical eligibility for promotion, in practice it set qualification criteria for promotion more stringent than the employee could meet.

---

himself and other employees who were in fact promoted — or even to prove that other employees were promoted at the time his own request for promotion was denied. We infer that in Pettit the court intended that if any other employees were promoted at roughly the time the plaintiff sought promotion and if these employees were distinctly better qualified, the employer would have to prove these facts as part of his rebuttal. This issue arises in text infra when we instruct the District Court in the present case on the possible elements of the agency's rebuttal.

The employer could support his rebuttal case by showing that any other employees who were promoted at approximately the time the plaintiff was denied promotion and who were not themselves victims of the pattern of sexual harassment in fact met these more stringent criteria. See note 18 supra.

Applying these principles, we remand the case to the District Court for further proceedings consistent with this opinion.

So ordered.

EEOC v. RATH PACKING CO.

U.S. Court of Appeals, Eighth Circuit (St. Louis)

EQUAL EMPLOYMENT OPPORTUNITY COMMISSION v. THE RATH PACKING COMPANY and DISTRICT LOCAL 431 AMALGAMATED MEATCUTTERS and BUTCHERS WORKMEN OF NORTH AMERICA, AFL-CIO, Nos. 84-1217, 84-1458, and 85-1501, March 20, 1986

CIVIL RIGHTS ACT OF 1964

1. Bankruptcy — Stay of proceedings ▸106.3601 ▸108.0422 ▸108.7371

Employer was not entitled to automatic stay of EEOC's Title VII action once it filed petition for reorganization under Chapter 11 of Bankruptcy Act, despite contention that action by EEOC, although a regulatory agency, is stayed by automatic stay provision because it is primarily directed to making aggrieved persons financially whole, since EEOC suit to enforce Title VII seeks to stop harm to public — invidious employment discrimination — that is as detrimental to welfare of United States as are violations of environmental protection and consumer safety laws, which are expressly exempt from automatic stay.

2. Bankruptcy — Stay of proceedings ▸106.3601 ▸108.0422 ▸108.7371

Federal district court did not abuse its discretion in refusing to grant employer discretionary stay of EEOC's Title VII action after employer filed petition for reorganization under Chapter 11 of Bankruptcy Act, despite employer's contention that stay should have been granted because its assets were diminished by litigation expenses, since Congress, by excepting certain actions from Act's automatic stay provision, implicitly recognized that litigation expenses alone do not justify stay of proceeding.

3. Bankruptcy ▸106.3601 ▸108.0422 ▸200.01 ▸250.101

Federal district court did not err when it entered $1 million judgment under Title VII against employer that is seeking reorganization under Chapter 11 of Bankruptcy Act, since entry of judgment for injunctive relief and back pay is permitted under 11 U.S.C. §362(b)(5); however, court's establishment of detailed plan for paying judgment contravened 11 U.S.C. §362(a) by requiring employer to pay judgment in five equal installments of principal with accrued interest, with first installment due one year later and failure to meet required installment resulting in acceleration of unpaid balance at option of EEOC, and by directing EEOC to formulate plan for disbursement of judgment proceeds and to set up claims system.

4. Bankruptcy ▸106.3601 ▸108.0422 ▸200.01

Establishment of plan by which employer, which is seeking reorganization under Chapter 11 of bankruptcy Act, is to pay $1 million judgment to EEOC under Title VII contravenes 11 U.S.C. §1129, since payment of EEOC's claim, which is unsecured, may not be given preference over claims of other creditors, and neither EEOC's promise not to collect judgment nor possibility that bankruptcy court will modify payment plan is sufficient to uphold plan.

5. Bankruptcy — Interest ▸108.0422 ▸106.3601 ▸210.451

Federal district court erred when it awarded EEOC postjudgment interest on back-pay award against employer that is seeking reorganization under Chapter 11 of Bankruptcy Act, since 11 U.S.C. §502(b) provides for nonaccrual of interest as of date of bankruptcy filing and disallowance of any claims for unmatured interest that become due after filing date.

6. Defense ▸108.736

Business necessity defense is appropriately raised when facially neutral employment practices have disproportionate impact on protected groups, whereas bona fide occupational qualification defense is defense to affirmative, deliberate discrimination on basis of sex.

7. Sex — Hiring — Defense ▸108.4111 ▸108.4290

Ruling that employer's subjective hiring practices were not justified by business necessity is not erroneous, where 95 percent of employer's employees were men, it was unable to identify criteria and qualifications that were considered in its hiring decisions, and it therefore could not establish that such criteria and qualifications were necessary to safety and efficiency of its operations.

8. Back pay ▸210.051

Federal district court did not err in failing to identify which specific factors it considered in awarding EEOC back pay under Title VII, since presumption in favor of back pay renders inapplicable to situation in which back pay is granted the rationale underlying requirement of statement of reasons for denial of back pay, which is to give reviewing court opportunity to determine if compelling reasons justify the denial.

9. Back pay ▸108.0422 ▸210.501

Federal district court did not, contrary to contention of employer that is seeking reorganization under Chapter 11 of Bankruptcy Code, fail to consider its ability to pay award, where, except for rounding award off, court approved and adopted special master's finding that factors militating against back-pay award were not of sufficient weight or so exceptional so as to overcome presumption in favor of back pay, and it specifically considered and overruled employer's objection to special master's recommendation in support of back pay.

10. Back pay — ▸210.106 ▸108.0422 ▸210.501

Federal district court did not abuse its discretion when it awarded back pay to EEOC in Title VII action against employer that is seeking reorganization under Chapter 11 of Bankruptcy Act, since impact of award on employer's employees, who are also its majority stockholders, is insufficient reason to deny back pay; employees were aware of litigation six years before they purchased their stock, and it is not inequitable that, having received benefits of ownership from continuation of their employment and compensation, they should share detriment resulting from award.

11. Evidence ▸108.8101

Federal district court did not abuse its discretion when it denied employer's motion under Rule 60(b)(2) of Federal Rules of Civil Procedure for post-judgment relief on grounds of newly discovered evidence, where report of employer's hiring practices and experiences for four-month period did not exist at time of trial but was formulated after trial, and evidence of hiring practices and experience after trial is not relevant to employer's liability prior to trial.

12. Sex — Nepotism ▸108.4127 ▸108.4290 ▸108.736

Federal district court applied wrong legal standard in determining that employer's policy of not hiring employee spouses was justified by business necessity, since court should have considered whether there was compelling need for policy, not just whether it was simply reasonable or designed to improve conditions.

13. Sex — Nepotism — Defense ▸108.4127 ▸108.4290

Federal district court erred in finding that employer's policy of not hiring employee spouses was justified by business necessity, where court's holding that management's perception that absenteeism by both spouses had disruptive effect upon plant operations was rationally predicated upon sound business interests contradicts its finding that spouses had lower absentee rates than nonspouses and that daily production was not detrimentally affected by minimal dual spouse absenteeism, rule prohibiting trading of vacation time and requirement that all employees indicate their preference in order of seniority eliminated vacation problems that had impact on efficiency of employer's production, and court, though considering employee morale to be crucial in business necessity analysis, did not require employer to demonstrate how staff morale affected safety or efficiency of employer's operations.

14. Sex — Nepotism ▸108.4127

Alleged problems associated with employee's supervision of spouse does not justify employer's rule prohibiting hiring of employee spouses, where nondiscriminatory alternative existed in that collective bargaining contract permitted employee to bid out of position if employee would be supervised by spouse, and employer also could have negotiated for right to assign employees so that they would not be supervised by spouses.

15. Sex — Nepotism ▸108.4127 ▸108.4290

Employer's rule prohibiting hiring of employee spouses is not justified by business necessity, despite employer's contention that rule is needed to prevent employee pressure to hire spouses, where employer failed to demonstrate how this pressure resulted in lower production or decreased safety, and it did not show that pressure could not have been alleviated by rule that did not have discriminatory impact.

16. Back pay — Interest ▸210.451 ▸108.0422

Federal district court did not abuse its discretion when it denied prejudgment interest on EEOC's back-pay award against employer that is seeking reorganization under Chapter 11 of Bankruptcy Act, where court properly weighed interests of discriminatees in make-whole relief against financial impact of prejudgment interest in excess of $1 million dollars on employer and its owner-employees, and it also properly considered delay and uncertainty in determining employer's back-pay liability.

17. Back pay — Interest ►210.451

Federal district court may not deny interest on Title VII back pay award simply because plaintiff requests interest at rate that court finds unreasonable, but it may grant interest at rate that it determines to be fair and equitable.

18. Seniority ►215.261

Federal district court abused its discretion when it denied retroactive seniority to women who were unlawfully denied employment, despite employer's assertion of delay in maximum productivity until training is completed and undefined effect on relationship of workers, where employer did not allege and court did not find that grant of such seniority would result in discharge of employees, and employer's assertion that imposition of such seniority would result in bumping of long-time employees to less desirable jobs, lower employee morale, labor-management problems and pressure and strain on employees encompass consequences that can be expected in almost all Title VII cases.

19. Statistics ►108.8128

General population statistics were appropriate in determining extent of employer's discrimination in view of its failure to identify any criteria used in selecting employees or any common qualifications or skills that they possessed.

20. Statistics 108.8128

Federal district court erred in relying on percentage of women employed in nondurable goods manufacturing category, rather than general population statistics, in determining extent of meat packing company's discrimination against women and amount of back pay, where finding that percentage of women employed in nondurable goods manufacturing category was appropriate population base because only these women would be interested in jobs with employer fails to take into account that its refusal to hire women kept number of female workers in this category lower than it would have been absent discrimination.

21. Sex — Hiring — Statistics ►108.4111 ►108.8128

Use of applicant flow data to determine whether employer's hiring practices discriminate against women is inappropriate, where employer was only one of few large employers in small community of 1500 persons and its employment record was known to community, there was uncontradicted testimony that women did not believe they would be hired by employer, and this perception was consistent with its hiring practices, which resulted in 95 percent of its work force consisting of men.

22. Remedy — Back Pay — Nonapplicants ►210.051

Women who did not apply for jobs with meat packing company are entitled to opportunity to prove that they were deterred from applying by company's discriminatory practices.

23. Costs ►108.905

EEOC is entitled to recover full costs incurred in litigating Title VII action against employer, where EEOC prevailed on all three of its claims, including claim on which federal district court's finding was reversed, and neither employer nor court identified any misconduct on EEOC's part that would warrant denial of costs.

Appeals from the U.S. District Court for the Southern District of Iowa (40 FEP Cases 559; 40 FEP Cases 574, 37 B.R. 614, and 40 FEP Cases 576). Affirmed in part, and reversed and remanded in part.

Lorraine C. Davis, Washington, D.C., for appellee.

Ronald R. Peterson, Chicago, Ill., and Steven A. Weidner, Waterloo, Iowa, for appellant.

Before LAY, Chief Judge, and ROSS and McMILLIAN, Circuit Judges.

Full Text of Opinion

McMILLIAN, Circuit Judge: — Rath Packaging Company (Rath) appeals and the Equal Employment Opportunity Commission (EEOC) cross-appeals from a final judgment entered in the District Court for the Southern District of Iowa in an action brought pursuant to 42 U.S.C. §2000e (1982) (Title VII). The district court found that Rath's subjective hiring practices resulted in discrimination against women and were not justified by business necessity. The district court upheld Rath's no-spouse rule as justified by business necessity. The district court awarded backpay, post-judgment interest and affirmative injunctive relief. EEOC v. Rath Packaging Co., No. 77-57-D, slip op. at 7 (S.D. Iowa Feb. 10, 1984).

For reversal Rath argues that (1) the action should have been automatically stayed under 11 U.S.C. §362(a) of the Bankruptcy Act, (2) the district court abused its discretion in denying a stay under 11 U.S.C. §105 and 28 U.S.C. §1651, (3) the district court's judgment violated 11 U.S.C. §§362(b)(5), 502(b) and 1129 because the judgment enforces a money judgment and imposes post-judgment interest, (4) the district court erred in finding a lack of business necessity for Rath's hiring practices, and (5) the district court abused its discretion in awarding backpay in light of Rath's precarious financial condition. Rath also appeals a final order entered on March 14, 1985, denying Rath's Fed. R. Civ. P. 60(b) motion.

EEOC on cross-appeal argues that the district court erred (1) as a matter of law and fact in concluding that Rath's no-spouse rule was justified by business necessity, (2) in denying retroactive seniority, prejudgment interest, and full costs to EEOC, and (3) in not calculating the class backpay award on the basis of the availability of female workers in the general population of Louisa County, Iowa.

For the reasons discussed below, we affirm in part, reverse in part and remand this case for further proceedings consistent with this opinion.

Rath, an Iowa corporation, is engaged in the business of slaughtering hogs and proceeding the meat products obtained from the hogs. Rath has its principal plant in Waterloo, Iowa, and a limited operation in Columbus Junction, Iowa. The Columbus Junction plant, the subject of this litigation, is divided into 12 departments: hog kill, hog cut, loading, sanitation, trim, inedible rendering, yards, smoking, curing, packing, maintenance and miscellaneous gang. More than half of the job classifications at the Columbus Junction plant for the period from September 1, 1970, to August 31, 1979, were in the kill and cut departments. These jobs were considered the least desirable jobs in the plant but were the highest paid.

Rath's Columbus Junction facility employed approximately 250 persons; 50% of the employees were related to one another and 95% were male. The population of Columbus Junction is approximately 1500 persons.

Stipulated statistics established that 554 persons applied to Rath for employment from January 1, 1973, to February 15, 1978. During this period seven (or 7.39%) of the 95 female applicants (who were not spouses of current employees) were hired. Twenty-six additional female applicants were denied employment because they were spouses of current employees. Information concerning applications filed after February 15, 1978, is not available.

The United Food and Commercial Workers,[1] AFL-CIO (formerly Amalgamated Meatcutters and Butchers Workmen of North America), District Local No. 431 (Union), was the exclusive bargaining representative for plant employees at the Columbus Junction plant. The collective bargaining agreements governing the plant required that where possible Rath would promote or transfer from within rather than hire from without. When a vacancy occurred, the vacancy was posted so that employees in that department could bid. If there were no bids, persons in other departments could bid. If no one in another department bid, then the employee with the least seniority in the department where the vacancy occurred was "forced to" the job. If there was no employee to "force to" the job, then a new employee was hired. Rath had no established procedure for giving notice of vacancies to the public.

Rath's office manager, Walter McFarland, was responsible for accepting and maintaining applications and selecting applicants for employment. The plant superintendent had the authority to overrule McFarland's choice of applicants but seldom did so. Rath had no written or otherwise established selection guidelines and McFarland was unable to identify what information was deemed significant in evaluating and selecting applicants. McFarland expressly discounted age, height, weight, prior experience, and work history as being critical in the selection of new employees. McFarland, however, stressed the importance of getting the right person for the job because the person could be assigned to any job in the plant.

In August 1973 Rath prospectively implemented a no-spouse rule prohibiting the employment of spouses of Rath employees. From approximately 1966 to the time of trial, Rath employed seven married couples at the Columbus Junction plant.

EEOC filed this suit in September 1977. The suit was based on a charge filed on December 15, 1975, by Mary Turner, who alleged that Rath unlawfully refused to employ her because of her sex. EEOC alleged in its complaint that Rath refused to hire women at its

---

[1] The Amalgamated Meat Cutters and Butchers Workmen of North America, District Local 431, AFL-CIO, was designated as a defendant in the complaint pursuant to Fed. R. Civ. P. 19(a)(2). The district court on September 12, 1979, granted the Union's motion for a partial summary judgment on the issue of liability. The Union was required to participate in a subsequent hearing on relief.

Columbus Junction plant and that Rath's policy of not hiring spouses of employees excluded a disproportionate number of women from employment. EEOC sought injunctive relief, full backpay with interest, and costs.

The action was bifurcated and separate trials on liability and relief were held. After a four day trial in July 1980 on liability, the district court found that Rath discriminated against women in hiring from 1971 forward and that three women who testified at trial established individual claims of disparate treatment. The district court concluded, however, that Rath had shown a business necessity for the no-spouse rule.

The case was referred to a special master in 1982 for relief proceedings. In January 1983 Rath closed its Columbus Junction plant.[2] In April of 1983 the trial on relief was held. The special master recommended a class backpay award of $1,015,901, injunctive relief, and retroactive seniority for rejected female applicants. The special master further recommended that prejudgment interest not be granted. No recommendation was made concerning costs because one item of costs was compensation for the services of the special master.

After the special master issued his report and recommendations, Rath filed a petition in the bankruptcy court for reorganization under Chapter 11 of the Bankruptcy Act. The district court held that Rath's bankruptcy petition did not automatically stay the Title VII proceedings, In re Rath Packing Co., 37 Bankr. 614, 616–17, 40 FEP Cases 574 (S.D. Iowa 1984), and accordingly proceeded to consider the special master's recommendations and to enter final judgment.

The district court adopted the special master's recommendations to grant injunctive relief and to deny prejudgment interest. The district court awarded class-based backpay ($1,000,000) and post-judgment interest but denied retroactive seniority. The district court ordered that costs be shared equally between EEOC and Rath.

Rath and EEOC subsequently appealed the judgment of the district court. On October 9, 1984, the appeal was argued before this court. In February 1985 Rath filed a Rule 60(b) motion and requested that its appeal before this court be held in abeyance pending a decision on the motion. On

February 22, 1985, this court ordered the district court to certify its ruling on the Rule 60(b) motion and ordered that the appeal be held in abeyance. On March 14, 1985, the district court denied Rath's 60(b) motion. On April 22, 1985, the order holding the appeals in abeyance was vacated, and the appeal from the denial of the 60(b) motion was consolidated with the pending appeals.

Automatic Stay Under 11 U.S.C. §362(a)

Rath argues that the district court erred in refusing to stay those portions of the Title VII proceedings related to backpay, seniority, and interest because §362(a) provides for an automatic stay of such proceedings. In support of its position, Rath argues that the automatic stay is one of the fundamental debtor protections provided by the Bankruptcy Act and is inapplicable only where a governmental unit sues to protect the public safety and health. Relying on Missouri v. Bankruptcy Court, 647 F.2d 768, 776 (8th Cir. 1981), cert. denied, 454 U.S. 1162 (1982), Rath argues that an action brought by EEOC, although a regulatory agency, is stayed by the automatic stay provision because it is primarily directed to making aggrieved persons financially whole.

EEOC argues that this action comes within the exception to the automatic stay provision because it is a Title VII action brought to enforce federal laws prohibiting discrimination in the work place. EEOC argues that suits under Title VII are guided by "an overriding public interest in equal employment opportunity asserted through direct federal enforcement." General Telephone Co. v. EEOC, 446 U.S. 318, 326, 22 FEP Cases 1196 (1980) (citations omitted). Section 362(a)[3] provides

---

[2] The Columbus Junction plant was closed in June 1978, reopened in September 1979, closed again in January 1983, reopened in July 1984, and closed in October 1984.

[3] 11 U.S.C. §362(a) provides:

(a) Except as provided in subsection (b) of this section, a petition filed under section 301, 302, or 303 of this title operates as a stay, applicable to all entities, of —

(1) the commencement or continuation, including the issuance or employment of process, of a judicial, administrative, or other proceeding against the debtor that was or could have been commenced before the commencement of the case under this title, or to recover a claim against the debtor that arose before the commencement of the case under this title;

(2) the enforcement, against the debtor or against property of the estate, of a judgment obtained before the commencement of the case under this title;

(3) any act to obtain possession of property of the estate or of property from the estate;

(4) any act to create, perfect, or enforce any lien against property of the estate;

(5) any act to create, perfect, or enforce against property of the debtor any lien to the extent that such lien secures a claim that arose before the commencement of the case under this title;

that filing a bankruptcy petition operates as an automatic stay of judicial proceedings against the debtor. "The general policy behind this section is to grant complete, immediate, albeit temporary relief to the debtor from creditors, and also to prevent dissipation of the debtor from creditors, and also to prevent dissipation of the debtor's assets before orderly distribution to creditors can be effected." Penn Terra Ltd. v. Department of Environmental Resources, 733 F.2d 267, 271 (3d Cir. 1984) (Penn Terra). However, actions by a government unit to enforce its police or regulatory powers are exempt from operation of the automatic stay provision under §362(b)(4).⁴ Thus,

where a governmental unit is suing a debtor to prevent or stop violation of fraud, environmental protection, consumer protection, safety, or similar police or regulatory laws, or attempting to fix damage for violation of such laws, the action or proceeding is not stayed under the automatic stay.

S.Rep. No. 989, 95th Cong., 2nd Sess. 52, reprinted in 1978 U.S. Code Cong. & Ad. News 5787, 5838; H. Rep. No. 595, 95th Cong., 2nd Sess. 343, reprinted in 1978 U.S. Code Cong. & Ad. news 5787, 6299.

No court has considered whether a suit by EEOC comes within the exception to the automatic stay. Courts have, however, considered whether actions brought by other types of regulatory agencies come within the automatic stay. The Sixth Circuit held that workers' compensation proceedings were not automatically stayed where the benefits were to be paid from an insurance fund or from security bonds which were not part of the debtor's estate. In re Mansfield Tire & Rubber Co., 660 F.2d 1108, 1115 (6th Cir. 1981). Proceedings brought under the Fair Labor Standards Act for the assessment of penalties for violation of child labor laws likewise were not stayed by the automatic stay provision. In re Tauscher, 7 Bankr. 918, 920, 24 WH Cases 1310 (Bankr. E.D. Wis.

1981). The Third Circuit has also held that an action seeking a preliminary injunction to correct violations of the state environmental protection statute was not stayed by the automatic stay provision. Penn Terra, 733 F.2d at 274. Lastly, NLRB proceedings, which are closely analogous to EEOC proceedings, have not been stayed by the automatic stay provision. Ahrens Aircraft, Inc. v. NLRB, 703 F.2d 23, 24, 112 LRRM 3298 (1st Cir. 1983); NLRB v. Evans Plumbing Co., 639 F.2d 291, 293, 106 LRRM 3059 (5th Cir. 1981) (per curiam); In re Bel Air Chateau Hospitals, Inc., 611 F.2d 1248, 1250-51, 104 LRRM 2976 (9th Cir. 1979). Contra In re The Theobald Industries, Inc., 16 Bankr. 547, 537 (Bankr. D.N.J. 1981).

[1] Rath, relying on this court's decision in Missouri v. Bankruptcy Court, 647 F.2d at 776, argues that under the reasoning of this case the EEOC proceeding should have been automatically stayed. We disagree. In Missouri v. Bankruptcy Court, a state regulatory agency attempted in state court to enforce Missouri's grain laws, which enforcement was in direct conflict with the bankruptcy court's orders. This court rejected the state's contention that the police power exception automatically applied because a state agency was involved. Instead we analyzed the purpose underlying the Missouri law and found that although the law might be "regulatory in nature, [it] primarily relate[s] to the protection of pecuniary interest in the debtors' property and not to matters of public safety and health." Id.

By contrast, "EEOC does not function simply as a vehicle for conducting litigation on behalf of private parties; it is a federal administrative agency charged with the responsibility of investigating claims of employment discrimination and settling disputes." Occidental Life Insurance Co. v. EEOC, 432 U.S. 355, 368, 14 FEP Cases 1718 (1977). Thus, "[w]hen the EEOC acts, albeit at the behest of and for the benefit of specific individuals, it acts also to vindicate the public interest in preventing employment discrimination." General Telephone Co. v. EEOC, 446 U.S. at 326. When EEOC sues to enforce Title VII it seeks to stop a harm to the public — invidious employment discrimination which is as detrimental to the welfare of the country as violations of environmental protection and consumer safety laws, which are expressly exempt from the automatic stay. We therefore hold that the automatic stay provision did not apply to this Title VII action brought by EEOC.

---

(6) any act to collect, assess, or recover a claim against the debtor that arose before the commencement of the case under this title;

(7) the setoff of any debt owing to the debtor that arose before the commencement of the case under this title against any claim against the debtor; and

(8) the commencement or continuation of a proceeding before the United States Tax Court concerning the debtor.

⁴ 11 U.S.C. §362(b)(4) provides:

(b) The filing of a petition under section 301, 302, or 303 of this title does not operate as a stay

. . .

(4) under subsection (a)(1) of this section, of the commencement or continuation of an action or proceeding by a governmental unit to enforce such governmental unit's police or regulatory power. . . .

Denial of a Discretionary Stay

Rath next argues that the district court abused its discretion in refusing to grant discretionary stay based on 11 U.S.C. §105 and 28 U.S.C. §1651. Rath argues that its assets were diminished by the litigation expenses and therefore a discretionary stay should have been granted. Further, Rath argues that the Columbus Junction plant closed during the pendency of the litigation and no decision had been made at the time of the trial whether it would reopen. Thus, Rath argues the injunctive relief sought was meaningless.

EEOC argues that the district court properly denied the discretionary stay because litigation fees do not threaten the estate of the bankrupt. Litigation fees, like other debts incurred by a bankrupt before its reorganization plan is filed or approved, are ultimately settled by the bankruptcy court. EEOC argues that Congress by providing for the exception to the automatic stay implicitly recognized that preservation of the estate of the debtor is not always the primary goal.

Section 105 [5] gives the bankruptcy court the power to issue orders necessary or appropriate to carry out the provisions of Title 11. The All Writs Act, 28 U.S.C. §1651,[6] authorizes bankruptcy courts to issue stays. "Stays or injunctions issued under these sections will not be automatic upon the commencement of a case, but will be granted or issued under the usual rules governing the issuance of injunctions." In re Vantage Petroleum Corp., 26 Bankr. 471, 476 (Bankr. E.D.N.Y. 1982). "[S]tays will be granted only if a party shows a necessity for a stay." In re Bel Air Chateau Hospitals, Inc., 611 F.2d at 1251; see In re Matter of Shippers Interstate Service, Inc., 618 F.2d 9, 13, 103 LRRM 2960 (7th Cir. 1980). These stays by definition are discretionary and this court will overturn the decision of the lower court only if there has been an abuse of discretion.

[2] We hold that the district court did not abuse its discretion in denying the request for a stay of the EEOC action. Congress by excepting certain actions from the automatic stay provision recognized that the debtor would likely incur litigation expenses as a result of any excepted lawsuit. Penn Terra, 733 F.2d at 278. Congress has therefore implicitly recognized that litigation expenses alone do not justify a stay of a proceeding. See In re Rath Packing Co., 38 Bankr. 552, 562-63, 116 LRRM 2039 (Bankr. N.D. Iowa 1984) (stay of NLRB proceedings denied).

Entry of Money Judgment

Rath next argues that the district court erred in entering the judgment against Rath because governmental units may not seek to enforce money judgments. Rath, relying on In re Mansfield Tire & Rubber Co., 660 F.2d at 1113, 1115, argues that the scope of the district court's order far exceeds the limited police power exception of 11 U.S.C. §362(b)(5). Rath argues that the district court order established a payment plan, imposed prejudgment interest, and elevated EEOC to the status of a favored creditor with 100% payment.

EEOC argues that the district court judgment does not violate §362(b)(5). Specifically EEOC argues that §362(b)(5) only prohibits actions to enforce or execute a money judgment, and the judgment in this case is not self-executing. Relying on Penn Terra, EEOC argues that it is the "seizure of a defendant debtor's property, to satisfy the judgment ... which is proscribed by subsection 362(b)(5)." 733 F.2d at 275. EEOC further asserts that during the pendency of the bankruptcy proceedings it will not file an action against Rath for contempt for failure to pay or otherwise attempt to actually obtain execution of the judgment.

Section 362(b)(5) [7] provides that the automatic stay does not apply to enforcement of a judgment, other than a money judgment, obtained in an action or proceeding by a governmental unit to enforce such governmental unit's police or regulatory powers. The reason for this ban against enforcement of money judgments is to prevent unfairness to a debtor's other creditors.

Since the assets of the debtor are in the possession and control of the bankruptcy court, and since they constitute a fund out

---

[5] 11 U.S.C. §105(a) provides: "(a) The bankruptcy court may issue any order, process, or judgment that is necessary or appropriate to carry out the provisions of this title."

[6] 28 U.S.C. §1651(a) provides: "(a) The Supreme Court and all courts established by Act of Congress may issue all writs necessary or appropriate in aid of their respective jurisdictions and agreeable to the usages and principles of law."

---

[7] 11 U.S.C. §362(b)(5) provides:
(b) The filing of a petition under section 301, 302, or 303 of this title does not operate as a stay

(5) under subsection (a)(2) of this section, of the enforcement of a judgment, other than a money judgment, obtained in an action or proceeding by a governmental unit to enforce such governmental unit's police or regulatory power....

of which all creditors are entitled to share, enforcement by a governmental unit of a money judgment would give it preferential treatment to the detriment of all other creditors.

H. Rep. No. 595, 95th Cong., 2nd Sess. 342-43 (1978); reprinted in 1978 U.S. Code Cong. & Ad. News 5787, 6299; S. Rep. No. 989, 95th Cong., 2nd Sess. 51-52 (1978), repringed in 1978 U.S. Code Cong. & Ad. News 5787, 5838.

[3] The entry of a judgment for injunctive relief and backpay is permitted under §362(b)(5), but the actual enforcement of the backpay judgment is not permitted. E.g., NLRB v. Evans Plumbing Co., 639 F.2d at 293; cf. In re Mansfield Tire & Rubber Co., 660 F.2d at 1115 (Industrial Commission of Ohio, Bureau of Workers Compensation, could adjudicate workers' compensation claims against the debtor and could order payment of the claims only because the claims were to be paid either from an insurance fund or surety bonds, neither of which were a part of the debtor's estate).

We hold that the district court did not err in entering a money judgment against Rath. The district court, however, went beyond the entry of a money judgment as permitted by §362(b)(5) and established a detailed payment plan. The judgment of February 10, 1984, not only awarded EEOC the sum of $1,000,000, but required Rath to repay the sum in five equal installments of principal with accrued interest, with the first installment due on February 10, 1985. Failure to meet a required installment results in acceleration of the unpaid balance at the option of EEOC. EEOC was also directed to formulate a plan for disbursement of judgment proceeds and to set up a claims system. This plan went beyond the entry of a money judgment and therefore violated 11 U.S.C. §362(a).

[4] Rath also argues that the establishment of a payment plan violates 11 U.S.C. §1129.[8] We agree. The bankruptcy court has the responsibility to confirm a reorganization plan and to distribute Rath's assets in accord with this plan. Payment of the EEOC claim, a pre-petition unsecured claim, may not be given preference over the claims of other creditors. Neither EEOC's promise not to collect the judgment nor the possibility that the bankrupt-

cy court will modify the payment plan is sufficient to correct the error.

[5] Rath further argues that the imposition of post-judgment interest is contrary to 11 U.S.C. §502(b) which prohibits the imposition of interest after the date of the bankruptcy filing. We agree that the district court erred in awarding post-judgment interest. Section 502(b)[9] provides that as of the date of the bankruptcy filing, interest will not accrue and any claims for unmatured interest which become due after the filing date shall be disallowed. Nicholas v. United States, 384 U.S. 678, 682 (1966); In re Boston & Maine Corp., 719 F.2d 493, 495 (1st Cir. 1983), cert. denied, 104 S.Ct. 1913 (1984). The purpose of this rule is stated in Vanston Bond Holders Protective Committee v. Green, 329 U.S. 160, 163-64 (1946):

Exaction of interest where the power of the debtor to pay even his contractual obligations is suspended by law, has been prohibited because it was considered in the nature of a penalty imposed because of a delay in prompt payment — a delay necessitated by law .... The delay in distribution ... is a necessary incident to the settlement of the estate ... it would be inequitable for anyone to gain an advantage or to suffer a loss because of such delay.

Subjective Hiring Practices

[6] Rath next argues that the district court erred in holding that there was no business necessity for Rath's subjective hiring practices. Rath had no established criteria for selecting employees. Rath argues that the positions, although unskilled in nature, require certain objective skills and experience because an employee might be forced to perform any job in the plant. Rath also argues that it should not be required to adopt what the court perceives to be the best hiring procedures rather than those which Rath has developed based on its experience. Lastly, Rath argues that the district court did not distinguish between the strict test of a bona fide

---

[8] 11 U.S.C. §1129(a)(1) provides: "(a) The court shall confirm a plan only if all of the following requirements are met: (1) The plan complies with the applicable provisions of the chapter."

[9] 11 U.S.C. §502(a), (b), (2) provides:
(a) A claim of interest, proof of which is filed under section 501 of this title, is deemed allowed, unless a party in interest, including a creditor of a partner in a partnership that is a debtor in a case under chapter 7 of this title, objects.
(b) Except as provided in subsections (f), (g), (h) and (i) of this section, if such objection to a claim is made, the court, after notice and a hearing, shall determine the amount of such claim as of the date of the filing of the petition, and shall allow such claim in such amount, except to the extent that —
* * *
(2) such claim is for unmatured interest. ...

occupational requirement and the less strict test of a valid business reason.[10]

EEOC argues that the district court's finding is supported by the overwhelming weight of the evidence and therefore is not clearly erroneous. EEOC argues that McFarland, the Rath official primarily responsible for hiring at Rath, was unable to articulate any particular qualifications or attributes he looked for in an applicant. EEOC also argues that Rath failed to establish that the subjective hiring procedures were necessary or essential and that there were no alternative practices with less discriminatory effect.

"[A]n employment practice which has a disparate impact on a group protected under Title VII is invalid unless the employer can prove the challenged practice is justified by a business necessity." Kirby v. Colony Furniture Co., 613 F.2d 696, 703, 21 FEP Cases 1179 (8th Cir. 1980). " 'The touchstone is business necessity and the practice must be shown to be necessary to safe and efficient job performance . . . .' " Id. (citations omitted). "The system in question must not only foster safety and efficiency, but must be essential to that goal." United States v. St. Louis-San Francisco R.R., 464 F.2d 301, 308, 4 FEP Cases 853 (8th Cir. 1972) (emphasis added), cert. denied, 409 U.S. 1116, 5 FEP Cases 299 (1973). A business practice may not be justified on the basis of business necessity if there exists a "nondiscriminatory alternative means of determining qualification." Id. at 309; see Dothard v. Rawlinson, 433 U.S. 321, 329, 15 FEP Cases 10 (1977).

[7] We hold that the district court did not err in holding that Rath's subjective hiring practices were not justified by business necessity. The undisputed evidence established that Rath's subjective hiring practices had a disparate impact on women. Ninety-five percent of Rath's employees were men. After EEOC established the disparate impact of the subjective hiring practices, Rath had the burden of producing evidence of business necessity and the burden of persuasion on that issue. Rath was unable to identify the criteria and qualifications which were considered in the hiring decisions. It follows therefore that Rath could not establish that these qualifications and criteria were necessary to the safety and efficiency of its operations. Rath's hiring practices, even if intended to select the best qualified person, were highly susceptible to abuse. While some subjectivity is inevitable in the hiring process, the total lack of objective criteria at Rath "could only reinforce the prejudices, unconscious or not, which Congress in Title VII sought to eradicate as a basis for employment." Stewart v. General Motors Corp., 542 F.2d 445, 451, 13 FEP Cases 1035 (7th Cir. 1976), cert. denied, 433 U.S. 919, 15 FEP Cases 31 (1977). " '[S]ex is the sole identifiable factor explaining the divergence in numbers of men and women selected by Rath during the relevant time frame.' " EEOC v. Rath Packing Co., No. 77-57-D, slip op. at 6 (liability order of April 22, 1981) (citation omitted).

Backpay Award

Rath next argues that the district court erred in awarding backpay. In support of this position, Rath argues that the district court failed to make findings concerning Rath's ability to pay or to articulate reasons for its decision. Rath also argues that the district court failed to consider the number of victims and the number of nonvictims affected and the economic circumstances of the industry.

Rath argues that it has experienced "horrendous losses" since 1977[11] and

---

[10] The district court correctly applied the business necessity test in this case. The business necessity defense and the bona fide occupational qualification (BFOQ) defense are both defenses to Title VII violations. The business necessity defense, however, is appropriately raised when facially neutral employment practices have a disproportionate impact on protected groups. The BFOQ defense on the other hand is a defense to affirmative deliberate discrimination on the basis of sex. Harriss v. Pan American World Airways, Inc., 649 F.2d 670, 674, 24 FEP Cases 947 (9th Cir. 1980); Garcia v. Gloor, 609 F.2d 156, 163, 21 FEP Cases 884 (5th Cir. 1980); see Dothard v. Rawlinson, 433 U.S. 321, 332, 15 FEP Cases 10 (1977) (BFOQ) (standard applied to regulation prohibiting employment of female guards in maximum security prison; business necessity test applied to height and weight regulation). Both defenses have been construed narrowly. Sex discrimination based on a BFOQ is permitted only where "reasonably necessary to the normal operation of that particular business." 42 U.S.C. §2000e(2)(e). A neutral employment practice may be justified by business necessity only if the practice not only fosters safety and efficiency but is essential to that goal. United States v. St. Louis-San Francisco R.R., 464 F.2d 301, 308, 4 FEP Cases 853 (8th Cir. 1972), cert. denied, 409 U.S. 1116, 5 FEP Cases 299 (1973).

[11] Rath argues that its financial position is precarious and a backpay award plus interest could result in the permanent closing of the Columbus Junction plant and the loss of jobs. Rath argues that it has had to resort to extraordinary means to secure even a limited line of credit (about $15 million), and that this credit and other loans made by Rath are secured by Rath's inventory, receivables, trademarks of the company, and real property. The company pension plan was terminated for financial reasons in 1982 and Rath continues to make sizable payments to reduce its obligations under the plan. Rath is also required to make cash deposits for performance bonds. The employees in 1983 deferred $2.50 each per hour in wages and made other concessions in order to sustain the company.

therefore does not have the ability to pay the award out of current resources, either borrowed or owned. Rath argues that the employees, the majority owners of the company, are the only ones who can provide funds to satisfy such an award and they have already made many financial sacrifices for the company.

Rath urges this court to review this issue because the issue is based almost entirely on the written record and not upon the testimony of witnesses. Lastly, Rath argues that it may have no forum to have this issue reviewed if this court does not review it because EEOC will argue in the bankruptcy court that the issue is "res judicata" and, secondly, the bankruptcy court may believe that it does not have the authority to modify the district court's order.

EEOC argues that the district court did not abuse its discretion in awarding backpay. EEOC argues that persons who have been denied employment because of discrimination are entitled under Title VII to backpay and backpay is to be denied only in extraordinary circumstances.

"The district court is obligated to grant a plaintiff who has been discriminated against . . . the most complete relief possible." Briseno v. Central Technical Community College Area, 739 F.2d 344, 347, 37 FEP Cases 57 (8th Cir. 1984); see Franks v. Bowman Transportation Co., 424 U.S. 747, 764, 12 FEP Cases 549 (1976). There is a strong presumption that persons who have been discriminated against are entitled under Title VII to backpay; this presumption can only be overcome "for reasons, which if applied generally, would not frustrate the central statutory purposes of eradicating discrimination throughout the economy and making persons whole for injury suffered through past discrimination." Albemarle Paper Co. v. Moody, 422 U.S. 405, 421, 10 FEP Cases 1181 (1975). "[S]pecial factors which justify not giving an award of class wide backpay have been narrowly construed," Kirby v. Colony Furniture Co., 613 F.2d at 699; see Wells v. Meyer's Bakery, 561 F.2d 1268, 1272, 15 FEP Cases 930 (8th Cir. 1977), and usually include circumstances where state legislation is in conflict with Title VII. Pettway v. American Cast Iron Pipe Co., 494 F.2d 211, 260, 7 FEP Cases 115 (5th Cir. 1974) (banc).

[8] We consider first Rath's argument that the district court was required to state its reasons in support of the award of backpay. Rath cites two district court cases for the proposition that a district court must state reasons for an award of backpay. Ingram v. Madison Square Garden Center, 482 F.Supp. 918, 921, 32 FEP Cases 538 (S.D.N.Y. 1979); Rios v. Enterprise Ass'n of Steamfitters Local 638, 400 F.Supp. 988, 991, 10 FEP Cases 1278 (S.D.N.Y. 1975). Rath also attempts to argue by analogy from other cases which state that a district court must identify the factors which justify the denial of backpay. The rationale, however, underlying the requirement for a statement of reasons for a *denial* of backpay does not exist where a district court grants backpay. A presumption exists in favor of backpay; backpay may be denied only if there are compelling reasons justifying the denial. Consequently, the district court is required to state reasons for the denial in order that a reviewing court may determine if compelling reasons exist. We hold that the district court did not err in failing to identify those specific factors it considered in awarding backpay.

[9] Rath next argues that the district court did not consider Rath's ability to pay prior to granting backpay. The record does not support Rath's assertion. The special master considered at length Rath's financial condition. The special master found that the factors militating against an award of backpay — (1) Rath's "precarious financial status and ongoing losses,"-(2) 60% of the shareholders are employees, and (3) Rath's stated inability to liquidate an award without further employee concessions — were not of sufficient weight or so exceptional that they overcame the presumption that backpay is one of the consequences of Title VII violations.

The district court approved and adopted the report and recommendation of the special master except as modified. The district court did not modify the special master's findings or recommendation on backpay except to round the backpay award off to $1,000,000. Further, the district court specifically considered and overruled Rath's objection to the special master's recommendation for backpay. EEOC v. Rath Packing Co., No. 77-57-D, slip op. at 7 (order of Feb. 10, 1984). Rath challenged the recommendation on the grounds that Rath was unable to pay the award and the award would have an adverse effect on the employees at the Columbus Junction plant. In response to this objection, the district court did not indicate that Rath's financial condition was not considered in making the backpay award. Rather, the district court expressly recognized that "[t]he effect of this backpay award can now be taken into consideration by the bankruptcy court." Id. at 3. The district court in the same order expressly considered Rath's financial condition in awarding post-judgment interest. Id. at 7. The district court denied prejudgment interest because of Rath's "precarious financial condition" and ordered installment payments of the award for the same reason. Id.

[10] We hold that the district court did not abuse its discretion in awarding backpay. Victims of employment discrimination are entitled to "make-whole" relief, which includes backpay. Backpay should not be denied simply because the employer, who has wronged the victims, will be adversely affected by the backpay award. See Frank v. Bowman Transportation Co., 424 U.S. at 774. The impact of the award on Rath's employees, who are also the majority stockholders, is an insufficient reason to deny backpay. These employees were aware of this litigation, which commenced in 1977, when they purchased their stock in 1983. In addition they received benefits from the purchase of the stock — the continuation of their employment and compensation. See In re Rath Packing Co., 36 Bankr. 979, 981, 115 LRRM 2717 (Bankr. N.D. Iowa 1984). It is not inequitable that the employee-shareholders, having received the benefits of ownership, should share the detriment resulting from the backpay award.

Denial of Rule 60(b) Motion

The district court denied Rath's Fed. R. Civ. P. 60(b) motion on the basis that the evidence offered by Rath did not constitute newly discovered evidence and "for other reasons expressed in [EEOC's] response to defendant's motion." The district court found that the evidence tendered as newly discovered evidence was formulated after the trial.

Rath argues that the district court abused its discretion in denying its motion. Rath submitted a report concerning its hiring procedures upon reopening its Columbus Junction facility in July 1984. The report covered the four months from the time the Columbus Junction facility opened in July 1984 to October 1984, when it closed again. Rath claims that the report reflects the actual level of interest of women in employment at Rath and the actual employment experience of women who accepted employment at Rath during this period.

EEOC argues that the motion was not filed within a reasonable time as required by the rule. The motion was filed seven months after the entry of judgment. EEOC also argues that the evidence was not newly discovered evidence because it was formulated after the trial and concerned only post-trial events, that is, Rath's hiring practices and experience after the trial. EEOC further argues that the evidence is neither probative of nor relevant to the issue of Rath's liability.

In order to obtain relief under Fed. R. Civ. P. 60(b) (2) on grounds of newly discovered evidence, the moving party must establish that (1) was discovered after trial, (2) it exercised diligence to obtain the evidence before trial, (3) the evidence is not merely cumulative or impeaching, (4) the evidence is material, and (5) the evidence is such that a new trial probably would produce a new verdict. Rosebud Sioux Tribe v. A. & P. Steel, Inc., 733 F.2d 509, 515 (8th Cir.), cert. denied, 105 S.Ct. 565 (1984). The district court's ruling on a motion for relief from judgment will be disturbed on appeal only if the district court abused its discretion. Pioneer Insurance Co. v. Gelt, 558 F.2d 1303, 1312 (8th Cir. 1977).

[11] We hold that the district court did not abuse its discretion in denying Rath's motion. The report of Rath's hiring practices and experience for the period of July through October 1984 was not evidence which was in existence at the time of the trial but was evidence which was formulated after the trial. Further evidence of Rath's hiring practices and experience after the trial is not relevant to the issue of Rath's liability prior to trial.

No-Spouse Rule (Cross-appeal)

EEOC on cross-appeal argues that the district court erred as a matter of law and fact in holding that Rath's no-spouse rule was not justified by business necessity. EEOC argues that the district court, although articulating the proper legal standard, in fact imposed a lighter burden on Rath than required by the law of this circuit. EEOC further argues that this finding is contrary to the record evidence and inconsistent with the district court's subsidiary findings.

The district court stated that "the issue the court must address is ... whether management's response to *perceived* production problems ... was *reasonable* ... and designed to improve conditions in the plant." EEOC v. Rath Packing Co., slip op. at 23 (order of Apr. 22, 1981) (emphasis added). The district court found that Rath was "unable to statistically corroborate its contention that production was adversely affected through the hiring of spouses." Id. The district court nonetheless ultimately concluded that Rath had demonstrated "an acceptable business-related basis for the rule," id. at 24, and that the "antispousal policy was enacted to achieve the interrelated business objectives of optimum production and employee performance." Id. at 20.

Rath urges this court to depart from its strict test of business necessity and to follow the less demanding standard applied by the Seventh Circuit in Yuhas v. Libbey-Owens-Ford Co., 562 F.2d 496, 16 FEP Cases 891 (7th Cir. 1977) (Yuhas), cert. denied, 435 U.S. 934, 17 FEP Cases 87 (1978), and by the district court in this case. Rath argues that the court in Yuhas correctly recognized that spousal relationships in the workplace create situations which are problematic for the employer and employees — problems of efficiency, productivity and ease of management. Rath argues that its no-spouse rule was directed at problems which had occurred when married couples worked at Rath; these problems were dual absenteeism, vacation scheduling, supervision, and employee pressure to hire spouses.

As we have previously stated, Title VII forbids the use of a facially neutral employment standard which disproportionately excludes a protected class from employment unless the employer shows that the standard is justified by business necessity. "[T]he employer must meet the burden of showing that any given requirement [has] ... a manifest relation to the employment in question.'" Dothard v. Rawlinson, 433 U.S. at 329, citing Griggs v. Duke Power Co., 401 U.S. 424, 432, 3 FEP Cases 175 (1971).

[T]he proper standard for determining whether "business necessity" justified a result which has a ... discriminatory result is not whether it is justified by routine business considerations but whether there is a *compelling need* for the employer to maintain that practice and whether the employer can prove there is no alternative to the challenged practice.

Kirby v. Colony Furniture Co., 613 F.2d at 705 n.6 (emphasis in original); see Gilbert v. City of Little Rock, 722 F.2d 1390, 1395, 33 FEP Cases 557 (8th Cir. 1983), cert. denied, 104 S.Ct. 2347, 34 FEP Cases 1312 (1984).

[12] We hold that the district court applied the wrong legal standard in determining whether the no-spouse rule was justified by business necessity. The district court did not consider whether there was a compelling need

for the no-spouse rule.[12] In order for Rath to prevail, the problem to be addressed by the no-spouse rule must be concrete and demonstrable, not just "perceived"; and the rule must be essential to eliminating the problem, not simply reasonable or designed to improve conditions. Jones v. Lee Way Motor Freight, Inc., 431 F.2d 245, 248, 2 FEP Cases 895 (10th Cir. 1970), cert. denied, 401 U.S. 954, 3 FEP Cases 193 (1971).

[13] Application of the proper legal standard to the district court's factual findings compels the conclusion that Rath failed to demonstrate that the no-spouse rule was justified by business necessity. Rath asserted that dual absenteeism was a problem when both spouses worked for Rath. The district court found, however, that from March 3, 1975, to May 31, 1978, "spouses exhibited a lower absentee rate than did non-spouses." EEOC v. Rath Packing Co., slip op. at 21 (order of Apr. 21, 1981). The district court noted that Rath was able to point to only one incident of habitual dual absenteeism. The district court further found that production records between 1975 and 1978 revealed that "daily production was not detrimentally affected by the minimal dual spouse absenteeism during this period." Id. The district court nonetheless held that "management's perception in 1973 of a disruptive effect upon plant operations ... [was] rationally predicated upon sound business interests." Id.

Secondly, Rath asserted that the presence of both spouses in the work force caused problems in scheduling vacations. The district court found that "the two most serious difficulties connected to spousal selection of vacation time were corrected when the company prohibited trading [of vacation time] in 1970 and initiated a policy in 1973 requiring all employees to indicate in the order of seniority their preference when canvassing is undertaken." Id. at 22. These two rules eliminated the vacation problems which

---

[12] The standard which this circuit applies in this case is consistent with the law in the majority of the other circuits. See Rowe v. Cleveland Pneumatic Co., 690 F.2d 88, 93–94, 29 FEP Cases 1682 (6th Cir. 1982); Jackson v. Seaboard Coastline R.R., 678 F.2d 992, 1016–17, 29 FEP Cases 442 (11th Cir. 1982); Williams v. Colorado Springs School Dist., 641 F.2d 835, 840–42, 25 FEP Cases 256 (10th Cir. 1981); Kinsey v. First Regional Sec., Inc., 557 F.2d 930, 837, 14 FEP Cases 1143 (D.C. Cir. 1977); Pettway v. American Cast Iron Pipe Co., 494 F.2d 211, 245–47, 7 FEP Cases 1115 (5th Cir. 1974); Robinson v. Lorillard Corp., 444 F.2d 791, 798, 3 FEP Cases 653 (4th Cir.), cert. denied, 404 U.S. 1006 (1971).

had an impact on the efficiency of Rath's production.

The district court, however, felt that the actual scheduling of vacations was not the only factor to be considered, but that employee morale was crucial in the business necessity analysis of the problem. The district court found that "spouses remained dissatisfied with the present procedure" and that disgruntled fellow workers often applied for vacation times sought by a less senior spousal employee in order to prevent a couple from securing a joint vacation. Id. The district court, however, did not require Rath to demonstrate how staff morale affected the safety or efficiency of Rath's operation. Staff discontent and reduced staff morale as a result of the scheduling of spouses' vacations may not be the basis for the no-spouse rule unless these problems affect the safety and efficiency of Rath's operation.

[14] Rath next asserts that the no-spouse rule was required in order to avoid problems associated with an employee's supervision of his or her spouse. Rath cited one instance where spousal supervision resulted in complaints of favoritism to and harassment of the supervised spouse. It is not sufficient that the rule be business-related; the rule must be essential to safety and efficiency. Jones v. Lee Way Motor Freight, Inc., 431 F.2d at 249. There must be no other available nondiscriminatory alternative to accomplish the legitimate business purpose. Dothard v. Rawlinson, 433 U.S. at 329. In this case a nondiscriminatory alternative existed. The collective bargaining agreement permitted an employee to bid out of a position where the employee would be supervised by a spouse. Rath also could have negotiated for the right to assign employees so that they would not be supervised by spouses.

[15] The last reason asserted by Rath for the no-spouse rule is employee pressure to hire spouses. Rath failed to demonstrate how this pressure resulted in lower production or decreased safety. Nor was there any showing by Rath that the pressure could not have been alleviated by a rule which did not have a discriminatory impact.

In summary, we hold that Rath failed to establish a business necessity for the no-spouse rule. Rath failed to show that the problems that Rath experienced in employing spouses had any demonstrable effect on safety and efficiency. Workers' morale, which Rath and the district court deemed crucial to the business necessity analysis, cannot justify implementing a discriminatory policy where the claimed dissatisfaction has not been shown to have resulted in reduced productivity, decreased job efficiency, or more dangerous working conditions.

We note further that Rath's reliance on Yuhas is misplaced. The Seventh Circuit in Yuhas upheld a no-spouse rule although the employer was unable to demonstrate that employment of spouses affected efficiency or safety. The court held that "(b)ecause the no-spouse rule plausibly improves the work environment, and because it does not penalize women on the basis of their environmental or genetic background," the rule was job related and did not violate Title VII. 562 F.2d at 500. The court stated however that its decision might have been different "if plaintiffs had shown that defendant historically employed more men than women . . . because it intentionally discriminated against women. [The court assumed] that the present disparity between men and women . . . was the result of noninvidious factors." Id. The standard articulated in Yuhas therefore would not be applicable to this case because the district court found Rath intentionally discriminated against women. This intentional discrimination against women resulted in Rath's employees being overwhelmingly male.

Denial of Prejudgment Interest (Cross-appeal)

EEOC argues that the district court erred in denying prejudgment interest because prejudgment interest, like backpay, is appropriate in order to promote the make-whole purpose of Title VII. EEOC further argues that the district court's decision, although discretionary, should be set aside because it was based on erroneous beliefs and an improper understanding of the law.

Rath argues that the district court did not abuse its discretion in denying prejudgment interest because there is no presumption in favor of prejudgment interest and interest should be denied where its exaction would be inequitable. Rath further argues that the district court's decision may only be set aside if there is no evidence in the record to support the district court's decision.

"Prejudgment interest serves at least two purposes: (1) it helps compensate plaintiffs for the true cost of money damages they have incurred, (2) where liability and the amount of damages are fairly certain, it promotes settlement and deters an attempt to benefit unfairly from the inherent delays of litigation." General Facilities v. National Marine Service, 664 F.2d 672, 674 (8th Cir. 1981); see Behlar v. Smith, 719 F.2d 950, 954, 33 FEP Cases 92 (8th Cir. 1983). The decision to award or deny prejudgment interest will be upheld unless the district court abuses its discretion. Earnhardt v. Puerto Rico, 744 F.2d 1, 3, 35 FEP Cases 1406 (1st Cir. 1984).

The district court in this case denied prejudgment interest because of Rath's precarious financial situation. The district court also found that (1) the interest rates which EEOC requested were rates which no member of the plaintiff class could reasonably have obtained had she possessed the funds, (2) the delay in determining Rath's backpay liability made an assessment of prejudgment interest would have required additional sacrifices by Rath employees. Report and Recommendation of Special Master, Sept. 30, 1983, at 41-43.

[16, 17] We hold that the district court did not abuse its discretion in denying prejudgment interest. The district court properly weighed the interest of the victims in make-whole relief against the financial impact of a prejudgment interest award in excess of one million dollars on Rath and its owner-employees.[13] The delay (although the fault of neither party) and the uncertainty in determining Rath's backpay liability, on which the interest is to be calculated, were also proper factors for the district court to consider. Heiar v. Crawford County, 746 F.2d 1190, 1201, 35 FEP Cases 1458 (7th Cir. 1984), cert. denied, 105 S.Ct. 3500, 37 FEP Cases 1883 (1985). We may not substitute our judgment for that of the district court in reconciling these competing interests.[14] Domingo v. New England Fish Co., 727 F.2d 1429, 1446, 34 FEP Cases 584 (9th Cir.) modified on

---

[13] EEOC indicates that prejudgment interest on the backpay actually awarded amounts to $988,272.00. This figure does not include interest on the additional backpay to be awarded as a result of our decision expanding the relevant labor pool and holding that the no-spouse rule was not justified by business necessity.

[14] The district court found that the interest rates requested by EEOC were rates which "no female employee could have reasonably obtained had she possessed the funds." We do not believe that a district court may deny prejudgment interest because the plaintiff requests interest at a rate which the court finds unreasonable. The district court may grant prejudgment interest at the rate which it determines to be fair and equitable. EEOC asserts that the rates used in computing the prejudgment interest were the IRS prime interest rates during the 1973 to 1980 period. We note that prejudgment interest awards based on the prime interest rates have been permitted by other courts. E.g., EEOC v. Wooster Brush Co., 727 F.2d 566, 33 FEP Cases 1823 (6th Cir. 1984); EEOC v. Pacific Press Publishing Ass'n, 482 F.Supp. 1291, 1319-20, 21 FEP Cases 848 (N.D. Cal. 1979), aff'd, 676 F.2d 1271, 28 FEP Cases 1596 (9th Cir. 1982).

other grounds, 742 F.2d 520, 37 FEP Cases 1303 (1984).

Denial of Retroactive Seniority (Cross-appeal)

The district court denied retroactive seniority because the "complexity of the problems accompanying retroactive seniority counsel against this particular remedy." The district court rejected the special master's finding that the problems envisioned by Rath — a delay in maximum productivity until training is completed and an undefined effect on the relationship of the workers — did not overcome the presumption in favor of retroactive seniority.

EEOC argues that the district court erred in denying retroactive seniority. Further, EEOC argues that diminution of seniority expectations of incumbent employees is clearly a usual and foreseeable impact of hiring claimants and giving them seniority. EEOC argues that this is not the type of unusual adverse impact contemplated by Franks v. Bowman Transportation Co., 424 U.S. at 774-75, justifying a denial of seniority.

Rath argues that the district court did not err because retroactive seniority would result in bumping of long time employees to less desirable jobs, increase the pressure and strain on employees, lower employee morale, and create labor management problems.

In Franks v. Bowman Transportation Co., the Supreme Court, in discussing retroactive seniority in Title VII cases, stated:

[I]n exercising their equitable powers, district courts should take as their starting point the presumption in favor of rightful-place seniority relief, and proceed with further legal analysis from that point; and ... such relief may not be denied on the abstract basis of adverse impact upon interests of other employees but rather only on the basis of unusual adverse impact arising from facts and circumstances that would not be generally found in Title VII cases.

Id. at 779 n.41 (citation omitted).

The Court further stated: "We find untenable the conclusion that this form of relief may be denied merely because the interest of other employees may thereby be affected." Id. at 774-76. "Adequate protection of ... rights under Title VII may necessitate ... some adjustment of the rights of [non-victim] employees. The Court must be free to deal equitably with conflicting interests of [non-victim] employees in order to shape remedies that will most effectively protect and address the rights of the ... victims of discrimination.' " Id. at 775-76 n.35 (citation omitted). Factors "such as the number of victims, the number of non-victim employees affected and the alternatives available to them and the economic circumstances of the industry," International Brotherhood of Teamsters v. United States, 431 U.S. 324, 376 n.62, 14 FEP Cases 1514 (1977) (citation omitted), should be considered by the district court in determining whether to grant retroactive seniority.

In striking this equitable balance between the interests of the victims of discrimination and incumbent employees, courts have primarily been concerned that retroactive seniority relief not result in the discharge of "innocent" incumbent employees. In Romasanta v. United Airlines, Inc., 717 F.2d 1140, 1147-56, 32 FEP Cases 1545 (7th Cir. 1983), the Seventh Circuit denied competitive retroactive seniority to a class of 1400 former employees. The court found that an award of competitive retroactive seniority would result in the discharge of hundreds of incumbent employees because there was a low attrition rate and a low growth rate in the company. Id.

The Ninth Circuit in Moore v. City of San Jose, 615 F.2d 1265, 22 FEP Cases 1053 (9th Cir. 1980), stated that some effects on incumbent employees are justified to achieve the goals of Title VII. Id. at 1271. The court further stated that the burden is on the employer to demonstrate some unusual adverse impact which would justify the denial of retroactive seniority. Id. The court noted that the award of retroactive seniority would not result in the discharge of incumbent employees and further that the small number of victims would not affect the seniority-based benefits of incumbent employees.

This court in Briseno v. Central Technical Community College Area, 739 F.2d at 348, held that the relief granted a Title VII plaintiff may be limited so that innocent employees will not be displaced. This court nonetheless recognized that a plaintiff is entitled to be placed in a comparable position with his or her seniority and other rights to be determined as of the date he or she was denied employment. Where no vacancy exists, the plaintiff in entitled to receive monthly payments equal to the difference between what plaintiff would receive in a comparable position and what the plaintiff earned in mitigation of damages. These payments should continue until the plaintiff is hired by the employer. Id.

[18] In the instant case, Rath did not allege nor did the district court find that the grant of retroactive seniority would result in the discharge of employees. Rath asserted that the imposition of retroactive seniority would result in the bumping of long time employees to less desirable jobs, lower employee morale, labor-management problems, and pressure and strain on employees. These consequences can be expected in almost all Title VII cases. Retroactive seniority, therefore, could never be imposed if such factors are sufficient to justify the denial of retroactive seniority.

We hold that the district court abused its discretion in denying retroactive seniority. Imposition of retroactive seniority is required in the present case in order to make the identified victims of the discrimination whole, and the district court offers no compelling reason for the denial of retroactive seniority.

Labor Force Statistics (Cross-appeal)

EEOC argues that the district court erred in refusing to use general population statistics to determine the number of women Rath would have hired absent discrimination and in determining the number of persons entitled to backpay. The district court used applicant flow data. EEOC argues that the qualifications for the positions at Rath are those which the general population possesses or can readily acquire. EEOC further argues that the number of women workers in the categories of nonfarm laborers and operatives in nondurable goods manufacturing and the number of women in Rath's applicant pool were depressed because of Rath's discrimination. EEOC argues that there was overwhelming evidence that women, in greater numbers than represented in these groups, were interested in employment at Rath because the pay was good and the plant was close to their homes.

Rath argues that the district court correctly required EEOC to define the available qualified work force in terms of those in the county who would actually be interested in jobs at Rath. Rath also argues that the applicant flow data is the best indicator of the extent of an employer's discrimination.

The district court in its opinion on liability found that "general population or civilian work force data" was appropriate to determine whether Rath discriminated against women and the number of persons affected by the discrimination because "entry level or unskilled positions was an issue and the necessary qualifications are those that many people possess or can readily acquire." EEOC v. Rath Packing Co., slip op at 6 (order of Apr. 22, 1981). In its later clarification order of December 1982, the district could held, however, that "general work force statistics have no probative value in determining whether [Rath's] . . . hiring practices adversely impacted against females." The district court reasoned that many persons engaged in jobs in nonmanufacturing industries would not be interested in employment at Rath because of the nature of the work. The district court held that the general work force statistics should not be used because in these statistics the number of women in nonmanufacturing industries was not separated from the number of women in nondurable goods manufacturing. The district court therefore relied on Rath's applicant flow data in determining liability and backpay.

A comparison of general population statistics with an employer's relevant work force is generally appropriate where the jobs in question do not require special qualifications. Hazelwood School District v. United States, 433 U.S. 299, 308 n. 13, 15 FEP Cases 1 (1977); International Brotherhood of Teamsters v. United States, 431 U.S. at 339-40 n.20; EEOC v. Radiator Specialty, 610 F.2d 178, 184, 21 FEP Cases 351 (4th Cir. 1979). The burden is on the defendant to establish that the positions in question require special qualifications which are not possessed or readily acquired by the general population. EEOC v. Radiator Specialty, 610 F.2d at 184. The district court, however, is afforded a great deal of discretion in determining the relevant labor market. Markey v. Tenneco Oil Co., 635 F.2d 497, 499, 24 FEP Cases 1675 (5th Cir. 1981).

[19] Rath failed to establish that the positions in question required special qualifications not possessed or readily acquired by the general population. As previously discussed, Rath could not identify any criteria it used in selecting employees or any common qualifications or skills that its employees possessed. Thus general population statistics were appropriate in determining the extent of Rath's discrimination against women and the amount of backpay. Hazelwood School District v. United States, 433 U.S. at 308 n.13; Kinsey v. First Regional Securities, Inc., 557 F.2d 830, 839, 14 FEP Cases 1143 (D.C. Cir. 1977); Kaplan v. International Alliance of Theatrical & Stage Employees, 525 F.2d 1354, 1358, 11 FEP Cases 872 (9th Cir. 1975); Par-

ham v. Southwestern Bell Telephone Co., 433 F.2d 421, 426, 2 FEP Cases 1017 (8th Cir. 1970).

[20] We hold that the district court erred in finding that the percentage of women employed in the nondurable goods manufacturing category was the appropriate population base because only these women would be interested in jobs at Rath. This finding rests on a faulty premise, that female representation in this category is a true indicator of women's interest in positions at Rath. The district court failed to consider the impact that Rath's discriminatory practices had on the size of this group. In 1978, 230 or approximately 45 percent of the women in the nondurable goods manufacturing category were employed by Rath. Rath's refusal to hire women, therefore, kept the number of women workers in this category lower than it would have been absent discrimination. If this category is used rather than general work force statistics in determining Rath's liability, Rath would benefit from its prior wrongful discrimination.

The use of Rath's applicant flow data is likewise inappropriate for the same reasons. Although applicant flow data is often the best indicator of the extent of an employer's discrimination, this is not the case where persons have been deterred from applying because of the employer's discriminatory practices.

The effects of and the injuries suffered from discriminatory employment practices are not always confined to those who are expressly denied a requested employment opportunity. A consistently enforced discriminatory policy can surely deter job applications from those who are aware of it and are unwilling to subject themselves to the humiliation of explicit and certain rejection. . . . The . . . message can be communicated by [the employer's] consistent discriminatory treatment of actual applicants . . . and even by the . . . composition . . . of [the] work force. . . .

International Brotherhood of Teamsters v. United States, 431 U.S. at 365.

This court has also recognized that "[t]he application process might itself not adequately reflect the actual potential applicant pool, since otherwise qualified people might be discouraged from applying because of a self-recognized inability to meet the very standards challenged as being discriminatory." Donnell v. General Motors Corp., 576 F.2d 1292, 1299, 17 FEP Cases 712 (8th Cir. 1978) citing Dothard v. Rawlinson, 433 U.S. at 330, cert. denied, 459 U.S. 844, 15 FEP Cases 10 (1982).

[21] In this case Rath's discriminatory practices deterred women from

applying for employment. See Donnell v. General Motors Corp., 576 F.2d at 1298. Rath was one of a few large employers in a small community of 1500 and its employment record was known in the community. There was uncontradicted testimony that women did not believe they would be hired at Rath. This perception was consistent with Rath's hiring practices. Only seven of the 95 women who applied from 1973–78 were hired; 157 of the 433 male applicants were hired. Ninety-five percent of Rath's work force was male. The use of Rath's applicant flow data to determine Rath's liability would not give an accurate picture of the number of women affected by Rath's discrimination.

[22] On remand, the district court should utilize general work force statistics to determine Rath's liability and to compute the backpay award. The district court must also afford nonapplicants the opportunity to prove that they were deterred from applying by Rath's discriminatory practices. This is not an easy burden for the nonapplicant. International Brotherhood of Teamsters v. United States, 431 U.S. at 367–68.

Inasmuch as the purpose of the nonapplicant's burden of proof will be to establish that [her] status is similar to that of the applicant, [she] must bear the burden of coming forward with the basic information about [her] qualifications that [she] would have presented in an application.... [T]he burden then will be on the employer to show that the nonapplicant was nevertheless not a victim of discrimination.

Id. at 369 n. 53.

Costs (Cross-appeal)

EEOC argues that the district court abused its discretion in allocating 50 percent of the costs to each party. Rath argues that both parties were partially successful and therefore the district court was correct in allocating the costs equally.

Fed. R. Civ. P. 54(d) provides that costs are to be allowed as a matter of course to the prevailing party unless the court otherwise directs. "A party who has obtained some relief usually will be considered the 'prevailing party' ... even if it has not succeeded on all of its claims." Superturf, Inc. v. Monsanto Co., 660 F.2d 1275, 1287 (8th Cir. 1981); see Coyne Delany Co. v. Capital Development Board, 717 F.2d 385, 390 (7th Cir. 1983). " '[T]he prevailing party is prima facie entitled to costs and it is incumbent upon the losing party to overcome that presumption ... [because] denial of costs

is in the nature of a penalty for some defection ... in the course of the litigation.' " Walters v. Roadway Express, Inc., 557 F.2d 521, 526, 96 LRRM 2006 (5th Cir. 1977) (citation omitted); see Chicago Sugar Co. v. American Sugar Refining Co., 176 F.2d 1 (7th Cir. 1949), cert. denied, 338 U.S. 948 (1950).

[23] EEOC is clearly the prevailing party in this lawsuit. EEOC was successful in the district court on two of its three claims: the disparate impact claim based on subjective hiring procedures and the disparate treatment claims. Our reversal of the district court on the third claim based on the no-spouse rule means that EEOC succeeded on all three claims. Neither Rath nor the district court identified any misconduct by EEOC which would warrant a denial of costs. Chicago Sugar Co. v. American Sugar Refinery Co., 176 F.2d at 11. We therefore hold that EEOC should be awarded full costs. We need not decide whether the district court's order equally dividing costs based on EEOC's partial success at the trial level was an abuse of discretion.

Accordingly, the judgment of the district court is affirmed in part and reversed in part, and this case is remanded for further proceedings consistent with this opinion.

Concurring and Dissenting Opinion

ROSS, Circuit Judge, concurring in part and dissenting in part: — I must respectfully disagree with the majority's view that the district judge abused his discretion in declining to award retroactive competitive seniority to the EEOC. Moreover, I do not think the district judge erred in his definition of the relevant available labor pool for purposes of determining liability and computing backpay. In all other respects, I concur in the majority's opinion.

Denial of Retroactive Seniority

I do not agree that the district judge abused his discretion in denying retroactive competitive seniority. "[T]he statutory scheme of Title VII 'implicitly recognizes that there may be cases calling for one remedy but not another, and * * * these choices are, of course, left in the first instance to the district courts.' " Franks v. Bowman Transportation Co., 424 U.S. 747, 779, 12 FEP Cases 549 (1976).

As the majority notes, Rath's opposition to full retroactive seniority is based among other concerns on the prospect that long-term employees will be bumped to less desirable jobs. We recognized in Briseno v. Central Technical Community College Area, ˉ739 F.2d 344, 348, 37 FEP Cases 57 (8th Cir. 1984), cited by the majority, that the choice of remedies discussed in Franks permits a district court to limit relief so that innocent incumbent employees will not be displaced. In Moore v. City of San Jose, 615 F.2d 1265, 1272, 22 FEP Cases 1053 (9th Cir. 1980), also cited by the majority, the Ninth Circuit noted that retroactive seniority in the circumstances of that case would cause no existing employees to lose their jobs, and "the number of returning employees was small enough that their impact on the seniority-based benefits of incumbent employees would be minimal."

Thus, while I am not opposed to an award of noncompetitive "benefit" seniority [1] to appropriately identified victims of Rath's discriminatory policies, I would affirm the district court's denial of competitive seniority in this case. In light of the number of persons now rightfully entitled to a place in Rath's work force as the result of the company's years of discriminatory hiring, as well as Rath's current financial status and the certainty that incumbents will be bumped to lower positions, I consider the district court's adjustment of the remedy to account for incumbent employees appropriate. The retention of a full work force by a company which has experienced "horrendous losses" since 1977 and which is presently in bankruptcy seems to me exceedingly unlikely. See Romasanta v. United Air Lines, Inc., 717 F.2d 1140, 1147-56, 32 FEP Cases 1545 (7th Cir. 1983), cert. denied, 104 S.Ct. 1928, 34 FEP Cases 920 (1984) (declining to award full, retroactive competitive seniority in light of the adverse impact on a substantial number of incumbent employees and certain economic con-

ditions adversely affecting the defendant company's potential for growth).

Labor Force Statistics

In Green v. Missouri Pacific Railroad Co., 523 F.2d 1290, 1293-94, 10 FEP Cases 1409 (8th Cir. 1975), we recognized that generally three kinds of statistical comparisons may be used to establish whether a challenged employment practice has a disproportionate impact on a protected group in violation of Title VII. Two of these procedures involve resort to general population figures. The first examines whether "[women] as a class (or at least [women] in a specified geographical area) are excluded by the employment practice in question at a substantially higher rate than [men]." Id. at 1293. Another involves comparing the composition of the employer's work force with the composition of the population at large. Id. at 1294. The procedure which does not rely on general population data and which the district court used "focuses on a comparison of the percentage of [male and female] job applicants actually excluded by the employment practice* * *." Id.

The district court considered the EEOC's evidence in support of its reliance on general population statistics defective:

> While the Court believes that general population or similar work force data may be appropriate under certain circumstances, the Court is of the opinion that the failure to break the work force statistics for Louisa [sic] County into the job categories of "durable goods manufacturing" or "nonmanufacturing" industries, eliminates any substantive probative value the statistics on the general population may have had. Because of the nature of the jobs offered by the Rath plant, the Court is of the opinion that many persons engaged in jobs in nonmanufacturing industries would not be attracted to that type of work, although it may also be questionable whether this type of work would be attractive to many in the durable goods manufacturing. Such statistics would have had more validity than the general population figures.

I agree with the district court's analysis. I cannot accept the unsubstantiated premise advanced by the EEOC that the entire female component of the Louisa County, Iowa work force would have been interested in or qualified to perform the hog slaughtering and processing jobs at Rath. See New York City Transit Authority v. Beazer, 440 U.S. 568, 586 n.29, 19 FEP Cases 149 (1979).

Although "a statistical showing of disproportionate impact [need not] always be based on an analysis of the characteristics

---

[1] "Benefit"-type seniority refers to the use of a worker's earned seniority credits in computing his level of economic "fringe benefits." Examples of such benefits are pensions, paid vacation time, and unemployment insurance. "Competitive"-type seniority refers to the use of those same earned credits in determining his right, relative to other workers, to job-related "rights" that cannot be supplied equally to any two employees. Examples can range from the worker's right to keep his job while someone else is laid off, to his right to a place in the punch-out line ahead of another employee at the end of a workday.
Franks v. Bowman Transp. Co., 424 U.S. 747, 782, n.1,12 FEP Cases 549 (1976) (Powell, J. concurring in part and dissenting in part).

of actual applicants," Dothard v. Rawlinson, 433 U.S. 321, 330, 15 FEP Cases 10, "evidence showing that the figures for the general population might not accurately reflect the pool of qualified job applicants' undermines the significance of such [general population] figures." Teamsters v. United States, supra, at 340 n.20.

I therefore consider the district court's use of applicant flow data appropriate.

RULON-MILLER v. IBM

California Court of Appeal, First District

RULON-MILLER v. INTERNATIONAL BUSINESS MACHINES CORPORATION, et al., No. A016455, November 29, 1984

WRONGFUL DISCHARGE

1. Restriction on employee relationships ▶515.3912 ▶200.1503 ▶290.05 ▶200.1542

Substantial evidence supports jury verdict that employee who was accused of conflict of interest because she dated competitor's employee was discharged wrongfully, rather than routinely reassigned as alleged by employer.

2. Invasion of employee privacy — Employer policy ▶200.1503 ▶450.1205 ▶200.155509 ▶215.25 ▶290.05

Employee who was discharged because her dating of competitor's employee allegedly constituted conflict of interest was entitled to rely on employer's policy that insures to employee both right of privacy and right to hold job even though "off-the-job behavior" might not be approved of by employee's manager, and record shows that employer did not interpret this policy to prohibit romantic relationships.

3. Conflict of interest — Invasion of employee privacy — ▶290.05 ▶215.25 ▶200.1542

Discharged employee's social relationship with competitor's employee did not create conflict of interest that interfered with discharged employee's duties where employee's primary job as seller of typewriters and office equipment did not give her access to sensitive information that could have been useful to competitors; employer's alternative contention that rumors of employee's romantic relationship had effect of diminishing morale of workers reporting to employee is without merit, where workers testified that rumors in no way impaired her abilities as manager.

4. Breach of implied covenant — Invasion of employee privacy — ▶290.05 ▶450.1205 ▶450.1203 ▶200.1542

In confrontation between discharged employee and her supervisor who accused employee of conflict of interest stemming from her romantic involvement with competitor's employee, employee's assertion of her right to be free of inquiries concerning her personal life was based on substantive direct contract rights that flowed to her from employer's overall policy prohibiting company interest in outside activities of its employees so long as activities did not interfere with work of employee. Duty of fair dealing portion of implied covenant of good faith and fair dealing in employee's contract of employment requires that employer apply equally to all employees any rules and regulations it has and that employees also be afforded benefit of their protection.

5. Contract principle — Tort remedy ▶400.01 ▶450.05 ▶450.01

Party to contract may incur tort remedies when, in addition to breaching contract, it seeks to shield itself from liability by denying, in bad faith and without probable cause, existence of contract. Denial of existence of contract without more, however, is not actionable in tort.

6. Tortious conduct — Breach of contract ▶200.1542 ▶400.01 ▶515.2101 ▶290.05

Supervisor who denied existence of employee's contractual right to privacy as derived from company policy and who alleged that employee was being discharged because her romantic relationship with competitor's employee created conflict of interest is liable in tort for attempt to shield himself from liability in bad faith and without probable cause. Lack of any evidence showing that company processes, customer lists, or financial information were passed on to competition leads to conclusion that no probable cause existed for conflict-of-interest charge, which jury found to be untrue.

7. Infliction of emotional distress — Punitive damages ▶400.03 ▶200.1542 ▶610.0307 ▶215.25

Award of $200,000 in punitive damages for intentional infliction of emotional distress upon employee who was discharged by supervisor allegedly because her romantic relationship with competitor's employee constituted conflict of interest was supported by jury finding that supervisor's conduct was so extreme and outrageous as to go beyond all possible bounds of decency. Supervisor's denial to employee of right to privacy granted to all other workers for conduct unrelated to her work was degrading to her as person, and his unilateral action in purporting to remove any free choice on her part to choose between her job and lover, which was contrary to his earlier assurances, also would support conclusions that supervisor's conduct was intended to emphasize that she was powerless to do anything to assert her

rights as employee, and such powerlessness is one of most debilitating
kinds of human oppression.

Appeal from the California Superior
Court, San Francisco County. Af-
firmed.
Cliff Palefsky (McGuinn, Hillsman
& Palefsky), San Francisco, Calif., for
appellee.
James J. Walsh (Pillsbury, Madison
& Sutro), San Francisco, Calif., for ap-
pellant.

Full Text of Opinion

RUSHING,* Judge: — International Business Machines (IBM) appeals
from the judgment entered against it
after a jury awarded $100,000 compen-
satory and $200,000 punitive damages
to respondent (Virginia Rulon-Miller)
on claims of wrongful discharge and
intentional infliction of emotional distress. Rulon-Miller was a low-level
marketing manager at IBM in its office products division in San Francisco. Her termination as a marketing
manager at IBM came about as a result of an accusation made by her immediate supervisor, defendant Callahan, of a romantic relationship with
the manager of a rival office products
firm, QYX.

FACTUAL BACKGROUND

IBM is an international manufacturer of computers, office equipment
and telecommunications systems. As
well, it offers broad general services in
the data processing field. It is reputed
to be the single most successful high
technology firm in the world. It is also
a major force in the low technology
field of typewriters and office equipment.

IBM is an employer traditionally
thought to provide great security to its
employees as well as an environment
of openness and dignity. The company
is organized into divisions, and each
division is, to an extent, independent
of others. The company prides itself on
providing career opportunities to its
employees, and respondent represents
a good example of this. She started in
1967 as a receptionist in the Philadelphia Data Center. She was told that
"career opportunities are available to

[employees] as long as they are performing satisfactorily and are willing
to accept new challenges." While she
worked at the data center in Philadelphia, she attended night school and
earned a baccalaureate degree. She
was promoted to equipment scheduler
and not long after received her first
merit award. The company moved her
to Atlanta, Georgia, where she spent
15 months as a data processor. She was
transferred to the office products division and was assigned the position of
"marketing support representative" in
San Francisco where she trained users
(i.e., customers) of newly-purchased
IBM equipment. Respondent was promoted to "product planner" in 1973
where her duties included overseeing
the performance of new office products in the marketplace. As a product
planner, she moved to Austin, Texas,
and later to Lexington, Kentucky.
Thereafter, at the urging of her managers that she go into sales in the office products division, she enrolled at
the IBM sales school in Dallas. After
graduation, she was assigned to San
Francisco.

Her territory was the financial district. She was given a performance
plan by her management which set
forth the company's expectations of
her. She was from time to time thereafter graded against that plan on a
scale of one through five with a grade
of one being the highest. After her first
year on the job, she was given a rating
of one and was felt by her manager to
be a person who rated at the top of
IBM's scale.

A little over a year after she began in
San Francisco, IBM reorganized its office products division into two separate functions, one called office systems and another called office
products. Respondent was assigned to
office systems; again she was given
ratings of one and while there received
a series of congratulatory letters from
her superiors and was promoted to
marketing representative. She was one
of the most successful sales persons in
the office and received a number of
prizes and awards for her sales efforts.[1] IBM's system of rewarding sa-
lespersons has a formalistic aspect

---

* Assigned by the Chairperson of the Judicial
Council.

[1] In 1978 she fulfilled her annual sales quota in
the fifth month of the year. She was given a
"Golden Circle Award" in her third year of sales
which is a recognition of superior sales by the
company. She had been a member of the "100
Percent Club" for each of the years that she was in
the San Francisco office.

about it that allows for subtle distinctions to be made while putting great emphasis on performance; respondent exercised that reward system to its fullest. She was a very successful seller of typewriters and other office equipment.

She was then put into a program called "Accelerated Career Development Program" which was a way of rewarding certain persons who were seen by their superiors as having management potential. IBM's prediction of her future came true and in 1978 she was named a marketing manager in the office products branch.

IBM knew about respondent's relationship with Matt Blum well before her appointment as a manager. Respondent met Blum in 1976 when he was an account manager for IBM. That they were dating was widely known within the organization. In 1977 Blum left IBM to join QYX, an IBM competitor, and was transferred to Philadelphia. When Blum returned to San Francisco in the summer of 1978, IBM personnel were aware that he and respondent began dating again. This seemed to present no problems to respondent's superiors, as Callahan confirmed when she was promoted to manager. Respondent testified: "Somewhat in passing, Phil said: I heard the other day you were dating Matt Blum, and I said: Oh. And he said, I don't have any problem with that. You're my number one pick. I just want to assure you that you are my selection." The relationship with Blum was also known to Regional Manager Gary Nelson who agreed with Callahan. Neither Callahan nor Nelson raised any issue of conflict of interest because of the Blum relationship.

Respondent flourished in her management position, and the company, apparently grateful for her efforts, gave her a $4,000 merit raise in 1979 and told her that she was doing a good job. A week later, her manager, Phillip Callahan, left a message that he wanted to see her.

When she walked into Callahan's office he confronted her with the question of whether she was *dating* Matt Blum. She wondered at the relevance of the inquiry and he said the dating constituted a "conflict of interest," and told her to stop dating Blum or lose her job and said she had a "couple of days to a week" to think about it.[2]

---
[2] Because of the importance of this testimony, we set it out verbatim. Respondent testified: "I walked into Phil's office and he asked me to sit down and he said: Are you dating Matt Blum?

"And I said, What? I was kind of surprised he would ask me and I said: Well, what difference

The next day Callahan called her in again, told her "he had made up her mind for her," and when she protested, dismissed her.[3] IBM and Callahan claim that he merely "transferred" respondent to another division.

DISCUSSION

[1] Respondent's claims of wrongful discharge and intentional infliction of emotional distress were both submitted to the jury. Appellant argues that the jury should not have been permitted to consider the issue of wrongful discharge because as a matter of law the offer of reassignment cannot be considered a wrongful discharge. In developing this argument, IBM attempts to change the nature of this case from one of wrongful termination into a debate about constructive discharge through an alleged administrative reassignment.

---
know, you are removed from management effective immediately.

"And I said: I think you are dismissing me.

"And he said: If you feel that way, give me your I.D. card and your key to the office [¶] I want you to leave the premises immediately.

"And I was just about to burst into tears, and I didn't cry at work, so I basically fled his office.

"I felt he dismissed me."

does it make if I'm dating Matt Blum? . . .

"And he said, well, something to the effect: I think we have a conflict of interest, or the appearance of a conflict of interest here.

"And I said: Well, gee, Phil, you've, you've pointed out to me that there are no problems in the office because I am dating Matt Blum, and I don't really understand why that would have any, you know, pertinency to my job. You said I am doing an okay job. I just got a raise.

"And he said: Well, I think we have a conflict of interest . . . .

"He said: No and he said: I'll tell you what. He said: I will give you a couple of days to a week. Think this whole thing over.

"I said: Think what over?

"And he said: You either stop dating Matt Blum or I'm going to take You out of your management job. "And I was just kind of overwhelmed."

[3] Respondent stated the next day she was again summoned to his office where Callahan sat ominously behind a desk cleared of any paperwork, an unusual scenario for any IBM manager.

She further testified: "I walked into Phil's office and he asked me to shut the door, and he said he was removing me from management effectively immediately. And I said: What?

"And he repeated it. And I was taken aback, I was a little startled, and I think I said: "Well, gee, I thought I had a couple of days to a week to think over the situation that we discussed yesterday.

"And he said: I'm making the decision for you.

"And I said: Phil, you've told me that I'm doing a good job. You told me that we are not losing anybody to QYX because I am dating Matt Blum, that we are not losing any equipment to QYX. I just don't understand what bearing dating has to do with my job.

"And he said: We have a conflict of interest. . . .

"I said: Well, what kind of a job would it be?

"And he said: Well, I don't have it, but it will be non-management. You won't be a manager again.

"Pardon me? . . .

"And I think I was getting very upset so I think I said something because of that respect for the individual tenet of IBM's that I really believed in I didn't think that he was following what I thought IBM, really did believe in. And he just said: You

The test for the court here is substantial evidence (see Neal v. Farmers Ins. Exchange (1978) 21 Cal.3d 910, 922) and without any question there was substantial evidence to support the jury verdict that the respondent was wrongfully discharged rather than routinely reassigned.

The initial discussion between Callahan and respondent of her relationship with Blum is important. We must accept the version of the facts most favorable to the respondent herein. (Nestle v. City of Santa Monica (1972) 6 Cal.3d 920, 925.) When Callahan questioned her relationship with Blum, respondent invoked her right to privacy in her personal life relying on existing IBM policies. A threshold inquiry is thus presented whether respondent could reasonably rely on those policies for job protection. Any conflicting action by the company would be wrongful in that it would constitute a violation of her contract rights. (Lord v. Goldberg (1889) 81 Cal.596; Pugh v. See's Candies, Inc. (1981) 116 Cal. App. 3d 311, 115 LRRM 4002.)

Under the common law rule codified in Labor Code section 2922, an employment contract of indefinite duration is, in general, terminable at "the will" of either party. This common law rule has been considerably altered by the recognition of the Supreme Court of California that implicit in any such relationship or contract is an underlying principle that requires the parties to deal openly and fairly with one another. (Seaman's Direct Buying Service, Inc. v. Standard Oil Co. (1984) 36 Cal.3d 752.) this general requirement of fairness has been identified as the covenant of good faith and fair dealing. (Tameny v. Atlantic Richfield Co. (1980) 27 Cal. 3d 167, 1 IER Cases 102.) The covenant of good faith and fair dealing embraces a number of rights, obligations, and considerations implicit in contractual relations and certain other relationships. At least two of those considerations are relevant herein. The duty of fair dealing by an employer is, simply stated, a requirement that like cases be treated alike. Implied in this, of course, is that the company, if it has rules and regulations, apply those rules and regulations to its employees as well as affording its employees their protection.

As can be seen from an analysis of other cases, this is not in any substantial way a variation from general contract law in California, for if an employee has the right in an employment contract (as distinct from an implied covenant), the courts have routinely given her the benefit of that contract.

(Rest. 2d Contracts, §81; 1A *Corbin on Contracts* (1963) §152, pp. 13-17; see also cases cited in Pugh, supra, 116 Cal.App.3d at p. 325.) Thus, the fair dealing portion of the covenant of good faith and fair dealing is at least the right of an employee to the benefit of rules and regulations adopted for his or her protection.

In this case, there is a close question of whether those rules or regulations permit IBM to inquire into the purely personal life of the employee. If so, an attendant question is whether such a policy was applied consistently, particularly as between men and women. The distinction is important because the right of privacy, a constitutional right in California (City and County of San Francisco v. Superior Court (1981) 125 Cal.App.3d 879, 883), could be implicated by the IBM inquiry. Much of the testimony below concerned what those policies were. The evidence was conflicting on the meaning of certain IBM policies. We observe ambiguity in the application but not in the intent. The "Watson Memo" (so called because it was singed by a former chairman of IBM) provided as follows:

"TO ALL IBM MANAGERS:

"The line that separates an individual's on-the-job business life from his other life as a private citizen is at times well-defined and at other times indistinct. But the line does exist, and you and I, as managers in IBM, must be able to recognize that line.

"I have seen instances where managers took disciplinary measures against employees for actions or conduct that are not rightfully the company's concern. These managers usually justified their decisions by citing their personal code of ethics and morals or by quoting some fragment of company policy that seemed to support their position. Both arguments proved unjust on close examination. What we need, in every case, is balanced judgment which weighs the needs of the business and the rights of the individual.

"Our primary objective as IBM managers is to further the business of this company by leading our people properly and measuring quantity and quality of work and effectiveness on the job against clearly set standard of responsibility and compensation. This is performance — and performance is, in the final analysis, the one thing that the company can insist on from everyone.

"We have concern with an employee's off-the-job behavior only when it reduces his ability to perform regular job assignments, interferes with the job performance of other employees, or if his outside behavior affects the reputation of the company in a major way. When on-the-job performance is acceptable, I can think of few situations in which outside activities could result in disciplinary action or dismissal.

"When such situations do come to your attention, you should seek the advice and counsel of the next appropriate level of management and the personnel department in determining what action — if any — is called for. Action should be taken only when a legitimate interest of the company is injured or jeopardized. Furthermore the damage must be clear beyond reasonable doubt and not based on hasty decisions about what one person might think is good for the company.

"IBM's first basic belief is respect for the individual, and the essence of this belief is a strict regard for his right to personal privacy. This idea should never be compromised easily or quickly.
"/s/ Tom Watson, Jr."

[2] It is clear that this company policy insures to the employee both the right of privacy and the right to hold a job even though "off-the-job behavior" might not be approved of by the employee's manager.

IBM had adopted policies governing employee conduct. Some of those policies were collected in a document known as the "Performance and Recognition" (PAR) Manual. IBM relies on the following portion of the PAR Manual:

"A conflict of interest can arise when an employee is involved in activity for personal gain, which for any reason is in conflict with IBM's business interests. Generally speaking, 'moonlighting' is defined as working at some activity for personal gain outside of your IBM job. If you do perform outside work, you have a special responsibility to avoid any conflict with IBM's business interests.

"Obviously, you cannot solicit or perform in competition with IBM product or service offerings. Outside work cannot be performed on IBM time, including 'personal' time off. You cannot use IBM equipment, materials, resources, or 'inside' information for outside work. Nor should you solicit business or clients or perform outside work on IBM premises.

"Employees must be free of any significant investment or association of their own or of their immediate family's [sic], in competitors or suppliers, which might interfere or be thought to interfere with the independent exercise of their judgment in the best interests of IBM."

This policy of IBM is entitled "Gifts" and appears to be directed at "moonlighting" and soliciting outside business or clients on IBM premises. It prohibits "significant investment" in competitors or suppliers of IBM. It also prohibits "association" with such persons "which might interfere or be thought to interfere with the independent exercise of their judgment in the best interests of IBM."

Callahan based his action against respondent on a "conflict of interest." But the record shows that IBM did not interpret this policy to prohibit a romantic relationship. Callahan admitted that there was no company rule or policy requiring an employee to terminate friendships with fellow employees who leave and join competitors.⁴ Gary Nelson, Callahan's superior, also confirmed that IBM had no policy against employees socializing with competitors.

This issue was hotly contested with respondent claiming that the "conflict of interest" claim was a pretext for her unjust termination. Whether it was presented a fact question for the jury.

Do the policies reflected in this record give IBM a right to terminate an employee for a conflict of interest? The answer must be yes, but whether respondent's conduct constituted such was for the jury. We observe that while respondent was successful, her primary job did not give her access to sensitive information which could have been useful to competitors. She was, after all, a seller of typewriters and office equipment. Respondent's brief makes much of the concession by IBM that there was no evidence whatever that respondent had given any information or help to IBM's competitor QYX. It really is no concession at all; she did not have the information or help to give. Even so, the question is one of substantial evidence. The evidence is abundant that there was no conflict of interest by respondent.

[3] It does seem clear that an overall policy established by IBM chairman Watson was one of no company interest in the outside activities of an employee so long as the activities did not interfere with the work of the employee. Moreover, in the last analysis, it may be simply a question for the jury to decide whether, in the application of these policies, the right was conferred on IBM to inquire into the personal or romantic relationships its managers had with others. This is an important question because IBM, in attempting to reargue the facts to us, casts this argument in other terms, namely, that it had a right to inquire even if there was no evidence that such a relationship interfered with the discharge of the employee's duties *because* it had the effect of diminishing the morale of the employees answering to the manager. This is the "Caesar's wife" argument; it is merely a recast of the principal argument and asks the same question in different terms.⁵

---

⁴ An interesting side issue to this point is that Blum continued to play on an IBM softball team while working for QYX.

⁵ What we mean by that is that if you charge that an employee is passing confidential information to a competitor, the question remains whether the charge is true on the evidence available to the person deciding the issue, in this case, the respondent's managers at IBM. If you recast this argu-

The same answer holds in both cases: there being no evidence to support the more direct argument, there is no evidence to support the indirect argument.

[4] Moreover, the record shows that the evidence of rumor was not a basis for any decline in the morale of the employees reporting to respondent. Employees Mary Hrize and Wayne Fyvie, who reported to respondent's manager that she was seen at a tea dance at the Hyatt Regency with Matt Blum and also that she was not living at her residence in Marin, did not believe that those rumors in any way impaired her abilities as a manager. In the initial confrontation between respondent and her superior the assertion of the right to be free of inquiries concerning her personal life was based on substantive direct contract rights she had flowing to her from IBM policies. Further, there is no doubt that the jury could have so found and on this record we must assume that they did so find.

The Claim of Instructional Error.

[5, 6] Appellant claims that the trial judge erred in instructing the jury with respect to the standard set forth in special instruction number 2. However, it is clear that the court's special instructions numbered 2 [definition of good cause], 33 [employer good faith in honest but mistaken belief], 22 [employer business judgment and sensitive positions] and 3 [factors for good faith discharge] adequately covered the issue and we discern no error in either the instructions or the standards to be applied by the jury. Indeed in the court's special instruction number 3 the jury was given seven factors that they could take into account in determining whether an employer acted in good faith or bad faith in discharging an employee from employment.[6]

ment in the form of the "Caesar's wife" argument attempted by IBM, it will be seen that exactly the same question arises, namely, "is it true?" Indeed, the import of the argument is that the rumor, or an unfounded allegation, could serve as a basis for the termination of the employee.

[6] The factors to be considered under the court's special instruction number 3 are (1) whether or not the employee was discharged for legitimate business and employment reasons; (2) whether or not the employee was discharged on a pretext, that is, for a false reason or motive put forth to hide the real one; (3) whether or not the employee was engaged in a sensitive or confidential management position; (4) whether or not the employee had a conflict of interest; (5) whether or not the employee's personal, private or social relationships endangered, injured or jeopardized the employer's legitimate business interests; (6) whether or not the employer violated, invaded or infringed upon the employee's personal privacy and personal, private and social relationships; (7) whether or not the employee was discriminated against by the

Thus the court instructed the jury on the several separate theories of law including the several factual accounts that gave support to plaintiff's claim for wrongful discharge including defendant's claim that such discharge was privileged.

In the recent case of *Seaman's Direct Buying Service, Inc. v. Standard Oil Co.*, supra, 36 Cal.3d 752, the Supreme Court noted that certain other contractual relationships characterized by elements of public interest, adhesion and fiduciary responsibility may well be subject to tort action for breach of the covenant of good faith and fair dealing. (36 Cal.3d at pp. 768-769.)

The court went on to suggest that an employment relationship might give rise to tort remedies because the "relationship has some of the same characteristics as the relationship between insurer and insured." (Id., at p. 769, fn. 6; see also *Wallis v. Superior Court* (1984) 160 Cal.App.3d 1109 [pension agreement held to contain characteristics which allow a tort cause of action for breach].)

The court found it unnecessary to directly address the issue, enunciating a broader principle that "... a party to a contract may incur tort remedies when, in addition to breaching the contract, it seeks to shield itself from liability by denying, in bad faith and without probable cause, that the contract exists." (Seaman's, supra, at p. 769.) The lesson to be derived seems to be that denial of the existence of a contract without more is not actionable in tort.

In the case at bar, Callahan *denied* the employment rights asserted by respondent. At the second meeting he "stonewalled" respondent when she insisted on her rights and then fired her when she persisted. The *conduct* of the breaching party is the focus of the tort, particularly where there is an attempt to shield oneself from liability, in bad faith and without probable cause. Here, the "conflict of interest" charge was untrue and was used as a pretext to legitimate the termination. "Probable cause" would have been some reasonable basis for assuming that a significant company interest was at stake. There is no such evidence claimed by IBM, but one can easily formulate a case where company processes, customer lists, financial information, etc., are passed to the competi-

employer because of that employee's sex, citing *Cleary v. American Airlines, Inc.* (1980) 111 Cal.App.3d 443, 1 IER Cases 122; *Pugh v. See's Candies, Inc.* supra, 116 Cal.App.3d 311, 115 LRRM 4002, and BAJI No. 12.98, as modified.

tion. It is the admitted absence of any such evidence that leads us to conclude there was no probable cause here. Thus, the charge was made in bad faith and without probable cause.

The jury was specifically instructed on "bad faith." (See special instruction No. 3, supra.) Moreover, in instruction number 33 the judge told the jury that "an employer who acts in good faith on an honest but mistaken belief that discharge of an employee is required by legitimate business interests has not committed a wrongful discharge of the employee." The failure to give such an instruction, tailored appropriately to the facts of the case, was the principal reason for the reversal in Seamans, supra, 36 Cal.3d at pp. 769-770.

Thus the principle enunciated in Seaman's, that a party to a contractual relationship may not, in denying the existence of the contract, do so in bad faith and without probable cause, focuses necessarily on the actual conduct of the breaching party. It is not so much the duty owed under the contract as the duty arising from the relationship of one party to another. (See Sloane v. Southern Cal. Ry. Co. (1896) 111 Cal. 668, 676, 677.) That duty, at least, is implied from the formulation of the tort, namely, to act without bad faith and with probable cause. Here, Callahan breached that duty. The issue put to the jury was whether the conflict of interest charge was a pretext for firing respondent. This question required the jury to decide if Callahan had any belief in the existence of such a breach of company policy. On this record, the jury found that he did not. The evidence supports the jury verdict.

Intentional Infliction of Emotional Distress

[7] The contract rights in an employment agreement or the convenant of good faith and fair dealing gives both employer and employee the right to breach and to respond in damages. Here, however, the question is whether if IBM elected to exercise that right it should also be liable for punitive damages, because of its intentional infliction of emotional distress. The issue is whether the conduct of the marketing

manager of IBM was "extreme and outrageous," a question involving the objective facts of what happened in the confrontation between the employee and employer as well as the special susceptibility of suffering of the employee.

The general rule is that this tort, in essence, requires the defendant's conduct to be so extreme and outrageous as to go beyond all possible bounds of decency, and to be regarded as atrocious and utterly intolerable in a civilized community. (Alcorn v. Anbro Engineering, Inc. (1970) 2 Cal.3d 493, 498-499, particularly at fn. 5 quoting Rest. 2d Torts § 46, comment d.)[8]

The question is reduced to the inquiry of whether Callahan's statements and conduct could be found by the jury to fall within doctrinal requirements. " 'It is for the court to determine whether on the evidence severe emotional distress can be found; it is for the jury to determine whether, on the evidence, it has in fact existed.' " (Fletcher v. Western National Life Ins. Co. (1970) 10 Cal.App.3d 376, 397.) "Where reasonable men may differ" the court must instruct the jury on the law and entrust the factual determination to it. (Fuentes v. Perez (1977) 66 Cal.App.3d 163, 172.) The finding on this cause of action as reflected herein is sufficient to support the award of punitive damages. (Fletcher, supra, at p. 404.)

The jury was entitled to consider the evidence of extreme and outrageous conduct in light of the June 7 exchange followed by Callahan's conduct and pretextual statements, as well as in light of express corporate policy as manifested by the Watson memo. Indeed, the concern of the Watson memo is also a right protected by law. As we earlier noted "the right of privacy is unquestionably a 'fundamental interest of our society' " (City and County of San Francisco v. Superior Court, supra, 125 Cal.App.3d 879,

---

' Knowledge was the logical equivalent of an intentional act in Seaman's. But as the Court pointed out, that there was knowledge by defendant is the beginning of the inquiry, not the end. If the jury in Seaman's had been instructed that it might infer culpable intent from conduct, the jury's verdict would have stood. Here, the jury was not in any such way misled. It was told it could infer wrongfulness by defendants from their conduct.

' See also Agarwal v. Johnson (1979) 25 Cal. 3d 932, 945-947 [employee subjected to racial epithets and profane insults]; Kelly v. General Telephone Co. (1982) 136 Cal.App.3d 278, 287 [false accusation of serious crime and alteration of personal records]; McGee v. McNally (1981) 119 Cal.App.3d 891, 896 [campaign of harassment designed to deprive plaintiff of his job and to replace him with a fellow worker]; Lagies v. Copley (1980) 110 Cal. App.3d 958 [attempt to undermine professional credibility as well as professional harassment]; Renteria v. County of Orange (1978) 82 Cal.App.3d 833, 21 FEP Cases 179 [rude and degrading treatment including surveillance and interrogation]; Toney v. State of California (1976) 54 Cal. App. 3d 779 [insidious racial harassment]; Hall v. May Department Store Co. (1978) 292 Or. 131, 635 P.2d 657 [threat of arrest with no evidence to support charge]; Rogers v. Loews L'Enfant Plaza Hotel (D.C. Cir. 1981) 526 F.Supp. 523, 529-531, 29 FEP Cases 828 [sexual harassment].

883.) It is guaranteed to all people by article I, section 1, of the state Constitution. So the question is whether the invasion of plaintiff's privacy rights by her employer, in the setting of this case, constitutes extreme and outrageous conduct. The jury by special verdict so found.

To determine if Callahan's conduct could reach the level of extreme, outrageous, and atrocious conduct, requires detailed examination. First, there was a decided element of deception in Callahan acting as if the relationship with Blum was something new. The evidence was clear he knew of the involvement of respondent and Blum well before her promotion. Second, he acted in flagrant disregard of IBM policies prohibiting him from inquiring into respondent's "off job behavior." By giving respondent "a few days" to think about the choice between job and lover, he implied that if she gave up Blum she could have her job. He then acted without giving her "a few days to think about it" or giving her the right to choose.

So far the conduct is certainly unfair but not atrocious. What brings Callahan's conduct to an actionable level is the way he brought these several elements together in the second meeting with respondent. He said, after calling her in, "I'm making the decision for you." The implications of his statement were richly ambiguous, meaning she could not act or think for herself, or that he was acting in her best interest, or that she persisted in a romantic involvement inconsistent with her job. When she protested, he fired her.

The combination of statements and conduct would under any reasoned view tend to humiliate and degrade respondent. To be denied a right granted to all other employees for conduct unrelated to her work was to degrade her as a person. His unilateral action in purporting to remove any free choice on her part contrary to his earlier assurances also would support a conclusion that his conduct was intended to emphasize that she was powerless to do anything to assert her rights as an IBM employee. And such powerlessness is one of the most debilitating kinds of human oppression. The sum of such evidence clearly supports the jury finding of extreme and outrageous conduct.

Accordingly we conclude that the emotional distress cause of action was amply proved and supports the award of punitive damages. (Neal v. Farmers Ins. Exchange, supra, 21 Cal.3d 910, 927-928).

The judgment is affirmed.

RACANELLI and HOLMDAHL, Judges, concur.

MERITOR SAVINGS BANK v. VINSON

Supreme Court of the United States

MERITOR SAVINGS BANK, FSB v. VINSON, et al., No. 84-1979, June 19, 1986

CIVIL RIGHTS ACT OF 1964

1. Scope ▸108.0401 ▸108.0407

Title VII is not limited to "economic" or "tangible" discrimination, since phrase "terms, conditions, or privileges of employment" evinces congressional intent to strike at entire spectrum of disparate treatment of men and women.

2. Sexual harassment ▸108.4159 ▸108.508

Title VII forbids sexual harassment, where Congress did not limit Title VII to "economic" or "tangible" discrimination, and EEOC guidelines specifying that sexual harassment is form of sex discrimination fully support view that harassment leading to noneconomic injury can violate Title VII.

3. Sexual harassment ▸108.4159 ▸108.508

EEOC guidelines concluding that "hostile environment" discrimination violates Title VII appropriately drew from, and were fully consistent with, existing caselaw, and, therefore, violation of Title VII may be established by proving that discrimination based on sex has created hostile or abusive work environment.

4. Sexual harassment ▸108.4159

Sexual harassment, to be actionable, must be sufficiently severe or pervasive to alter conditions of victim's employment and to create abusive working environment.

5. Sexual harassment — Defense ▸108.4159 ▸108.4290

Fact that sex-related conduct was "voluntary" in sense that complainant was not forced to participate against her will is not defense to sexual harassment Title VII action; correct inquiry is whether complainant by her conduct indicated that alleged sexual advances were unwelcome, not whether her actual participation in sexual intercourse was voluntary.

6. Sexual harassment — Evidence ▸108.4159 ▸108.8101

Evidence of complainant's sexually provocative speech or dress is not irrelevant in determining whether she found particular sexual advances unwelcome.

7. Sexual harassment — Liability of employer ▸108.4159 ▸108.0403

Congress wanted courts to look to agency principles for guidance in determining whether employer is liable for supervisor's sexual harassment, even though such common-law principles may not be transferable in all their particulars to Title VII, since Congress' decision to define "employer" to include any "agent" of an employer surely evinces intent to place some limits on acts of employees for which employers are to be held responsible.

8. Sexual harassment — Liability of employer ▸108.4159 ▸108.0403

Court of appeals erred in concluding that employers are always automatically liable for sexual harassment by their supervisors regardless of circumstances of particular case, but absence of notice to employer does not necessarily insulate that employer from liability.

9. Sexual harassment — Defense ▸108.4159 ▸108.4290

Mere existence of grievance procedure and policy against discrimination, coupled with complainant's failure to invoke that procedure, does not insulate employer from liability for employer's sexual harassment, although these facts are relevant to determination of issue.

———

On writ of certiorari to the U.S. Court of Appeals for the District of Columbia Circuit (36 FEP Cases 1423, 753 F.2d 141). Affirmed and remanded.

See also 23 FEP Cases 37; 27 FEP Cases 948; and 37 FEP Cases 1266, 760 F.2d 1330.

F. Robert Troll (Charles H. Fleischer, Randall C. Smith, and Ross, Marsh & Foster, with him on brief), Washington, D.C., for petitioner.

Patricia J. Barry, Grover City, Calif. (Catharine A. MacKinnon, Mill Valley, Calif., with her on brief), for respondents.

Charles Fried, Solicitor General, W. Bradford Reynolds and Richard K. Willard, Assistant Attorneys General, Carolyn B. Kuhl, Deputy Solicitor General, Albert G. Lauber, Jr., Assistant to the Solicitor General, John F. Cordes and John F. Daly, U.S. Department of Justice, and Johnny J. Butler, Acting General Counsel, filed brief for United States and EEOC, as amici curiae, seeking reversal.

Robert T. Thompson, Dannie B. Fogleman, and Susan L. Hartzoge (Thompson, Mann and Hutson), Washington, D.C. (Stephen A. Bokat, Washington, D.C., of counsel), filed brief for Chamber of Commerce of the United States, as amicus curiae, seeking reversal.

Robert E. Williams, Douglas S. McDowell, and Garen E. Dodge (McGuiness & Williams), Washington, D.C., filed brief for Equal Employment Advisory Council, as amicus curiae, seeking reversal.

William B. Harvey and Michael B. Rosen, Boston, Mass., filed brief for Boston University, as amicus curiae, seeking reversal.

Michael H. Salsbury, David E. Zerhusen, and Herbert F. Janick III (Jenner & Block), Washington, D.C., filed brief for Members of Congress, as amici curiae, seeking affirmance.

S. Beville May and Alison J. Bell (Choate, Hall & Stewart), Boston, Mass., field brief for Women's Bar Association of Massachusetts, Minnesota Women Lawyers, Inc., Women Lawyers Association of Michigan, and Colorado Women's Bar Association, as amici curiae, seeking affirmance.

Laurie E. Foster and Ellen M. Saideman (Lord, Day & Lord), New York, N.Y., filed brief for Working Women's Institute and 11 other organizations, as amici curiae, seeking affirmance.

Stephen N. Shulman, Lynda S. Mounts, and Sally J. Schornstheimer, Washington, D.C. (Rosemary C. Byrne, Jeanne P. Bolger, Barbara A. Solomon, and Cadwalader, Wickersham & Taft, New York, N.Y., of counsel), filed brief for Women's Bar Association of the State of New York, as amicus curiae, seeking affirmance.

Linda R. Singer, Gail E. Ross, and Joanne L. Hustead (Goldfarb & Singer), Washington, D.C., Anne E. Simon and Nadine Taub, New York, N.Y., Judith Levin (Rabinowitz, Boundin, Standard, Krinsky & Lieberman, P.C.), New York, N.Y., and Barry H. Gottfried (Fisher, Wayland, Cooper & Leader), Washington, D.C., filed brief for Women's Legal Defense Fund and 18 other organizations, as amici curiae, seeking affirmance.

Marsha F. Berzon, San Francisco, Calif., Debra F. Katz, Washington, D.C., Joy L. Koletsky, Washington, D.C., and Laurence Gold, Washington, D.C. (Winn Newman, Washington, D.C., and Sarah E. Burns, Washington, D.C., of counsel), filed brief for AFL-CIO and three other organizations, as amici curiae, seeking affirmance.

W. Cary Edwards, Attorney General of New Jersey, James J. Ciancia, Assistant Attorney General, Susan L. Reisner and Lynn B. Norcia, Deputy Attorneys General, attorneys general of seven other states, and general counsel of Pennsylvania Human Relations Commission, filed brief for New Jersey, seven other states, and Pennsylvania Human Relations Commission, as amici curiae, seeking affirmance.

Before BURGER, Chief Justice, and BRENNAN, WHITE, MARSHALL, BLACKMUN, POWELL, REHNQUIST, STEVENS, and O'CONNOR, Justices.

Full Text of Opinion

JUSTICE REHNQUIST delivered the opinion of the Court.

This case presents important questions concerning claims of workplace "sexual harassment" brought under Title VII of the Civil Rights Act of 1964, 78 Stat. 253, as amended, 42 U.S.C. §2000e et seq.

I

In 1974, respondent Mechelle Vinson met Sidney Taylor, a vice president of what is now petitioner Meritor Savings Bank (the bank) and manager of one of its branch offices. When respondent asked whether she might obtain employment at the bank, Taylor gave her an application, which she completed and returned the next day; later that same day Taylor called her to say that she had been hired. With Taylor as her supervisor, respondent started as a teller-trainee, and thereafter was promoted to teller, head teller, and assistant branch manager. She worked at the same branch for four years, and it is undisputed that her advancement there was based on merit alone. In September 1978, respondent notified Taylor that she was taking sick leave for an indefinite period. On November 1, 1978, the bank discharged her for excessive use of that leave.

Respondent brought this action against Taylor and the bank, claiming that during her four years at the bank she had "constantly been subjected to sexual harassment" by Taylor in violation of Title VII. She sought injunctive relief, compensatory and punitive damages against Taylor and the bank, and attorney's fees.

At the 11-day bench trial, the parties presented conflicting testimony about Taylor's behavior during respondent's employment.* Respondent

---

* Like the Court of Appeals, this Court was not provided a complete transcript of the trial. We therefore rely largely on the District Court's opinion for the summary of the relevant testimony.

testified that during her probationary period as a teller-trainee, Taylor treated her in a fatherly way and made no sexual advances. Shortly thereafter, however, he invited her out to dinner and, during the course of the meal, suggested that they go to a motel to have sexual relations. At first she refused, but out of what she described as fear of losing her job she eventually agreed. According to respondent, Taylor thereafter made repeated demands upon her for sexual favors, usually at the branch, both during and after business hours; she estimated that over the next several years she had intercourse with him some 40 or 50 times. In addition, respondent testified that Taylor fondled her in front of other employees, followed her into the women's restroom when she went there alone, exposed himself to her, and even forcibly raped her on several occasions. These activities ceased after 1977, respondent stated, when she started going with a steady boyfriend.

Respondent also testified that Taylor touched and fondled other women employees of the bank, and she attempted to call witnesses to support this charge. But while some supporting testimony apparently was admitted without objection, the District Court did not allow her "to present wholesale evidence of a pattern and practice relating to sexual advances to other female employees in her case in chief, but advised her that she might well be able to present such evidence in rebuttal to the defendants' cases." Vinson v. Taylor, 22 EPD ¶30708, pp. 14688-14689, 23 FEP Cases 37, 38-39, n. 1 (D DC 1980). Respondent did not offer such evidence in rebuttal. Finally, respondent testified that because she was afraid of Taylor she never reported his harassment to any of his supervisors and never attempted to use the bank's complaint procedure.

Taylor denied respondent's allegations of sexual activity, testifying that he never fondled her, never made suggestive remarks to her, never engaged in sexual intercourse with her and never asked her to do so. He contended instead that respondent made her accusations in response to a business-related dispute. The bank also denied respondent's allegations and asserted that any sexual harassment by Taylor was unknown to the bank and engaged in without its consent or approval.

The District Court denied relief, but did not resolve the conflicting testimony about the existence of a sexual relationship between respondent and Taylor. It found instead that

"If [respondent] and Taylor did engage in an intimate or sexual relationship during the time of [respondent's] employment with [the bank], that relationship was a voluntary one having nothing to do with her continued employment at [the bank] or her advancement or promotions at that institution." Id., at 42 (footnote omitted).

The court ultimately found that respondent "was not the victim of sexual harassment and was not the victim of sexual discrimination" while employed at the bank. Id., 43.

Although it concluded that respondent had not proved a violation of Title VII, the District Court nevertheless went on to address the bank's liability. After noting the bank's express policy against discrimination, and finding that neither respondent nor any other employee had ever lodged a complaint about sexual harassment by Taylor, the court ultimately concluded that "the bank was without notice and cannot be held liable for the alleged actions of Taylor." Id., at 42.

The Court of Appeals for the District of Columbia Circuit reversed. 243 U.S. App. D.C. 323, 753 F.2d 141, 36 FEP Cases 1423 (1985). Relying on its earlier holding in Bundy v. Jackson, 205 U.S. App. D.C. 444, 641 F.2d 934, 24 FEP Cases 1155 (1981), decided after the trial in this case, the court stated that a violation of Title VII may be predicated on either of two types of sexual harassment: harassment that involves the conditioning of concrete employment benefits on sexual favors, and harassment that, while not affecting economic benefits, creates a hostile or offensive working environment. The court drew additional support for this position from the Equal Employment Opportunity Commission's Guidelines on Discrimination Because of Sex, 29 CFR §1604.11(a) (1985), which set out these two types of sexual harassment claims. Believing that "Vinson's grievance was clearly of the [hostile environment] type," 243 U.S. App. D.C., at 327, 753 F.2d, at 145, 36 FEP Cases, at 1426, and that the District Court had not considered whether a violation of this type had occurred, the court concluded that a remand was necessary.

The court further concluded that the District Court's finding that any sexual relationship between respondent and Taylor "was a voluntary one" did not obviate the need for a remand. "[U]ncertain as to precisely what the [district] court meant" by this finding, the Court of Appeals held that if the evidence otherwise showed that "Taylor made Vinson's toleration of sexual harassment a condition of her employment," her voluntariness "had no materiality whatsoever." Id., at 328, 753 F.2d at 146, 36 FEP Cases, at 1427. The court then surmised that the District Court's finding of voluntariness might have been based on "the voluminous testimony regarding respondent's dress and personal fantasies," testimony that the Court of Appeals believed "had no place in this litigation." Id., at 328, n.36, 753 F.2d, at 146, n.36, 36 FEP Cases, at 1427.

As to the bank's liability, the Court of Appeals held that an employer is absolutely liable for sexual harassment practiced by supervisory personnel, whether or not the employer knew or should have known about the misconduct. The court relied chiefly on Title VII's definition of "employer" to include "any agent of such a person," 42 U.S.C. §2000e(b), as well as on the EEOC guidelines. The court held that a supervisor is an "agent" of his employer for Title VII purposes, even if he lacks authority to hire, fire, or promote, since "the mere existence — or even the appearance — of a significant degree of influence in vital job decisions gives any supervisor the opportunity to impose on employees." 243 U.S. App. D.C., at 332, 753 F.2d, at 150, 36 FEP Cases, at 1430.

In accordance with the foregoing, the Court of Appeals reversed the judgment of the District Court and remanded the case for further proceedings. A subsequent suggestion for rehearing en banc was denied, with three judges dissenting. 245 U.S. App. D.C. 1330, 760 F.2d 1330, 37 FEP Cases 1266 (1985). We granted certiorari, 474 U.S. —— (1985), and now affirm but for different reasons.

II

Title VII of the Civil Rights Act of 1964 makes it "an unlawful employment practice for an employer ... to discriminate against any individual with respect to his compensation, terms, conditions, or privileges of employment, because of such individual's race, color, religion, sex, or national origin." 42 U.S.C. §2000e-2(a)(1). The prohibition against discrimination based on sex was added to Title VII at the last minute on the floor of the House of Representatives. 110 Cong. Rec. 2577-2584 (1964). The principal argument in opposition to the amendment was that "sex discrimination" was sufficiently different from other types of discrimination that it ought to receive separate legislative treatment. See id., at 2577 (Statement of Rep. Celler quoting letter from United States Department of Labor); id., at 2584 (statement of Rep. Green). This argument was defeated, the bill quickly passed as amended, and we are left with little legislative history to guide us in interpreting the Act's prohibition against discrimination based on "sex."

Respondent argues, and the Court of Appeals held, that unwelcome sexual advances that create an offensive or hostile working environment violate Title VII. Without question, when a supervisor sexually harasses a subordinate because of the subordinate's sex, that supervisor "discriminate[s]" on the basis of sex. Petitioner apparently does not challenge this proposition. It contends instead that in prohibiting discrimination with respect to "compensation, terms, conditions, or privileges" of employment, Congress was concerned with what petitioner describes as "tangible loss" of "an economic character," not "purely psychological aspects of the workplace environment." Brief for Petitioner 30-31, 34. In support of this claim petitioner observes that in both the legislative history of Title VII and this Court's Title VII decisions, the focus has been on tangible, economic barriers erected by discrimination.

[1, 2] We reject petitioner's view. First, the language of Title VII is not limited to "economic" or "tangible" discrimination. The phrase "terms, conditions, or privileges of employment" evinces a congressional intent "to strike at the entire spectrum of disparate treatment of men and women' " in employment. Los Angeles Department of Water and Power v. Manhart, 435 U.S. 702, 707, n.13, 17 FEP Cases 395, 398 (1978), quoting Sprogis v. United Air Lines, Inc., 444 F.2d 1194, 1198, 3 FEP Cases 621, 623-624 (CA7 1971). Petitioner has pointed to nothing in the Act to suggest that Congress contemplated the limitation urged here.

Second, in 1980 the EEOC issued guidelines specifying that "sexual harassment," as there defined, is a form of sex discrimination prohibited by Title VII. As an "administrative interpretation of the Act by the enforcing agency," Griggs v. Duke Power Co., 401 U.S. 424, 433-434, 3 FEP Cases 175, 179 (1971), these guidelines, " 'while not controlling upon the courts by reason of their authority, do constitute a body of experience and informed judgment to which courts and litigants may properly resort for guidance,' " General Electric Co. v. Gilbert, 429 U.S. 125, 141-142, 13 FEP Cases 1657, 1664 (1976), quoting Skidmore v. Swift & Co., 323 U.S. 134, 140, 4 WH Cases 866 (1944). The EEOC guidelines fully support the view that harassment leading to noneconomic injury can violate Title VII.

In defining "sexual harassment," the guidelines first describe the kinds of workplace conduct that may be actionable under Title VII. These include "[u]nwelcome sexual advances, requests for sexual favors, and other verbal or physical conduct of a sexual nature." 29 CFR §1604.11(a) (1985). Relevant to the charges at issue in this case, the guidelines provide that such sexual misconduct constitutes prohibited "sexual harassment," whether or not it is directly linked to the grant or denial of an economic *quid pro quo*, where "such conduct has the purpose or effect of unreasonably interfering with an individual's work performance or offensive working environment." §1604.11(a)(3).

[3] In concluding that so-called "hostile environment" (i.e., non *quid pro quo*) harassment violates Title VII, the EEOC drew upon a substantial body of judicial decisions and EEOC precedent holding that Title VII affords employees the right to work in an environment free from discriminatory intimidation, ridicule, and insult. See generally 45 Fed. Reg. 74676 (1980). Rogers v. EEOC, 454 F.2d 234, 4 FEP Cases 92 (CA5 1971), cert. denied, 406 U.S. 957, 4 FEP Cases 771 (1972), was apparently the first case to recognize a cause of action based upon a discriminatory work environment. In Rogers, the Court of Appeals for the Fifth Circuit held that a Hispanic complainant could establish a Title VII violation by demonstrating that her employer created an offensive work environment for employees by giving discriminatory service to its Hispanic clientele. The court explained that an employee's protections under Title VII extend beyond the economic aspects of employment:

"[T]he phrase 'terms, conditions or privileges of employment' in [Title VII] is an expansive concept which sweeps within its protective ambit the practice of creating a working environment heavily charged with ethnic or racial discrimination .... One can readily envision working environments so heavily polluted with discrimination as to destroy completely the emotional and psychological stability of minority group workers ...." 454 F.2d. at 238, 4 FEP Cases, at 95.

Courts applied this principle to harassment based on race, e.g., Firefighters Institute for Racial Equality v. St. Louis, 549 F.2d 506, 514-515, 14 FEP Cases 1486, 1493 (CA8), cert. denied sub nom. Banta v. United States, 434 U.S. 819, 15 FEP Cases 1184 (1977); Gray v. Greyhound Lines, East, 178 U.S. App. D. C. 91, 98, 545 F.2d 169, 176, 13 FEP Cases 1401, 1406 (1976), religion, e.g., Compston v. Borden, Inc.,

424 F.Supp. 157, 17 FEP Cases 310 (SD Ohio 1976), and national origin, e.g., Cariddi v. Kansas City Chiefs Football Club, 568 F.2d 87, 88, 16 FEP Cases 462, 462-463 (CA8 1977). Nothing in Title VII suggests that a hostile environment based on discriminatory *sexual* harassment should not be likewise prohibited. The guidelines thus appropriately drew from, and were fully consistent with, the existing caselaw.

Since the guidelines were issued, courts have uniformly held, and we agree, that a plaintiff may establish a violation of Title VII by proving that discrimination based on sex has created a hostile or abusive work environment. As the Court of Appeals for the Eleventh Circuit wrote in Henson v. Dundee, 682 F.2d 897, 902, 29 FEP Cases 787, 791 (1982):

"Sexual harassment which creates a hostile or offensive environment for members of one sex is every bit the arbitrary barrier to sexual equality at the workplace that racial harassment is to racial equality. Surely, a requirement that a man or woman run a guantlet of sexual abuse in return for the privilege of being allowed to work and make a living can be as demeaning and disconcerting as the harshest of racial epithets."

Accord, Katz v. Dole, 709 F.2d 251, 254-255, 31 FEP Cases 1521, 1523 (CA4 1983); Bundy v. Jackson, 205 U. S. App. D. C. 444, 641 F.2d 934, 944, 24 FEP Cases 1155, 1160 (1981); Zabkowicz v. West Bend Co., 589 F.Supp. 780, 35 FEP Cases 610 (ED Wisc. 1984).

[4] Of course, as the courts in both Rogers and Henson recognized, not all workplace conduct that may be described as "harassment" affects a "term, condition, or privilege" of employment within the meaning of Title VII. See Rogers v. EEOC, supra, at 238, 4 FEP Cases, at 95 ("mere utterance of an ethnic or racial epithet which engenders offensive feelings in an employee" would not affect the conditions of employment to sufficiently significant degree to violate Title VII); Henson, supra, at 904, 29 FEP Cases, at 793 (quoting same). For sexual harassment to be actionable, it must be sufficiently severe or pervasive "to alter the conditions of [the victim's] employment and create an abusive working environment." Ibid. Respondent's allegations in this case — which include not only pervasive harassment but also criminal conduct of the most serious nature — are plainly sufficient to state a claim for "hostile environment" sexual harassment.

The question remains, however, whether the District Court's ultimate finding that respondent "was not the victim of sexual harassment," 22 EPD ¶30708, at 14692-14693, 23 FEP Cases, at 43, effectively disposed of respondent's claim. The Court of Appeals recognized, we think correctly, that this ultimate finding was likely based on one or both of two erroneous views of the law. First, the District Court apparently believed that a claim for sexual harassment will not lie absent an *economic* effect on the complainant's employment. See ibid. ("It is without question that sexual harassment of female employees in which they are asked or required to submit to sexual demands as a *condition to obtain employment or to maintain employment or to obtain promotions* falls within protection of Title VII.") (emphasis added). Since it appears that the District Court made its findings without ever considering the "hostile environment" theory of sexual harassment, the Court of Appeals' decision to remand was correct.

[5] Second, the District Court's conclusion that no actionable harassment occurred might have rested on its earlier "finding" that "[i]f [respondent] and Taylor did engage in an intimate or sexual relationship ..., that relationship was a voluntary one." Id., at 14692, 23 FEP Cases, at 42. But the fact that sex-related conduct was "voluntary," in the sense that the complainant was not forced to participate against her will, is not a defense to a sexual harassment suit brought under Title VII. The gravamen of any sexual harassment claim is that the alleged sexual advances were "unwelcome." 29 CFR §1604.11(a) (1985). While the question whether particular conduct was indeed unwelcome presents difficult problems of proof and turns largely on credibility determination committed to the trier of fact, the District Court in this case erroneously focused on the "voluntariness" of respondent's participation in the claimed sexual episodes. The correct inquiry is whether respondent by her conduct indicated that the alleged sexual advances were unwelcome, not whether her actual participation in sexual intercourse was voluntary.

[6] Petitioner contends that even if this case must be remanded to the District Court, the Court of Appeals erred in one of the terms of its remand. Specifically, the Court of Appeals stated that testimony about respondent's "dress and personal fantasies," 243 U.S.App.D.C. at 328, n. 36, 753 F.2d, at 146, n.36, 36 FEP Cases, at 1427, which the District Court apparently admitted into evidence, "had no place in this litigation." Ibid. The apparent ground for this conclusion was that respondent's voluntariness *vel non* in submitting to Taylor's advances was

immaterial to her sexual harassment claim. While "voluntariness" in the sense of consent is not a defense to such a claim, it does not follow that a complainant's sexually provocative speech or dress is irrelevant as a matter of law in determining whether he or she found particular sexual advances unwelcome. To the contrary, such evidence is obviously relevant. The EEOC guidelines emphasize that the trier of fact must determine the existence of sexual harassment in light of "the record as a whole" and "the totality of circumstances, such as the nature of the sexual advances and the context in which the alleged incidents occurred." 29 CFR §1604.11(b) (1985). Respondent's claim that any marginal relevance of the evidence in question was outweighed by the potential for unfair prejudice is the sort of argument properly addressed to the District Court. In this case the District Court concluded that the evidence should be admitted, and the Court of Appeals' contrary conclusion was based upon the erroneous, categorical view that testimony about provocative dress and publicly expressed sexual fantasies "had no place in this litigation." 243 U. S. App. D. C., at 328, n. 36, 753 F.2d, at 146, n. 36, 36 FEP Cases, at 1427. While the District Court must carefully weigh the applicable considerations in deciding whether to admit evidence of this kind, there is no *per se* rule against its admissibility.

III

Although the District Court concluded that respondent had not proved a violation of Title VII, it nevertheless went on to consider the question of the bank's liability. Finding that "the bank was without notice" of Taylor's alleged conduct, and that notice to Taylor was not the equivalent of notice to the bank, the court concluded that the bank therefore could not be held liable for Taylor's alleged actions. The Court of Appeals took the opposite view, holding that an employer is strictly liable for a hostile environment created by a supervisor's sexual advances, even though the employer neither knew nor reasonably could have known of the alleged misconduct. The court held that a supervisor, whether or not he possesses the authority to hire, fire, or promote, is necessarily an "agent" of his employer for all Title VII purposes, since "even the appearance" of such authority may enable him to impose himself on his subordinates.

The parties and *amici* suggest several different standards for employer liability. Respondent, not surprisingly, defends the position of the Court of Appeals. Noting that Title VII's definition of "employer" includes any "agent' of the employer, she also argues that "so long as the circumstance is work-related, the supervisor is the employer and the employer is the supervisor." Brief for Respondent 27. Notice to Taylor that the advances were unwelcome, therefore, was notice to the bank.

Petitioner argues that respondent's failure to use its established grievance procedure, or to otherwise put it on notice of the alleged misconduct, insulates petitioner from liability for Taylor's wrongdoing. A contrary rule would be unfair, petitioner argues, since in a hostile environment harassment case the employer often will have no reason to know about, or opportunity to cure, the alleged wrongdoing.

The EEOC, in its brief as *amicus curiae*, contends that courts formulating employer liability rules should draw from traditional agency principles. Examination of those principles has led the EEOC to the view that where a supervisor exercises the authority actually delegated to him by his employer, by making or threatening to make decisions affecting the employment status of his surbordinates, such actions are properly imputed to the employer whose delegation of authority empowered the supervisor to undertake them. Brief for United States and Equal Employment Opportunity Commission as *Amicus Curiae* 22. Thus, the courts have consistently held employers liable for the discriminatory discharges of employees by supervisory personnel, whether or not the employer knew, should have known, or approved of the supervisor's actions. E.g., Anderson v. Methodist Evangelical Hospital, Inc., 464 F.2d 723, 725, 4 FEP Cases 987, 988 (CA6 1972).

The EEOC suggests that when a sexual harassment claim rests exclusively on a "hostile environment" theory, however, the usual basis for a finding of agency will often disappear. In that case, the EEOC believes, agency principles led to

"a rule that asks whether a victim of sexual harassment had reasonably available an avenue of complaint regarding such harassment, and, if available and utilized, whether that procedure was reasonably responsive to the employee's complaint. If the employer has an expressed policy against sexual harassment and has implemented a procedure specifically designed to resolve sexual harassment claims, and if the victim does not take advantage of that procedure, the employer should be shielded from liability absent actual knowledge of the sexually hostile environment (obtained, e.g., by the filing of a charge with the EEOC or a comparable state agency). In all other cases, the employer will be liable if it has actual knowledge of the harassment or if, considering all the facts of the case, the victim in question had no reasonably available avenue for making his or her complaint known to appropriate management officials." Brief for United States and Equal Opportunity Employment Commission as *Amici Curiae*, 26.

As respondent points out, this suggested rule is in some tension with the EEOC guidelines, which hold an employer liable for the acts of its agents without regard to notice. 29 CFR §1604.11(c) (1985). The guidelines do require, however, an "examin[ation of] the circumstances of the particular employment relationship and the job [f]unctions performed by the individual in determining whether an individual acts in either a supervisory or agency capacity." Ibid.

This debate over the appropriate standard for employer liability has a rather abstract quality about it given the state of the record in this case. We do not know at this stage whether Taylor made any sexual advances toward respondent at all, let alone whether those advances were unwelcome, whether they were sufficiently pervasive to constitute a condition of employment, or whether they were "so pervasive and so long continuing ... that the employer must have become conscious of [them]," Taylor v. Jones, 653 F.2d 1193, 1197-1199, 28 FEP Cases 1024, 1027 (CA8 1981) (holding employer liable for racially hostile working environment based on constructive knowledge).

[7, 8] We therefore decline the parties' invitation to issue a definitive rule on employer liability, but we do agree with the EEOC that Congress wanted courts to look to agency principles for guidance in this area. While such common-law principles may not be transferable in all their particulars to Title VII, Congress' decision to define "employer" to include any "agent" of an employer, 42 U.S.C. §2000e(b), surely evinces an intent to place some limits on the acts of employees for which employers under Title VII are to be held responsible. For this reason, we hold that the Court of Appeals erred in concluding that employers are always automatically liable for sexual harassment by their supervisors. See generally Restatement (Second) of Agency §§219-237 (1958). For the same reason, absence of notice to an employer does not necessarily insulate that employer from liability. Ibid.

[9] Finally, we reject petitioner's view that the mere existence of a grievance procedure and a policy against discrimination, coupled with

respondent's failure to invoke that procedure, must insulate petitioner from liability. While those facts are plainly relevant, the situation before us demonstrates why they are not necessarily dispositive. Petitioner's general nondiscriminaton policy did not address sexual harassment in particular, and thus did not alert employees to their employer's interest in correcting that form of discrimination. App. 25. Moreover, the bank's grievance procedure apparently required an employee to complain first to her supervisor, in this case Taylor. Since Taylor was the alleged perpetrator, it is not altogether surprising that respondent failed to invoke the procedure and report her grievance to him. Petitioner's contention that respondent's failure should insulate it from liabilty might be substantially stronger if its procedures were better calculated to encourage victims of harassment to come forward.

IV

In sum, we hold that a claim of "hostile environment" sex discrimination is actionable under Title VII, that the District Court's findings were insufficient to dispose of respondent's hostile environment claim, and that the District Court did not err in admitting testimony about respondent's sexually provocative speech and dress. As to employer liability, we conclude that the Court of Appeals was wrong to entirely disregard agency principles and impose absolute liability on employers for the acts of their supervisors, regardless of the circumstances of a particular case.

Accordingly, the judgment of the Court of Appeals reversing the judgment of the District Court is affirmed, and the case is remanded for further proceedings consistent with this opinion.

It is so ordered.

Concurring Opinions

JUSTICE STEVENS, concurring.

Because I do not see any inconsistency between the two opinions, and because I believe the question of statutory construction that JUSTICE MARSHALL has answered is fairly presented by the record, I join both the Court's opinion and JUSTICE MARSHALL's opinion.

JUSTICE MARSHALL, with whom JUSTICE BRENNAN, JUSTICE BLACKMUN, and JUSTICE STEVENS join, concurring in the judgment.

I fully agree with the Court's conclusion that workplace sexual harassment is illegal, and violates Title VII. Part III of the Court's opinion, however, leaves open the circumstances in which an employer is responsible under Title VII for such conduct. Because I believe that question to be properly before us, I write separately.

The issue the Court declines to resolve is addressed in the EEOC Guidelines on Discrimination Because of Sex, which are entitled to great deference. See Griggs v. Duke Power Co., 401 U.S. 424, 433-434, 3 FEP Cases 175, 179 (1971) (EEOC Guidelines on Employment Testing Procedures of 1966); see also ante, at 6. The Guidelines explain:

"Applying general Title VII principles, an employer . . . is responsible for its acts and those of its agents and supervisory employees with respect to sexual harassment regardless of whether the specific acts complained of were authorized or even forbidden by the employer and regardless of whether the employer knew or should have known of their occurrence. The Commission will examine the circumstances of the particular employment relationship and the job functions performed by the individual in determining whether an individual acts in either a supervisory or agency capacity.

"With respect to conduct between fellow employees, an employer is responsible for acts of sexual harassment in the workplace where the employer (or its agents or supervisory employees) knows or should have known of the conduct, unless it can be shown that it took immediate and appropriate corrective action." 29 CFR §§1604.11(c), (d) (1985)

The Commission, in issuing the Guidelines, explained that its rule was "in keeping with the general standard of employer liability with respect to agents and supervisory employees. . . . [T]he Commission and the courts have held for years that an employer is liable if a supervisor or an agent violates the Title VII, regardless of knowledge or any other mitigating factor." 45 Fed. Reg. 74676 (1980). I would adopt the standard set out by the Commission.

An employer can act only through individual supervisors and employees; discrimination is rarely carried out pursuant to a formal vote of a corporation's board of directors. Although an employer may sometimes adopt company-wide discriminatory policies violative of Title VII, acts that may constitute Title VII violations are generally effected through the actions of individuals, and often an individual may take such a step even in defiance of company policy. Nonetheless, Title VII remedies, such as reinstatement and backpay, generally run against the employer as an entity.[1] The question thus arises as to the circumstances under which an employer will be held liable under Title VII for the acts of its employees.

The answer supplied by general Title VII law, like that supplied by federal labor law, is that the act of a supervisory employee or agent is imputed to the employer.[2] Thus, for example, when a supervisor discriminatorily fires or refuses to promote a black employee, that act is, without more, considered the act of the employer. The courts do not stop to consider whether the employer otherwise had "notice" of the action, or even whether the supervisor had actual authority to act as he did. E.g., Flowers v. Crouch-Walker Corp., 552 F.2d 1277, 1282, 14 FEP Cases 1265, 1268 (CA7, 1977); Young v. Southwestern Savings and Loan Assn., 509 F.2d 140, 10 FEP Cases 522 (CA5 1975); Anderson v. Methodist Evangelical Hospital, Inc., 464 F.2d 723, 4 FEP Cases 987 (CA6 1972). Following that approach, every Court of Appeals that has considered the issue has held that sexual harassment by supervisory personnel is automatically imputed to the employer when the harassment results in tangible job detriment to the subordinate employee. See Horn v. Duke Homes, Inc., Div. of Windsor Mobile Homes, 755 F.2d 599, 604-606, 37 FEP Cases 228, 231-233 (CA7 1985); Vinson v. Taylor, 243 U.S. App. D.C. 323, 329-334, 753 F.2d 141, 147-152, 36 FEP Cases 1423, 1427-1431 (1985); Craig v. Y&Y Snacks, Inc., 721 F.2d 77, 80-81, 33 FEP Cases 187, 189-190 (CA3 1983); Katz v. Dole, 709 F.2d 251, 255, n.6, 31 FEP Cases 1521, 1524 (CA4 1983); Henson v. City of Dundee, 682 F.2d 897, 910, 29 FEP Cases 787, 798 (CA11 1982); Miller v. Bank of America, 600 F.2d 211, 213, 20 FEP Cases 462, 463-464 (CA9 1979).

The brief filed by the Solicitor General on behalf of the EEOC in this case suggests that a different rule should apply when a supervisor's harassment "merely" results in a discriminatory work environment. The Solicitor General concedes that sexual harassment that affects tangible job benefits is an exercise of authority delegated to the supervisor by the employer, and thus gives rise to employer liability. But, departing from the EEOC Guidelines, he argues that the case of a supervisor merely creating a discriminatory work environment is different because the supervisor "is not exercising, or threatening to exercise, actual or apparent authority to make personnel decisions affecting the victim." Brief for United States and EEOC as Amici Curiae 24. In the latter situation, he concludes, some further notice requirement should therefore be necessary.

The Solicitor General's position is untenable. A supervisor's responsibilities do not begin and end with the power to hire, fire, and discipline employees, or with the power to recommend such actions. Rather, a supervisor is charged with the day-to-day supervision of the work environment and with ensuring a safe, productive, workplace. There is no reason why abuse of the latter authority should have different consequences than abuse of the former. In both cases it is the authority vested in the supervisor by the employer that enables him to commit the wrong: it is precisely because the supervisor is understood to be clothed with the employer's authority that he is able to impose unwelcome sexual conduct on subordinates. There is therefore no justification for a special rule, to be applied only in "hostile environment" cases, that sexual harassment does not create employer liability until the employee suffering the discrimination notifies other supervisors. No such requirement appears in the statute, and no such requirement can coherently be drawn from the law of agency.

Agency principles and the goals of Title VII law make appropriate some limitation on the liability of employers for the acts of supervisors. Where, for example, a supervisor has no authority over an employee, because the two work in wholly different parts of the employer's business, it may be improper to find strict employer liability. See 29 CFR §1604.11(c) (1985). Those considerations, however, do not justify the creation of a special "notice" in hostile environment cases.

Further, nothing would be gained by crafting such a rule. In the "pure"

---

[1] The remedial provisions of Title VII were largely modeled on those of the National Labor Relations Act (NLRA). See Albemarle Paper Co. v. Moody, 422 U.S. 405, 419, and n. 11, 10 FEP Cases 1181, 1188 (1975); see also Franks v. Bowman Transportation Co. 424 U.S. 747, 768-770, 12 FEP Cases 549, 557-558 (1976).

[2] For NLRA cases, see, e.g., Graves Trucking, Inc. v. NLRB, 692 F.2d 470, 111 LRRM 2862 (CA7 1982); NLRB v. Kaiser Agricultural Chemical, Division of Kaiser Aluminum & Chemical Corp., 473 F.2d 374, 384, 82 LRRM 2455 (CA5 1973); Amalgamated Clothing Workers of America v. NLRB, 124 U.S. App. D.C. 365, 377, 365 F.2d 898, 909, 62 LRRM 2431 (1966).

hostile environment case, where an employee files an EEOC complaint alleging sexual harassment in the workplace, the employee seeks not money damages but injunctive relief. See Bundy v. Jackson, 205 U.S. App. D.C. 444, 446, 641 F.2d 934, 946, n.12, 24 FEP Cases 1155, 1162 (1981). Under Title VII, the EEOC must notify an employer of charges made against it within 10 days after receipt of the complaint. 42 U.S.C. §2000e-5(b). If the charges appear to be based on "reasonable cause," the FEOC must attempt to eliminate the offending practice through "informal methods of conference, conciliation, and persuasion." Ibid. An employer whose internal procedures assertedly would have redressed the discrimination can avoid injunctive relief by employing these procedures after receiving notice of the complaint or during the conciliation period. Cf. Brief for United States and EEOC as *Amici Curiae* 26. Where a complainant, on the other hand, seeks backpay on the theory that a hostile work environment effected a constructive termination, the existence of an internal complaint procedure may be a factor in determining not the employer's liability but the remedies available against it. Where a complainant without good reason bypassed an internal complaint procedure she knew to be effective, a court may be reluctant to find constructive termination and thus to award reinstatement or backpay.

I therefore reject the Solicitor General's position. I would apply in this case the same rules we apply in all other Title VII cases, and hold that sexual harassment by a supervisor of an employee under his supervision, leading to a discriminatory work environment, should be imputed to the employer for Title VII purposes regardless of whether the employee gave "notice" of the offense.

Appendix B

Corporate Policies

Rainier National Bank

Steelcase, Inc.

RAINIER NATIONAL BANK:

POLICY ON RECRUITING AND SELECTING EMPLOYEES

Rainier's recruiting and selection procedures provide a framework for filling positions with qualified candidates.

Rainier is an equal opportunity employer that selects qualified internal and external applicants to fill positions without regard to age, sex, marital status, race, religion, color, national origin, veteran status or sensory, mental or physical handicaps.

EMPLOYMENT OF RELATIVES

Rainier welcomes the opportunity to hire qualified relatives and friends of present employees. Problems may arise, however, when a new or existing employee works in an area in proximity to his or her relative or a person to whom he or she is closely attached. These problems relate to the strong emotional bonds which may exist between relatives or close friends. When such emotional bonds exist, the reality or appearance of improper influence or favor presents a problem. When such a work problem exists, Rainier follows these guidelines:

- Any direct supervisor-subordinate relationship between relatives is prohibited.

- Any indirect supervisor-subordinate relationship between relatives is prohibited except with the express approval of the division head.

- Any job assignment affecting relatives which may jeopardize Rainier's security is prohibited. An example of this situation is where an auditor is assigned to audit a branch where a relative works.

- Any working relationship between relatives which appears to present a potential or actual morale problem for the relatives or for other employees must be approved by the division head.

If any of these situations occur, the employees involved will be asked to resolve the problem by a certain date. If the employees are unable to reach a resolution, the options available to the company include:

- Transfer of one or both employees;
- Reorganization; or
- Request for resignation.

Although the above guidelines mention only relatives, similar actions may be required to separate close friends.

Reprinted by permission of Rainier National Bank

STEELCASE, INC.

EMPLOYEE SPONSORSHIP POLICY FOR PRODUCTION EMPLOYEES

Full-Time Production Hiring

PURPOSE

To maximize the overall effectiveness of the manufacturing process at Steelcase by giving proper consideration to the ability, potential and compatibility of people being hired into full-time production jobs. To satisfy company, legal, employee and community interests when hiring new employees to full-time production jobs.

POLICY

A pool of 300 to 500 prospective full-time production employees will be established, maintained and utilized to provide a ready source of potential full-time production employees. This pool will be the sole source of our new full-time production hires. All hiring procedures will comply with the company Equal Employment Opportunity policy (#201).

Management accepts only as many applicants as have a reasonable chance for employment in the foreseeable future.

Hiring from the pool of applicants is based on ability, potential and the needs of the hiring plant. Employee seniority is used only to sponsor an applicant for consideration for the pool.

A retiree who did not use his or her sponsorship prior to retiring may sponsor a son or daughter only. To do so, the retiree should contact the supervisor of hourly/skilled trades employment. The retiree's sponsored son or daughter will be considered for the pool in line with the number of years seniority he or she had with Steelcase.

If the spouse of a Steelcase employee is submitted for sponsorship to the pool, an agreement must be reached that if employed both spouses cannot work in the same plant nor attempt to transfer to that plant once employed.

A sponsored applicant may be perceived as not being a fit for Steelcase based on information gathered during the screening process. To make sure this sponsored applicant is given every consideration his or her file will be reviewed by a committee made up of representatives as follows:

- A representative from employment
- A plant manager
- A superintendent
- A representative from employee relations

A former employee of Steelcase being considered for rehire will also be reviewed by this committee. To be considered, a former employee must apply for rehire through one of the designated sources.

This committee will meet as needed to make the final decision regarding the disposition of the sponsored applicant. The sponsored applicant will be sent a letter telling him or her whether he or she is a part of the full-time production hiring pool. If the applicant is turned down, the sponsoring employee's sponsorship eligibility will be treated as if he or she had elected not to sponsor an applicant.

If, after a sponsored applicant becomes a part of the hiring pool, that applicant withdraws himself or herself from the hiring pool the sponsoring employee's sponsorship eligibility will be treated as if he or she had elected not to sponsor an applicant.

Eligibility

To be considered for entry into the pool, all prospective employees must:

- Be 18 years of age (or 17 years of age with a high school diploma) and physically and mentally capable of doing the assigned work or learning it within a reasonable period of time.
- Have one year's work experience in any type of work or at least one summer (3 months) at Steelcase.
- Represent the only sponsorship from his or her family household (i.e., if husband and wife work for Steelcase, they can jointly sponsor only one person).

Selection of the Pool

The production hiring pool will be established through the following sources:

- Employee sponsorship. Each active full-time employee with 15 years or more seniority and in good standing can sponsor one applicant for pool consideration. The applicant must meet all of the eligibility requirements listed above. An eligible employee may elect not to sponsor anyone when his or her opportunity arises. If, in the future, he or she chooses to sponsor someone, the employee can do so when additional people are required for the pool. The application will be considered in line with the sponsor's seniority.

If the need for applicants exceeds the numbers available through sponsorship by employees with 15 years or more seniority, employees with fewer than 15 years seniority will become eligible to sponsor applicants, again, on a seniority basis. The process will continue down the seniority list until all active full-time employees have had an opportunity to sponsor an applicant. No employees will be able to sponsor a second applicant, regardless of their seniority, until all active full-time employees have had an opportunity to sponsor an applicant.

- Other sources. Management prerogative on special needs cases and hardship cases and recommendations from selected community agencies will be used to fill the pool in order to meet affirmative action requirements and fulfill community and other unusual special needs commitments.

DISCUSSION

Past practice has been to fill approximately 80% of the open positions through employee sponsorship and approximately 20% from other sources.

Because of the number of people on the seniority roles compared to the number of new employees required, each employee will probably have only one opportunity during his or her employment at Steelcase to sponsor an individual for the production hiring pool.

RESPONSIBILITIES

- *Manufacturing management* estimates the number of additional full-time production employees needed each year.
- A *committee of human resources personnel* screen the applicants for the pool.
- *Employment* notifies current employees when they become eligible to sponsor an applicant to the pool and assigns prospective employees from the pool to a plant requiring additional employees.

- *Manufacturing management and employee relations within a hiring plant* assign new employees to a division and department.
- The *supervisor of hourly/skilled trades employment* processes sponsorships by retired full-time employees who did not use their sponsorship before retiring.
- A *committee* consisting of the *plant manager, superintendent,* and representatives from *employment* and *employee relations* reviews and decides cases in which the sponsored applicant is a former Steelcase employee, or in which questions arise as to the sponsored applicant's suitability for Steelcase employment.

Reprinted by permission of Steelcase, Inc.

Appendix C

Nepotism Regulations For Federal Employees

(5 CFR Ch. 1, Sections. 310.101 = 310.202, 1-1-87 Edition)

Subpart A = Restrictions on the Employment of Relatives

Section 310.101 Coverage.
This subpart applies to appointment, employment, promotion, or advancement in (a) the competitive service; and (b) the excepted service in the executive branch.

Section 310.102 Definitions.
In this subpart:
(a) "Relative" means father, mother, son, daughter, brother, sister, uncle, aunt, first cousin, nephew, niece, husband, wife, father-in-law, mother-in-law, son-in-law, daughter-in-law, brother-in-law, sister-in-law, stepfather, stepmother, stepson, stepdaughter, stepbrother, stepsister, half brother, or half sister.
(b) "Public official" means an officer, a member of the uniformed services, an employee, and any other individual, in whom is vested the authority by law, rule, or regulation, or to whom the authority has been delegated, to appoint, employ, promote, or advance individuals, or to recommend individuals for appointment, employment, promotion, or advancement.
(c) "Chain of Command" is the line of supervisory personnel that runs from a public official to the head of his agency.

Section 310.103 Restrictions.
(a) A public official shall not advocate one of his relatives for appointment, employment, promotion, or advancement to a position in

his agency or in an agency over which he exercises jurisdiction or control.

(b) A public official shall not appoint, employ, promote, or advance to a position in his agency or in an agency over which he exercises jurisdiction or control:

(1) One of his relatives; or

(2) The relative of a public official of his agency, or of a public official who exercises jurisdiction or control over his agency, if the public official has advocated the appointment, employment, promotion, or advancement of that relative.

(c) For the purpose of this section, a public official who recommends a relative, or refers a relative for consideration by a public official standing lower in the chain of command, for appointment, employment, promotion, or advancement is deemed to have advocated the appointment, employment, promotion or advancement of the relative.

(d) This section does not prohibit the appointment in the competitive service of a preference eligible if (1) his name is within reach for selection from an appropriate certificate of eligibles and (2) an alternative selection cannot be made from the certificate without passing over the preference eligible and selecting an individual who is not a preference eligible.

Subpart B = Emergency Exceptions

Section 310.201 Coverage.

This subpart applies to an office, agency, or other establishment in the executive, legislative or judicial branch of the Federal Government, and in the government of the District of Columbia.

(5 U.S.C. 3110)

Section 310.202 Exceptions.

When necessary to meet urgent needs resulting from an emergency posing an immediate threat to life or property, or a national emergency as defined in the Federal Personnel Manual, a public official may employ relatives to meet those needs without regard to the restrictions in section 3110 of title 5, United States Code, and this part. Appointments under these conditions are temporary not to exceed 1 month, but may be extended for a second month if the emergency need still exists.

(5 U.S.C. 1104; Pub. L. 95-454, sec. 3 (5))

[44 FR 54692, Sept. 21, 1979]

Anti-Nepotism Guidelines

By Joan G. Wexler
Associate Dean and Professor of Law
Brooklyn Law School
Brooklyn, N.Y.

Introduction

Traditionally, anti-nepotism rules were designed to prevent the hiring of incompetent relatives. With the entrance of women into the workforce in unprecedented numbers, corporate policies against nepotism are now being applied in situations not contemplated by their drafters — for example, when employees at the same workplace marry, a husband or wife seeks employment at the place where his or her spouse already works, or a married couple applies jointly for employment with the same employer. Although many anti-nepotism policies limit the employment of other relatives in addition to spouses, because of their potential discriminatory impact on women, it is no-spouse rules that are most frequently challenged in court. As a result, these rules should be re-evaluated by employers and fair and clear written standards should be established to govern this aspect of employment relations.

The following guidelines address legitimate employer concerns, but do not unduly hinder married couples in their employment choices. If an employer wishes to have a broader anti-nepotism policy that affects relatives or other relationships between employees, the guidelines can be easily adapted.

General Policy

Employers should neither deny nor grant employment benefits on the basis of a person's marital status or marital relationship. If an individual fulfills all objective job-related qualifications, marital status should not be a deterrent or an advantage to employment unless it is justified by a business or ethical necessity.

Employment of a Spouse or a Married Couple

1. Do not make any employment decision, including placement, hiring, salary, or promotion based on whether the person's spouse is employed by you or whether you are considering hiring that spouse.

2. For reasons of business necessity, you may refuse to place one spouse under the direct supervision of the other spouse. Indirect supervision of the other spouse, such as where one spouse is a department head and other supervisory personnel are between that position and the spouse's position, should not prevent the employment of either spouse.

3. Only compelling and overriding business reasons of safety, security, supervision, or morale constitute business necessity. Mere business convenience is insufficient. For example, if promotion, salary, disciplinary, or removal decisions concerning the supervised spouse can be made by another supervisor or by a supervisors' committee that does not include the spouse, no business necessity exists.

4. Keep in mind that business necessity is a limited exception to the general rule of non-discrimination. The burden will be on you, the employer, to show that such discrimination is justified. You should be able to demonstrate that the alleged hazards of the employment situation are greater for spouses than for other persons.

5. Employers of attorneys and others whose conduct is guided by professional codes of ethics should take such codes into account in making employment decisions. Because the ethical-defense exception is a limited one, you will have the burden of proving that a decision not to hire a spouse is based solely on such ethical codes and any interpretive decisions of them.

6. If you would have hired an applicant, but did not because of the existence of a business necessity or ethical necessity defense, you should inform the married couple of your decision and the reasons for it. Give them the option to choose which spouse should be employed.

Employment of People Who Marry After They are Hired

1. The marriage of current employees that results in one spouse working under the direct supervision of the other spouse may justify a change in their employment. In determining whether a business necessity to make such a change exists, give particular consideration to the length of time the supervisor-supervisee relationship existed

prior to the marriage and to the work performance of the individuals involved during that time.

2. If the marriage of current employees results in both spouses working in the same department or division, you should be able to demonstrate business necessity to justify any change in placement. To determine whether business necessity exists, give particular consideration to the past work performance and job levels of the individuals. Moreover, it is best to have a suitable trial period of employment (after the marriage) to determine whether any potential problems actually occur.

3. When an alternative placement is necessary, offer a transfer within the company to a position with a similar salary and promotional opportunity. Give the spouses the option as to which spouse should be transferred, unless a business necessity exists to do otherwise. Terminate an employee only when no other option exists and, again, give the spouses the option to choose which spouse must leave your employ.

* * *

Office Romance Guidance

By Nancy Woodhull
President, USA Today/Gannett New Media
Research & Development Division, Gannett Co., Inc.

Male-female relationships in the office should be managed like other close relationships. They are the same as a father-and-son team, or two male co-workers who have been friends since boyhood. All are alliances that could be perceived as affecting the power structure. Co-workers might fear that the formal and informal communication networks of the organization will be bypassed. The effect of the alliance must be managed well.

Here are some do's and don'ts for employers and employees in such situations:

DO:

1. *Have an open door policy.* Circulate among employees so you can hear their concerns. Open communication helps you to monitor situations that might affect the workplace.

2. *Discuss with the people in the relationship* what effect their alliance will have on the people for and with whom they work.

3. *Encourage the couple's co-workers* to have one-on-one conversations with you. You can use these talks to determine what bothers them about the alliance.

4. *Decide on a plan* that will give the couple, the employer, and the co-workers the result they want. In most cases, everyone probably wants to be part of a team where people are judged by the results they produce and not who they know.

DON'T:

1. *Ban such relationships.* With more women entering the workforce, more people will find their partners in life among partners in business.

2. *Ignore the relationship.* Instead, manage the effect of the relationship as you would manage the effects of anything else in the workplace.

3. *Allow the couple to isolate themselves.* Encourage them to continue individually to have strong interaction with others in the workplace.

4. *Separate the couple* by moving one member to a new job. Let the facts be the judge. If, by allowing them to work together, you cannot achieve the results everyone wants, it will be obvious that a new course of action is needed.

* * *

Appendix F

Model Corporate Policy On Sexual Harassment

Kaleel Jamison Associates

Reprinted by permission

SEXUAL HARASSMENT POLICY, PHILOSOPHY AND PROCEDURES

Section I - The Law

The primary basis for action against employers is Section 703 of Title VII of the 1964 Civil Rights Act (as amended), which prohibits discrimination on the basis of sex in employment and provides legal authority for the following guidelines:

Unwelcome sexual advances, requests for sexual favors, and other verbal or physical conduct of a sexual nature constitute sexual harassment when:

(1) submission to such conduct is made either explicitly or implicitly a term or condition of an individual's employment,

(2) submission to or rejection of such conduct by an individual is used as the basis for employment decisions affecting such individual, or

(3) such conduct has the purpose or effect of unreasonably interfering with an individual's work performance or creating an intimidating, hostile, or offensive working environment.

The guidelines impose absolute liability on employers for the acts of supervisors regardless of whether the conduct was known to, or authorized or forbidden by, the particular employer.

Similarly, under the guidelines an employer may be liable for acts in the workplace committed by non-employees if the employer knew, or should have known, of the conduct and failed to take appropriate corrective action.

In addition to establishing standards for imposing liability, the guidelines make employers responsible for developing programs to prevent sexual misconduct in the workplace.

Under the guidelines, an employer must also thoroughly investigate all complaints alleging sexual harassment and all instances potentially constituting harassment that come to the employer's attention through means other than formal complaints. Following an investigation, an employer is required to take immediate and appropriate corrective action to remedy any illegality detected and prevent its recurrence. Failure to do so constitutes a violation of Title VII as interpreted by the Equal Employment Opportunity Commission.

Section II - Why This Issue is Important to us at

  A. Mutual Respect, Self Respect, and Teamwork

      In the modern world women and men work together--and the numbers
      of women in the workplace are steadily increasing. Individuals
      do not leave their sexuality at home when they come to work. We
      do not want, nor expect, women and men in the organization to be
      separated by invisible walls. We do want policies and practices
      that are dedicated to eliminating reprehensible behavior and
      facilitating healthy working relationships.

      We want women and men to come to work in   as individuals
      assured that they will face neither discrimination or favoritism
      based on sex or any factor other than qualifications and performance.
      We encourage and hope to have warm, collegial, supportive relation-
      ships between employees of both genders at all levels. Where
      sexual harassment is an obstacle to such relationships we want
      it eliminated.

  B. Off the Premises

      We are neither able nor desirous of legislating morals. What
      "consenting adults" do off Company property, on their own time,
      is their own business--unless the conduct affects their per-
      formance at work or affects the work of others. When work
      performance suffers, sexual activity becomes company business.
      When the consequences of off-the-job relationships intrude into
      the workplace, i.e., job-related discrimination, favoritism, or
      disruption in the workplace, it becomes company business.

Section III - The Policy

It is   policy to maintain a discrimination-free work environment
for all employees. Part of maintaining a good working atmosphere includes
freedom from unwelcomed sexual advances as well as a workplace free of
harassment based on age, race, religion, physical ability, or national
origin. Therefore, it is important for all employees to know and understand that no form of harassment will be tolerated. The following describes
the Policy regarding Sexual Harassment:

  A. Not to tolerate sexual harassment as a form of behavior in the
      work environment.

  B. Affirmatively to dissuade such practices through communication,
      training and other appropriate methods to sensitize the population
      to sexual harassment issues.

C. To investigate all observed or reported instances, and take corrective action. Where a clear infringement of the rights of others and policy violations is determined, appropriately to discipline the offender, making discipline consistent with the offense. Appropriate discipline may range from counseling and reprimand; through pay reduction, change in classification or reassignment to another area; to discharge in cases of gross misconduct or repeated offenses.

D. To base all decisions pertaining to hiring, promotion, training, layoffs and other personnel practices on uniformly applied standards of ability, training, experience, past performance, and other job-related factors and to maintain such standards at a consistently high level for the healthy growth of the business in a highly competitive economy.

E. To provide processes for employees that experience or see a violation of the Sexual Harassment Policy which protect confidentiality, shield the individual from recrimination, and allow for corrective action to be instituted.

F. To inhibit in no way nor restrict the relationships of women and men employees within appropriate modes of behavior - but rather to welcome, encourage and support teamwork and mutual respect among all employees.

This policy prohibits discrimination for or against an employee on the basis of conduct not related to work performance, such as the taking or refusal to take a personnel action, including promotion of employees who submit to sexual advances or refusal to promote employees who resist or protest sexual overtures.

Any violation of this policy will receive prompt and appropriate action. Any employee or prospective employee who experiences harassment or intimidation should immediately contact their supervisor or the Employee Responsibility and Development function.

Section IV - Definitions

A. Sexual Attraction

Sexual attraction is a situation in which one person experiences exhilaration toward another, without the desire to diminish the other.

Attraction between individuals - whether one way or mutual - is a fact of life that cannot be stopped. Flirtation - signaling an attraction and seeking to advance a relationship - takes many courses. Sexual attraction can show itself along a wide range of experiences-- from a simple feeling of appreciation, to falling in love. At both ends of that range, sexual attraction can be a straightforward, natural exchange between two people. What characterizes sexual attraction is consent, and increased self-esteem on the part of both people. People who experience such attraction should pay particular attention to:

- appropriate public behavior
- the effect of their feelings on business decisions
- whether any resulting behavior or relationship is
  likely to be disruptive to the productivity of the
  organization.

B. Sexual Harassment

Sexual harassment is differentiated from attraction and flirtation
and can be generally defined as follows: Sexual Harassment is a
form of employee misconduct which is demeaning to another person
and undermines the integrity of the employment relationship.

All employees must be allowed to work in an environment free from
unsolicited and unwelcome sexual overtures. Sexual harassment is
unwelcome sexual attention which causes the recipient distress
and results in an inability on the part of the recipient to
function effectively in the performance of job requirements. It
is characterized by repetition and often by a component of abuse
of power. Sexual harassment does not refer to occasional com-
pliments. It refers to behavior which is not welcome, which is
personally offensive, which debilitates morale, and which therefore
interferes with the work effectiveness of its recipient. Sexual
harassment may occur between employees regardless of their
relationship, that is, it is not limited to supervisor-subordinate
relationships. Sexual harassment may include actions such as:

- sex-oriented verbal "kidding" or abuse
- subtle pressure for sexual activity
- physical contact such as patting, pinching or
  constant brushing against another's body
- demands for sexual favors, accompanied by implied
  or overt promises of preferential treatment or threats
  concerning an individual's employment status.

C. Unintentional Sexual Harassment

There is occasionally confusion about behavior that may originate
in sexual attraction and be intended to convey appreciation. In
fact, such behavior may be experienced by the recipient as sexual
harassment. The initiator may be feeling sexually attracted to
another person, but because of unequal rank, the recipient may be
under constraint and not let the initiator know that the attention
is unwanted. There is always the possibility that even simple
admiration expressed by the person of higher rank can cause the
other person unintended distress and a resultant impairment of
job performance. Whenever there is an inequality in rank, the
person of higher rank must be especially sensitive to the
possibility that admiration could be experienced as harassment.

B. Initiation Rites Could Lead to Sexual Harassment

Many work groups have special jokes and pranks that they
play on a new person joining the unit. These are often
ways of testing the person before they become fully included.
If the testing is done fairly to all new people it results in
individuals becoming a member of the unit. If the testing is
done only to specific individuals, it is harassment designed
to keep them out or to make it more difficult for the new
person to join. If the initiation is different for women
than it is for men, or if the normal initiation rites have
sexist aspects then it is sexual harassment.

Section V - Responsibilities

A. All Employees

All employees are responsible to assure that no sexual
harassment occurs in

B. Supervisors, Union Representatives and Managers

1. Supervisors, union representatives, and managers are
    accountable for prevention and correction of sexual
    harassment occurrences in their areas of responsibility.

2. Managers and supervisors at all levels are responsible
    for making sure that employees in their areas of
    responsibility are aware of this policy, for assuring
    that all personnel decisions in their areas are in
    accordance with this policy, for initiating corrective
    action when offenses are observed or reported, and for
    determining the corrective action when offenses merit
    such.

C. Employees who have experienced or seen a violation of
    Sexual Harassment Policy

Any employee who believes that she or he has been the
recipient of sexual harassment or who is aware of an
occurrence of sexual harassment has an obligation and
a duty to report the potential policy violation so that
corrective action may be taken, as appropriate. Such
individuals are also encouraged to seek corrective
action by:

    - Confronting the individual instigating the harassment.
    - Reporting such conduct immediately to their supervisors.

D. Employee Responsibility and Development Area:

1. The Employee Responsibility and Development area is responsible for providing the following regarding the Sexual Harassment Policy:

    a. Educating employees,
    b. Developing processes for conducting investigations of violation and for determing corrective action when violations merit such,
    c. Informing employees of their responsibility to report violations,
    d. Establishing the corrective action process,
    e. When warranted to counsel employees and to provide assistance in the addressing of a real or perceived violation of the Sexual Harassment Policy.

2. The Employee Responsibility and Development area will review the corrective action of all cases where sexual harassment has been determined.

3. The Employee Responsibility and Development area will keep records of Sexual Harassment Policy violations and investigations in cases where sexual harassment has been determined.

4. The Employee Responsibility and Development area will be available for consultation with supervisors, managers, union representatives, and other employees regarding the Sexual Harassment Policy.

Section VI - Procedure for Addressing Possible Sexual Harassment Policy Violations

A. Steps

Step 1: Possible Violation of Sexual Harassment Policy

The person who experienced, or saw, a violation
of the Sexual Harassment Policy (to be referred to
as: recipient) has a responsibility to tell the
individual who is believed to, or who did, violate
the sexual harassment policy to stop.

Step 2: Informing The Initiating Supervisor

The recipient informs her/his direct supervisor
(to be referred to as: initiating supervisor)
that a potential violation of the policy has
occurred.

This is the final step, if the person who is
believed to have violated the Sexual Harassment
Policy stops, and if the situation does not
warrant further corrective action.

Step 3: Initiating Supervisor's Role

If the person who is believed to have violated
the Sexual Harassment Policy does not stop, or
if the possible violation warrants further corrective
action, the initiating supervisor is to inform her/his
manager regarding the violation of policy.

Step 4: Initiating Supervisor's Role

The initiating supervisor is to report the alleged
violation to the supervisor of the possible violator
(to be referred to as: responsible supervisor) and
request that an investigation be undertaken.

Step 5: Responsible Supervisor's Role

a. If the person who is believed to have violated
the Sexual Harassment Policy is exempt:

The responsible supervisor is to investigate
the allegation, to determine whether a
violation occurred, and take corrective
action as necessary.

b. If the person who is believed to have violated
the Sexual Harassment Policy is non-exempt:

1. The responsible supervisor contacts Employee Responsibility and Development regarding the allegation for consultation and/or involvement.

2. The responsible supervisor contacts the union representative regarding the allegation.

3. The responsible supervisor holds a meeting with a union representative and the employee whose behavior is in question to investigate the potential policy violation.

4. The responsible supervisor determines if a violation occurred and takes corrective action as necessary.

Step 6: Feedback Loop

a. The responsible supervisor will send to the union, when a non-exempt employee is involved, a copy of a written statement documenting the process, findings and action taken.

b. The responsible supervisor is to inform the initiating supervisor regarding finds and action taken.

c. The initiating supervisor is to inform:

   (1) The recipient regarding findings and action taken.
   (2) Their manager regarding findings and action taken.

d. If corrective action has been taken by the responsible supervisor, appropriate written documentation is to be sent to the Employee Responsibility and Development area.

Note:

1. If the person who is believed to have violated the Sexual Harassment Policy is the recipient's supervisor, the recipient is to inform her or his next level supervisor that a potential violation of the Policy has occurred. That supervisor becomes the initiating/responsible supervisor and is to follow the steps accordingly.

2. It is the intent of this procedure to resolve any suspected violations at the lowest possible level with the fewest people involved.

3. At any time in the process the Employee Responsibility and Development area can be contacted by any of the employees involved, or the Employee Responsibility and Development area can initiate involvement at anytime.

4. In addition to the Employee Responsibility and Development area, any of the employees involved can contact line personnel areas for assistance.

5. It is the responsibility of supervisory, management personnel and union representatives to maintain the highest degree of confidentiality throughout the process.

B. Flow Chart

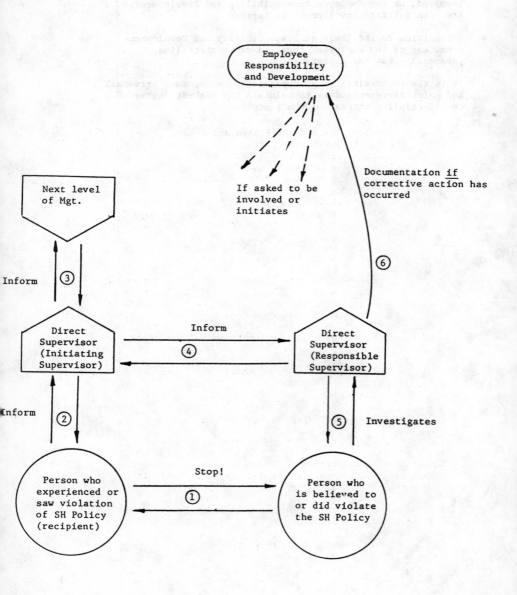

Section VII - Sexual Harassment Corrective Action Categories

A. Category I - Infractions: Most Serious

Incidents of sexual harassment which involved explicit or
implicit threats, or which state or imply that sexual
cooperation will have any effect on the individual's
employment assignment, compensation, advancement, career
development, or any other condition of employment, will
result in suspension and/or immediate discharge. Such
incidents include, but are not limited to:

- Statements or implications that an individual's
  "sexual cooperation" will have any effect on the
  individual's employment, assignment, compensation,
  advancement, career development, or any other
  condition of employment.
- Offensive, threatening or abrasive physical contact,
  e.g., patting, touching.
- Repeated flirtation, advances, propositions, and
  the repeated posting of sexually suggestive pictures
  or objects after previous corrective action has been
  instituted.

B. Category II - Infractions: Next Most Serious

Incidents of sexual harassment which do not involve explicit
or implicit threats and which do not state or imply that
sexual cooperation will have any effect on the individual's
employment, assignment, compensation, advancement, career
development, etc., will result in the violator receiving a
write-up or warning. Such incidents include, but are not
limited to:

. Explicit threatening or degrading verbal abuse of a
  suggestive or sexual nature,
. Persistent invitations,
. Sexually explicit or degrading jokes,
. Excessive comments about a person's body.

C. Category III - Infractions: Less Serious

Incidents in this category will result in the violator
receiving counseling or write-up. Such incidents include,
but are not limited to:

. Pictures and representations in general display which
  although not sexually explicit are suggestive and
  offensive.
. Failure to report any Category I violation of the
  Sexual Harassment Policy.

DATE DUE

GAYLORD			PRINTED IN U.S.A.

Order these other BNA Special Reports:

Timely reporting and key documents on important issues such as pregnancy disability, parental leave, reproductive hazards, and discrimination.
Single copy price: $65
Order #BSP-66

Reveals staffing strategies that can make your operation more productive. Learn about flextime, subcontracting, work-sharing, home-work, temporary help, and more.
Single copy price: $50
Order #45-LDSR-47

Explores approaches many organizations are taking toward child and dependent care, parental leave, alternative work schedules, and employee assistance programs.
Single copy price: $40
Order #45-LDSR-37

From early alcohol counseling programs to broad EAPs that cover all sorts of human problems: gambling, financial, legal, housing, eating disorders, smoking and drug abuse.
Single copy price: $50
Order #BSP-59

To order these BNA Special Reports, call TOLL FREE 1-800-372-1033.

A supplement to BNA publications.